LONDON GUNNERS

THE STORY OF THE H.A.C.
SIEGE BATTERY IN ACTION

THE BATTERY (RIGHT AND LEFT SECTIONS), GORENFLOS, MAY, 1918

LONDON GUNNERS

THE STORY OF THE H.A.C.
SIEGE BATTERY IN ACTION

BY

W. R. KINGHAM, M.A.

(EX-GUNNER, H.A.C.)

WITH A FOREWORD BY
THE EARL OF DENBIGH, C.V.O., A.D.C., T.D.
COLONEL COMMANDING THE HONOURABLE ARTILLERY COMPANY

WITH ILLUSTRATIONS AND MAPS

SECOND AND CHEAPER EDITION

METHUEN & CO. LTD.
36 ESSEX STREET W.C.
LONDON

First Published . . November 1919
Second and Cheaper Edition November 1919

TO THE MEMORY OF
MY GALLANT BROTHER PHIL

PREFACE

THIS book arose out of a desire on the part of my comrades, as of myself, that some written record should be left of our life in Flanders and France. Notes of all kinds, official details, and human memories were freely placed at my disposal, and the result at least ought to be, not only an accurate history of our particular battery, but, as well, a representative account of life in a howitzer battery on active service. While every assistance has been rendered by our officers, I must emphasise the fact that I have written throughout on my own responsibility, and in a mere gunner's spirit.

Colonel the Earl of Denbigh, besides contributing the foreword, has shown a personal interest in the work for which I should like here to express the gratitude which I feel to him.

In connection with the composition of the book, I keenly appreciate encouragement given, in one form or another, by nearly every member of the Battery. Did not a brother's love, and an admiration that is not partial, lead me to try, in my poor way, to honour as noble a lad as ever lived, I should have been proud to dedicate this book to that goodly company of men with whom I went through war's dangers.

I must express my particular obligations to F. Godden and C. T. Skilbeck, in whose constant support I have prized the fruits of a friendship for which, if for nothing else, I should have reason to thank my Army life ; to Major Spooner, Major Edmondson, Major Knox, and Captain Chattey, for the help they ever gave me, when, at hours seasonable and unseasonable, I assailed them ; to A. S. Challis, my artistic coadjutor, as gifted and generous as valiant ; to R. W. Bartlett, W. P. Lewis, and H. W. Upperton, for tangible aid, rendered in various ways ; and to those other men of E Sub., Usher, Vokins, Bocking, Gibbs and the rest, who in our bare billets at Beauvois assisted me unfailingly with counsel and friendly jibe, and, not least, by exempting from the common labours of plate-washing and porridge-making one happy in being their friend, if not in being their chronicler.

W. R. KINGHAM

September 1919.

CONTENTS

CHAPTER I

ix

FOREWORD

By the Earl of Denbigh, C.V.O. A.D.C., T.D., Colonel Commanding Honourable Artillery Company

THE H.A.C. is a Corps unlike any other in the British Empire. To begin with, its origin dates from the reign of Henry VIII, if not from a much earlier period, and is anterior to that of any other unit of the British Army. It exists by virtue of a special Royal Warrant, and is governed under its own special set of H.A.C. regulations. Candidates for membership, having first passed the military tests as to health and measurements, are then brought before the Court of Assistants, a Committee annually elected in normal times from amongst the officers, N.C.O.s, privates, and members of the Veteran Company, for which latter status a qualification of seven years' efficient service on the active list of the Regiment is necessary. Each candidate is proposed and seconded, and the Court, having satisfied themselves by searching inquiry that he is desirable as a member, proceed to ballot for him. If he is then duly elected, he pays his two guineas' entrance fee, takes the Oath of Allegiance, and is duly posted to whichever unit of the Regiment he prefers. The net result of all this was that the Regiment, on the outbreak of war, was composed

of an educated set of men, mostly following business
or professional avocations, with a very great pride in
their Corps, a high sense of duty and " esprit de corps,"
and whom it was a pleasure to work with and a privilege
to command. As the result of twenty-six and a half
years in active command of the Regiment I have
always complete confidence that, if a party of H.A.C.
men are given a job to carry out, it will be done to
the very best of their ability.

On mobilisation in 1914 the Regiment consisted of
two excellent horse artillery batteries, " A " and " B,"
and a half-battalion of infantry well known for its
general smartness and efficiency and of high repute for
its musketry. The numerical strength was 740, being
160 under establishment.

Within two days we had hundreds of applicants
clamouring for admission, and amongst them a large
proportion of former members. As a result the batteries
were soon up to full strength, besides reserves ; the
half-battalion was expanded to a full battalion and,
not long after, a Second Battalion was sanctioned and
duly formed.

Early in September 1914 the two batteries, " A "
and " B," were included, under my command, in the
Artillery Force of the 2nd Mounted Division, and we
proceeded to Egypt in April, 1915. The Division,
having become much dispersed, was broken up in
March, 1916, and my appointment as C.R.A. came
to an end. I then returned to England and was
appointed to supervise the training and equipping of
various 2nd Line Territorial horse artillery batteries,
amongst which were the two 2nd Line horse artillery

H.A.C. batteries, which had been formed during the past year. During this time, the remarkable development of siege artillery in the field had taken place, and one day in the summer of 1916 my then Adjutant, Capt. A. J. Edmondson, said to me, " Why not have an H.A.C. Siege Battery ? " " Why not ? " said I; and, on my suggesting this to the War Office, the proposal was welcomed,for the other H.A.C. units, both artillery and infantry, had already been of great service in providing from their ranks a large number of men for commissions as very useful officers.

So the H.A.C. Siege Battery was born, and it was given the official number 309, which in itself was evidence of the progress made in creating this new force of siege artillery.

It is of interest to examine the following list of typical professions from which many members of the battery were drawn :

Bank Cashiers	.	.	. 5	Fine Art Dealer .	.	. 1
Bank Clerks	.	.	. 26	Civil Servant	.	. 2
Clerks (various)	.	.	. 9	Master Tailor	.	. 1
Engineers	.	.	. 8	Drapers	.	. 4
Undergraduates	.	.	. 4	Plate Glass Merchant .		. 1
Schoolmaster	.	.	. 1	Corn and Coal ditto	.	. 2
Schoolboy	.	.	. 1	Real Estate	.	. 1
Shipowner	.	.	. 1	Detective P.C. .	.	. 1
Students, Medical, etc.		.	. 6	Printers	.	. 2
Insurance Officials	.		. 5	Jeweller .	.	. 1
Farmers	.	.	. 3	Ecclesiastical Artist .		. 1
Commercial Travellers		.	. 4	Manufacturer's Agent		. 2
Secretary Ltd. Co.	.		. 1	Merchant .	.	. 1
Director ditto	.	.	. 1	Architect and Surveyor		. 3
Produce Broker	.	.	. 1	No occupation	.	. 4
Authors	.	.	. 3	Brewers	.	. 2
Journalist	.	.	. 1	Antique Dealer	.	. 1
Solicitors	.	.	. 3			

Capt. Edmondson was given command as Major, and right well he trained his command when it went away to an instruction camp.   Having carried out most creditable practice at Lydd, it was duly equipped and went to France early in 1917, where it was straightway sent to get its baptism of fire in the cauldron of Ypres.

The daily life of the members, their feelings under fire and their various experiences are well told in this interesting book by one who served throughout in the ranks.

I remember, when the H.A.C. sent a battery to the South African War, as the artillery of the City of London Imperial Volunteers, a book was written by one of the wagon-drivers entitled, " In the Ranks of the C.I.V."   The author was Mr. Erskine Childers, who later on produced that remarkable volume, " The Riddle of the Sands," which attracted so much attention at the time.   The former book was particularly interesting, as it recounted simply impressions and experiences in the South African War from an artillery driver's point of view.   It is no disparagement of such drivers to say that, up to then, they had not as a rule been possessed of literary gifts, so this work was rather a novelty.   In the recent European cataclysm, however, all classes have been found in the ranks, and many a book has been written embodying the thoughts and adventures of the private soldier.

At one period of the war, the prevailing infantry fable was to the effect that the artillery, who were of necessity a bit further back, had quite a " soft job " compared to theirs.   Very possibly, in that awful

winter of 1914–15, when the infantry had in many
cases to reach the front line over open, unprotected,
and fireswept ground, and then on arrival had to exist
in icy mud up to their knees, or even higher, the lot of
the artillery was in some ways preferable. Later on
in the campaign, however, the artillery had too often
a very bad time, particularly under the influence of
counter-battery work ; they also remained in action
positions for long spells at a time.

Reading of the doings of 309 Siege Battery, one is
struck by the never-failing good-humour which always
obliterated the effect of individual " grousers " who
are found wherever the British soldier exists. It was
reckoned by the authorities as a particularly good
battery, hard-working, cheerful under difficulties, well-
disciplined and capable of making things most unpleasant for the Boche by its accurate shooting. Its
casualties were continuous and considerable, and in
Lieut. Edmondson (a younger brother of the first C.O.)
and Lieut. Glover especially, it lost two splendid
officers who had set a fine example to all. The total
number posted to the battery was 401, and of these
39 were killed (including 5 officers), and 70 were
wounded, of whom 6 were officers. Thirty-one left the
battery to take up commissions in other batteries.

To my mind, far more might have been made of the
H.A.C. as a serving O.T.C. than was actually the case.
At one period of the war, after the terrible Somme fighting, the officer question in the Army became critical. I
suggest, with much respect, that some of the measures
then taken to secure officers were most unfortunate.
Commanding Officers were ordered to submit a certain

number of names for commissions every month, whether they had suitable men for officer rank or not. Some of them have told me how they used to protest against being compelled to forward the names of men who they felt were absolutely unsuitable, or whom they knew nothing of, through the fact of the individuals having only joined the units a few days previously.

For a long time the H.A.C. units, composed largely of men who might have been most usefully commissioned, were not allowed to forward more names than other units, which were composed of an entirely different type, and in which candidates for commissions were few and far between. It is notorious that at one period of the war many men who became officers were no more fitted to command, lead and care for men than they were to command a battleship. Some people seem to think that any man who is possessed of education is fit to be an officer, others that some dashing act of personal bravery or leadership in a hard fight should necessarily be rewarded with a commission. Many other qualifications are, however, required for the production of a good officer. A proper sense of duty, honour, and discipline, coupled with technical knowledge, a cool head in danger and a capacity for looking after the comfort and health of their men when not engaged in actual fighting, should always be regarded as essential requirements. Some of these qualities were too often wanting in many officers commissioned under the stress of war at a particular period.

In the H.A.C., Commanding Officers were always told to be most careful in their recommendations, and

I think that our promoted men have done very well on the whole, judging from the many reports that have reached me. I feel certain, if there had been more elasticity about the system, and if the authorities had not insisted for so long on treating all Regiments alike, that a good deal more, over and above the 4,000 that we actually sent for commissions, might have been made of the H.A.C. for the purpose of providing useful officers.

What the future of the Regiment will be I do not yet know, but however it may be composed I believe in maintaining a very high sense of what is called " esprit de corps " as a foundation for anything. It is then the duty of those in command, by maintaining a high military efficiency, to prevent " esprit de corps " from degenerating into that bastard variety known by the detestable word " swank." For this I have no sympathy.

I trust that those who served with the 309 (H.A.C.) Siege Battery will never regret having joined the Regiment, and that they will always do their best to maintain its traditions in the same way and with the same spirit that the H.A.C., as a whole, displayed in the Great War.

DENBIGH

October 5th, 1919.

b

LIST OF ILLUSTRATIONS

LIST OF MAPS AND PLANS

THE BATTERY, PRIOR TO EMBARKATION FOR FRANCE

LONDON GUNNERS

THE STORY OF THE H.A.C.
SIEGE BATTERY IN ACTION

CHAPTER I

THE BREAKING-IN AT YPRES

THE Honourable Artillery Company, of the City of London, has a long and varied history; its Siege Battery has a short but, let us hope, a not unworthy one. The outbreak of the war in 1914 found the Company represented by an infantry battalion and two batteries of Horse Artillery. The battalion crossed to France in September 1914, and in April 1915 the batteries went to Egypt; and soon a second battalion and two more horse batteries were raised, which in due course went over to France. Many men trained with our horse batteries eventually obtained commissions in the Royal Field Artillery, and, largely in order that the Company might similarly supply officers—much needed at the time—for the Royal Garrison Artillery, it was proposed in October 1916 that we should ourselves raise a siege battery—as a unit, that is, of the R.G.A. The approval of the War Office was quickly obtained, and in November some eighty men were selected as the nucleus of the H.A.C. (309) Siege

1

Battery. Five months' training followed in various
camps—our Headquarters in Finsbury Pavement,
Ewshott, Bordon, Aldershot, Lydd, Codford—and on
April 26th, 1917, the battery, with its four 6-inch
howitzers and equipment, landed at Le Havre, and
on May 4th went up the line, as one of the five batteries comprised in the 88th Heavy Artillery Group.

It was a battery absolutely new to the field of war ;
none of us, with the exception of two or three officers,
had had any experience on active service, so that its
history is, in one aspect, an estimate of the adapta-
bility of the ordinary city man to such novel and
hateful conditions as those of modern warfare. Busi-
ness-men and bank-clerks we were for the most part,
with a few farmers and a few students and a stray
schoolmaster or two. For nearly three years we
had heard of war and its terrors ; its glamour had
long since ceased to attract ; we were content to
be taking part in it at last, and merely hoped that
fortitude would be ours sufficient to bear whatever
trials this strange experience might have in store for
us. We didn't know what it was like to have shells
dropping near us—we hoped there wouldn't be too
many ; we didn't know what number of us would be
still in action after a week or so—we hoped a good
many. As we waited about, that afternoon of
May 5th, by Poperinghe station, there stole on our
ears the sound of distant guns : eerie, insistent, the
first faint rumbling of the reality of war. We listened
to it with awe, realising that we stood now on the
brink of the cauldron into which so many millions of
men had been thrown : we were being ushered into

the field of blood. Familiarity with war may later
have made us smile at the remembrance of such
thoughts—yet did they not truly represent the life
before us ?

We marched out of Poperinghe soon after five in
the evening, to follow in the track of hundreds of
thousands of our predecessors along that famous
" Pop."-Ypres road : that splendid avenue giving
how untrue an impression of the area into which it
led ! Already at Pop. we had seemed to be within
the war zone ; we heard of the bombing and shelling
to which the town was frequently subjected, and
there too, obsolete but grimly suggestive, was still
to be seen the " Wind Dangerous " board, relic of the
days of cloud-gas. We knew not—how should we,
utterly fresh as we were ?—when danger might
befall us, and as we went along we noted with strained
senses the trees, here and there, damaged by shell
fire, or saw for the first time puffs of German anti-
aircraft shells breaking round our airmen in the
distance. Some would keep on talking about these
things ; others of us resented their loquacity, feeling
ourselves merely in the mood for silent forebodings,
another matter over which in after days we were
willing to laugh at ourselves. In time fatigue and
hunger induced their usual apathy ; indeed, we were
nearly all old soldiers enough by now to forget everything else when food was to be obtained, so that
when at length, halting at Vlamertinghe Windmill,
seven kilos from Pop., we were issued out bread and
butter and hot tea, we ate and drank ravenously,
and became cheerful and vigorous again. " Vlam.,"

with its ruined church and abandoned houses, gave
us our first substantial illustration of the damage of
war.

Major Edmondson and Captain Knox, who had
gone on in advance to the position, returned to us
here to arrange for guides for us ; and we were ordered
to put on our steel helmets and wear gas-masks at
the alert—an order which, as every soldier knows,
can usually be safely disregarded for a long time after
it is issued ; but which, as every soldier knows, when
heard for the first time, entirely puts the wind up a
man, seeming to indicate the very approach of horrible
dangers. And then, having set off again in the
direction of Ypres—it was eight o'clock now, and
dusk—we were instructed that a distance of fifty
yards must be left between each section of fours.
An ominous precaution this ! and we wondered what
we, individually, should do when that expected shell
fell in between us and the men fifty yards in front
of us. Should we have a miraculous escape ? Or
would it leave us prone on the roadside ? Well,
well—we learnt later that they didn't often drop
just where you happened to be. But we suspected
otherwise this first night. Marching on, we saw
continued evidence of the ravages of war—gaping
shell-holes ; torn and grisly spectral forms which
proved, as we came up to them, to be shattered trees.
We noted all these things with silent disapproval.
At length a huge brick building loomed ahead of us,
battered and ragged, its many windows looking like
sightless eyes : it was Ypres Asylum ; we passed it
on our left, and the ruined town itself lay in front of

THE " BARONIAL HALL," YPRES

us. This destruction even beyond what we had
conceived—each house nothing but a broken piece
of wall and a mass of bricks or brick-dust—had been
done by incessant shell-fire. What wonder that a
certain apprehension seized us, as, hesitatingly, in
our long intervals, we stepped out between the lines
of débris?

And just then—ah! that sudden, growing roar
above us! that dreadful shriek! it was upon us, our
very selves! CRASH! The air quivered with rage,
throbbed almost as if it were some far-extending lyre
struck by a giant hand; mud, splinters hummed past
us, who had instinctively crouched down or thrown
ourselves full length on the ground as the explosion
took place. No, we were not hurt! Was it credible?
But what an escape! Our nerves were horribly
jangled—and then, almost before we had pulled ourselves together, again that roar, that crash! "Clear
off the road—take shelter anywhere!" some one
shouted, and we dashed to any shelter near at hand—
deep ditch, even a roofless house, cellars, some into
the strong Asylum dug-outs. Fritz sent more shells
over in rapid succession. Some of our comrades
were scores of yards away from us; yet they and we
thought the same shells were about to drop on us
both! We laughed at this, too, afterwards. For
nearly half an hour this trial to our nerves continued.
People in Blighty want to know, "How did you feel
when you were first under fire?" Well, we crouched
and quivered as they came over, and thought it
atrocious luck that we should be caught there just
where the shells were falling, while a few hundred

yards away we should have been in no danger ; and
very sad it seemed that our active service should be
terminated on this, its very first day. Yet when at
length the bombardment ceased, almost as suddenly
as it began, our active service was not terminated,
we were all unscathed, and marvellous it appeared to
us. We discovered afterwards that what we had
been through was Fritz's nightly " strafe " of the
road, which, with more experience, we should have
avoided. The leading sections of the battery had
indeed arrived at the position we were to occupy, just
as the strafe started ; but we, when we at length
felt equal to coming out on to the road again, had no
idea where to make for, until, to our relief, we heard
through the darkness the voice of Major Edmondson,
who had guessed what our feelings would be, and
come in the strafe to direct us. At length, then, we
straggled up to our position. But we felt no inclination at all to explore it that night. What was welcome
to us was to be hailed by our advance party from the
dug-outs, to realise, as we stumbled over the masses
of brick to these, that they were very solid and very
strong, and so to turn into what appeared a veritable
sanctuary. To the fleshly part of us it was a bit hard
to have, later on, to come out to unload the lorries, but
anyhow, we got down into our blankets by midnight,
and had a free night for rest, if not for sleep.

This, then, was active service ! We were not
enchanted with it, as we lay on the floor or on the
rabbit-wire beds in these little curved dug-outs, four
or five feet high. From every quarter of the surrounding country in turn seemed to come the bang of gun-

fire, making us wonder if men ever got to sleep up the line. Close and rather noisome was the atmosphere; racketing noise and danger were all about; and the only alleviating circumstances were, that we were all in it together, and fatigue—fatigue after the strain of the long day, which did at length send us to sleep.

We looked about us with eager curiosity in the morning. So here we were in Ypres, added to those many thousands who had already fought in this tormented city! Our dug-outs and gun-platforms, we discovered, made a fairly compact position, 200 or 300 yards to the west of the Cloth Hall. Bricks, broken walls, and shell-holes—it was, of course, amongst these that we found ourselves. An advance party had been sent up a week or so before the battery arrived, but it had had very little to do, as we were simply taking over the position from another battery. The " Walker " dug-outs, on the left, occupied by C and D Subs.,[1] had extraordinarily thick walls—a shell of concrete enclosing four feet of earth—and were proof against all but very big shells. Originally they were inside the ruins of an old building, but these had gradually fallen away, leaving the whitish concrete uncamouflaged, a good mark for the Boche. Twice while we occupied them he dropped 5·9's right

[1] A 4-gun Siege Battery is divided into two sections, right and left, which in turn consist each of two sub-sections ("Subs."), one for each gun. A 6-gun battery has an additional section, the centre. When at full strength there are about eighteen gunners in each Sub. Officers, batmen, signallers, observers, cooks, a sanitary expert, *et hoc genus omne* bring the total personnel of a 4-gun up to 137, of a 6-gun to 180,

on them, but thanks to their splendid stability the
shells did no more than break the outer layer of
concrete, and we quickly made good the damage by
dropping flints into the cavities and hardening them
together with mortar. The dug-outs occupied by
A and B Subs., at the right rear of the position, were
not quite so strong in structure, but very strong by
position ; they were built in the cellar space of an
old Convent Hall, known familiarly to us as the
" Baronial Hall." Of the roof only a few beams
remained, but much of the wall still stood, and
sheltered our dug-outs, which themselves were built
of elephant iron,[1] strengthened with rubble and
several layers of sand-bags. The feeling of security
we had that first night when we stepped into the
dug-outs, we never lost during the whole of our stay
at Ypres; their strength was the one feature which
made the strain of life in that shell-swept city bearable.

The four guns were placed in the garden of
the convent, each being camouflaged under a framework of corrugated iron, on which brick rubble was
thrown, so that, seen from an aeroplane, they resembled
the neighbouring ruins. There was indeed every
need to conceal our presence, for three other batteries
had in turn been shelled out of this very position.
The garden was now, of course, a place of little but
refuse-heaps and huge shell-holes ; yet here and
there bloomed unexpectedly ferns, lilies-of-the-valley,
stocks—blessed traces of the fragrance and beauty
of another life than this.

The Boche, except for including us impartially in

[1] Very strong, curved strips of corrugated iron.

YPRES: C SUB. GUN KNOCKED OUT

YPRES: OUR FURNITURE REPOSITORY

his area-strafes,[1] allowed us some time to settle down,
and we fell into a routine of work. We paraded after
breakfast, and were assigned our particular task—
on the guns, or some " fatigue." The gun position
had to be cleared as far as possible ; there were
always sandbags to be filled to strengthen dug-outs,
canteen, and cook-house ; and as soon as we started
shooting there was, of course, much work to be done
preparing the shells. Artillery work isn't merely a
matter of laying[2] the gun and firing the shell, as some
do think. Those are the " posh " jobs, and when in
action, the " layer " and the " No. 2," who " pulls
off,"[3] may sometimes be looked at enviously by the
rest of the team, who swing the 100-lb. shells about.
But all the team help in the preparations. The shells
have to be carried from the lorries to the side of the
gun—what a " sweat " ! At Ypres it meant stumbling
twenty or thirty yards with them over heaps of
rubble. Then they have to be cleaned with a brush
or sandbag, for it's risking an accident to put them
into the gun with too much mud on. (Some men too
will never forgive me if I do not mention that famous
word " grummets "—strips of oakum around the
driving band of the shell, which, of course, have to
be taken off now.) And then comes the " fusing "—
that is, putting into the nose of the shell the fuse,
which, on impact, fires the high explosive in the shell,
and which, being sensitive, it is not judged wise to

---

[1] Area-strafe—a general bombardment of a large area, a thousand yards or more square.

[2] " Laying," *i.e.* training the gun on the target.

[3] " Pulling off," jerking a cord (lanyard) hooked on to the firing cartridge, and so firing the gun.

insert in the shell until this is actually by the gun. Some of these things we did during the day, for we discovered, perhaps to our surprise, that it was possible to move about in the daylight without getting killed every moment; but very quickly it appeared that the night, too, must be yielded without murmur to the clamant demands of warfare, for the cover of darkness, screening their big bulk from Boche observation, was nearly always necessary when lorries or guns came up to or went from the position. Three of our guns were brought in the night after we had arrived, and then it was heaving at the drag-ropes and striving at the hand spikes till past midnight for us. But on most nights men would be working till a couple of hours later than this, bringing up shells. Then, of course, each gunner in his turn had to go on guard for three or four hours during the night. However, one could not "grouse" on the whole, for there was very little night firing, and, with breakfast at eight, one could generally get six or seven hours of uninterrupted sleep.

One or two illusions commonly entertained were soon dispelled. There was that of many of our dear relatives and omniscient friends at home: "Oh, you'll be all right out there, old man! The artillery aren't in any danger, you know—they're miles behind the line." On this point the melancholy record of our casualties, like those of other siege batteries, speaks for itself. But on the other hand, the picture of the front some of us may have had in our minds, as an area under a continuous storm of shell-fire, was at once seen to be false. True, at Ypres, as in the

salient generally, one could hardly ever cast a look
round without seeing somewhere a shell burst. But
the Boche was aiming at some definite and limited
target, and keeping more or less to it, so that we soon
learned that one could remain perfectly undisturbed
a couple of hundred yards away from a spot that he
was shelling for hours. This fact it is which dictates
one's action when the Boche starts to shell one's own
position : if working "in battle order," the shoot
must at all costs be carried on, casualties being disregarded ; but if not, why then, choosing the proper
moment, in between the rounds coming over, off one
dashes some little distance to a flank, and waits there
until the trouble has subsided. As the song of siege
batteries goes :

> " When we hear the sound of a German shell
> Off to the flank we clear like Hell—
> No battery ever runs half so well
> As . . . ."

(At Ypres, however, it was generally into our dug-
outs that we cleared, owing to their exceptional
strength.)

The first week or so, when no shells fell about our
position, the chief excitement was theirs who were
detailed each day to fetch our water supply. This
came from the reservoir by the Prison—a spot well
known to the Boche—so that often the men on the
water fatigue had a windy journey dodging his shells.
It was a good distance to carry water, and soon it
came about that a dozen men were washing in one
half-bucketful. Poor city men, erstwhile so immacu-
late ! Quite early Greenwood, the dispatch rider,

ran into plenty of shelling. There was one day in
particular when he had to take a message to Group
Headquarters at the same time as the Boche was
putting down a couple of hundred shells on the area.
He had to leave his motor-cycle by the roadside while
he crawled up a ditch to the Group habitation ; but he
managed to avoid the bursts, delivered his message,
and was highly commended. However, Group at
once 'phoned through to us that no more messengers
were to be sent until the bombardment had ceased.

It was on May 10th that we started our deeds of
prowess and fired our first shot, and soon we were
steadily engaged in heavy firing, in preparation, it
was understood, for some big attack of ours that was
impending. Once or twice a day all four gun-teams
would be turned out, to send off any number from
20 to 100 rounds per gun ; and often, in the hours
near midnight, our battery would join with apparently
every other battery in the town in a short, sharp
bombardment, intended to interfere with the enemy's
arrangements, and particularly with his transport
behind the lines. What was being effected, some of
us soon asked ourselves, with this continued output
of shells ? No doubt they burst upon a few Boches,
or messed up a little his sandbags or concreting, but
day after day was spent in the same spot, at the same
work ; there seemed no real gain. Was it merely a
huge game, devastating but futile, between us and
the Boche all the time ? We had then to remind
ourselves that modern warfare was indeed largely
stationary, yet that steady bombardment such as we
were taking part in did immeasurably increase the

enemy's difficulties, and contribute greatly to success
when in the end an advance was attempted.

The 6-inch howitzer has a range of 10,000 yards,
and it is only on the rarest occasions that the gunners
see their own shells burst. Observation of the effects
of our shooting is generally secured from a special
Observation Post (O Pip) some thousands of yards
in front of the guns. Our very first shoot was a
" calibration " shoot—a shoot, that is, to test the
guns, and discover, by observing the bursts, what
discrepancy there is between their nominal and their
actual efficiency. On this occasion the O.P. was
" Hussar Farm," in front of St. Jean, and the journey
of a couple of miles there was naturally rather windy
for the untried men (two or three signallers and an
observer), though the leadership of the Major, with
his little cane, of course gave them confidence. The
road that led to the O.P. was under machine-gun fire,
so the little party went the usual roundabout route,
keeping as far as possible under the lee of ruined
houses, and longing even for this imperfect shelter as
they did the last hundred yards merely under the
cover of a hedge. However, the O.P. itself was safe
enough—a concrete dug-out camouflaged amidst the
farm ruins ; and very interesting it was, looking
through the apertures in the wall, to see here and
there the turned-up earth which marked the German
front line ; very interesting, too, to see shells bursting
by some stumps of trees near the so-called " Rectory,"
to realise that it was one's own chums who were
putting these over, and then to 'phone down corrections to them till the succeeding bursts seemed actually

on the target. There were great yarns to be told of
the shooting and the country when the observing
party returned in the evening to the battery.

Various O.P.s were used from Ypres, O.P.s with
picturesque names which recall to officers and signallers windy journeys, if interesting days—Haslar
House, Hell-fire Corner (a concrete erection that a
Boche O.K.[1] once rudely shook, along with its inmates),
and Paradise Alley, which was in our front-line trenches.
We were firing on German trenches in these days.
Four hundred shells in a steady stream on a strip of
trench as many yards long! As our O.P. party saw,
and directed, their going over, they felt sure the
Boche in that area was having a thin time. One
trench in particular, " Caliban Trench," must have
been practically obliterated, if we could judge from
the heaps of débris that were flung up in the air.
But undoubtedly the most interesting shoot was one,
observed by the Major from a sap-head in front
of our trenches, on a fortified shell-crater. It was
some fifty yards to the left of the sap-head, so naturally he started the battery shooting well to the left,
and gradually brought the bursts right up to the
crater—a rather eerie proceeding, guiding them so
near to oneself: they sounded, of course, just like
Boche shells roaring through the air and bursting
close enough to damage one, friends as they were, if
one exposed oneself. While ranging, the Major saw
a Boche crawl into the crater, on some errand or
other, and he then put a round into the crater. Poor
Boche! However, the enemy were not long in

[1] That is, of course, a shell right on the target.

retaliating. They began to strafe with " pip-squeaks,"
the observing party had to retreat to the trench,
and the Major had to stop smoking, his pipe having
been knocked out of his mouth by a shell-splinter.

There was another method of observing and directing our shoots, particularly those on enemy batteries,
and this, of course, was by aeroplane. We would be
informed that an " aeroplane shoot " would take place
at a certain hour, and would groan, for it was a shoot
of scores of rounds, and meant more shell-humping,
more fusing; generally, too, it was at about five in
the morning, and the dawn had no attraction for us.
Then, turning out on the gun at the appointed time,
we would have often to wait an hour or two for our
tardy coadjutor. Happy, indeed, were the caitiffs
amongst us, if visibility was bad and the shoot " off " !
However, generally we got the message, " Your
aeroplane is just going up," and there it at length
appeared—a speck hovering high up in the sky,
apparently over our front line, and now and then
attracting a burst of anti-aircraft fire. The method
of communication adopted was as follows : the 'plane
sent its messages through by wireless to our wireless
operator, but it received messages from us by means
of great letters laid out on the ground and forming
part of a code. Thus it would first send through an
inquiry as to whether we were ready, and we should
put out the letter L, meaning " ready to engage
target." Later, perhaps, we might have occasion to
put out H, " Your signals weak," or V, " Repeat," or
T2, " Go home for two hours." These great letters,
three yards long, were laid out in a field in front of

Ypres Prison, and it was difficult to conceal them
from prowling Boche aeroplanes; so it was sometimes " diamond cut diamond " in the way of aeroplane shoots. Our men had often to avail themselves of the shelter of the shell-holes in the field.
Twice R.F.A. batteries near the prison requested us
not to put the letters out because of the fire they
were drawing. Now and then the signallers on duty
were forced to clear from those shell-holes, which were
becoming too hot quarters, and as they fled, the
Boche shells, falling about them, gave them that
unpleasant feeling as if the long-visioned Boche was
following up their retreat.

In the gun-work itself it was amusing to see how
the formal drill that we had learned in England was
almost wholly discarded. There, each gun was served
by ten men, each man had his number, each number
its proper position, its appointed work. Nos. 4 and 5,
for instance, and they alone, carried up the shell in
the tray; Nos. 3 and 5, and they alone, rammed it
home. But here—well, I'm not even sure that these
numbers just given are right ; for we soon left off
troubling about numbers. With the exception of
No. 1, the N.C.O. in charge, and No. 2, everybody did
what he could to get the gun into position, everybody
jumped about quickly doing the work that lay to his
hand, and we became bustling, efficient gun-crews
instead of polished automata. Heavy though the
work was to men unused to manual labour, we went
at it with vigour, at the gun-work even with zest, and
were not without commendation from the Major.
Now, too, the war standards of values replaced those

THE WATER-TOWER, YPRES

of the parade ground. Men who in Blighty had been
" ticked off " as untidy, or even " wash-outs," showed
themselves now sound, practical men, and established
reputations that they always maintained, while it
happened that some of their one-time mentors quite
failed to come up to expectations. That classification,
too, which is bound to be made in warfare—" windy "
and " not windy "—was made with us ; and here too,
as has been the case in every unit at the front, there
were many surprises. Quiet, easy-going people, others
with the indifferent, half-cynical outlook that city
life perhaps develops—it was men of these and other
equally unmilitary types who showed up curiously
well by contrast with others who had swaggered it
boldly till the test came.

And after a time the test did come ; hostile fire
became a bugbear ; and the question was put to the
proof how a unit of untried men could stand the
continuous strain of life under shell-fire. At first it
was merely our share of the " area-strafes " and the
surplus from other batteries' quantum of shelling that
we suffered from ; in particular there was a 60-pounder
battery at our rear that the Boche seemed to have
" well taped," treating it frequently to a two or three
hours' slow shoot. Over they would come, methodi-
cally, in salvos of two, and those that fell short were
our portion. It was apparently from one of these
shells that Mould, the first of our men to be hit, was
wounded (May 11th). After a little time, however,
our position seemed to be discovered. We had been
doing a shoot—a good shoot, too—for the report was
that we had set on fire a dump, which burned for two

2

days after ; but apparently a Boche 'plane was up while
we were firing, for in the evening shells started coming
over all about our guns and dug-outs. No deluding
ourselves that these were meant for other targets !
It was only a twenty minutes' strafe, and no one was
hurt ; but ruefully we had to reflect that the Boche
had spotted us, and that at any time now he might
catch us when we were out in the open. However,
the position had to be retained at any risk, for being
at the time the most forward siege battery position
in the sector, it was a particularly favourable one for
getting on to certain Boche trenches.

A day or two later the Boche started early. About
five in the morning he opened out on the 60-pounders,
gave them the usual couple of hours' strafe, and then
shortened on to us. He was indeed ranging by aeroplane on us, and our wireless operators picked up
corrections that the Boche 'plane was giving to its
guns. There came a direct hit on one of our Walker
dug-outs, and the German word " Gut " was picked
up on the wireless, and then a little later came the
German equivalent to our " O.K." It must have
been worth an " O.K." if the aviator actually saw
C Sub.'s gun, for, both its wheels knocked off, it lay
in the débris like a whale stranded on its belly.
Through the whole morning and until nearly four
o'clock that slow fire was kept up on our area, and we
sat imprisoned in our dug-outs—anxious enough at
the beginning, for this was in a way our first systematic
strafing—and then, as the hours went on, and we
weren't damaged, growing a little more settled under
the regular bursts that rocked us like a ship in a

storm; at length we became tired with the strain, and quite indifferent. One or two men slipped out and brought back bully and bread for our dinner; and in the middle of the afternoon, what was not the surprise, the joy, and the admiration of the bored men in the dug-outs when Sergeant Williams and Challis and Gillot came along with dixies of tea which they had taken it on themselves to make in the flimsy cook-house ? Bastow previously had shown great coolness in fetching water for Mr. Mortleman, who was suffering from shell-shock.

Whit-Sunday, May 27th, was another day of strafe. Fritz was shelling in the early morning, and as the men were getting up, a shell hit the wall of the old hall. Immediately a cry was heard outside, and Brownsill and others rushed out to give help. Heller, the medical orderly, was already on the spot, merely in his shirt, supporting a figure covered with brick-dust. It was poor Burningham, the limber-gunner, who had been out, in his conscientious way, attending to his limber, and was badly wounded and uncon-scious. They carried him along to the dressing-station in the Prison, where he died an hour after-wards. For most of that day the Boche kept up his fire. The next day was quieter, but on the 29th, in the evening, the Boche shelled us again, damaged A gun, and set fire to the old convent building which had served as an ammunition dump. The 1,200 cartridges and the fused shells had to be moved from the burning building—a ticklish job—but safely accomplished.

But indeed at any time now a salvo might come

over to shake us up, the precursor of an hour or two's
bombardment of our position, and then there was
nothing for it but to sit tight. On Sunday, June 3rd,
we were firing morning and afternoon ; unfortunately,
a Boche balloon was up, and their guns got on
us as soon as we started the afternoon shoot. A shell
dropped outside D Sub. dug-out, wounding Trice
and Earley, who were inside, and Barrett, who was
shaving outside. Earley died soon afterwards—
a fine type of lad, much esteemed, much regretted by
his companions. Group were advised of the situation, but answered that the shoot we were engaged
on was an important one, and must be continued, so
our men had to stick on the gun (for there was only
one in action, the other three having previously been
" knocked out "), although there were frequent bursts
of fire all round. After some time a near burst caught
T. H. Green and killed him, and slightly wounded
two or three other men, and Group, on being informed
of this, allowed the position to be cleared. During
this trying experience Corporal Vassie had led and
encouraged his men well ; but immediately on retiring
to the dug-out he collapsed with shell-shock, and the
others had to hold him down. Williams, that out-
standing figure in these days, Heller, Bishop, Gillot—
these were men who were particularly remembered
afterwards for their coolness in taking the wounded,
both our own and some infantrymen, along the
dangerous ways to the Prison dressing-station. That
night the Boche sent over gas-shells, so that after the
worries of the day, we were kept awake, with gas-
masks on, for three or four hours in the darkness.

The steady fire in the vicinity prevented any wireless mast from being put up ; the wire was fixed to old walls, but was soon cut, and was then attached to a forlorn apple-tree in a garden behind the Hall. So, too, the signallers were nearly always busy repairing their local wires.   An officer would try to 'phone through to Group, and fail : " Line gone dis.[1] again." And out from the dug-out the signallers on duty must go, and, keeping a sharp look-out and ears alert for shells, must trace the line till the cut was found and the damage repaired.

The section stores, to the left of the position, were knocked out ; part disappeared into thin air ; part were buried in the ground, from which they had to be dug up.

The strain of life was indeed becoming intense now. One felt a natural reluctance to leave the dug-outs, yet, once outside, felt utterly careless as to whether the Boche should start shelling or not ; and yet again the fear of a sudden burst near by took half one's attention off the work on hand.   It was fine, sunny weather this May time ; but one came out into the warmth and brightness only to see bricks, débris, hopelessness everywhere.   If one forgot one's surroundings, and for a moment the sunshine cheered body and mind, a crash ! somewhere near, and the sight of a fog of brickdust would inevitably spoil the beauty of the morning.   Nature, indeed, was allowed to give but little relief from the strain ; we went back as quickly as possible to our dungeon-like dug-outs.

Happily for us it was realised by the authorities

[1] *I.e.*, disconnected.

that the Boche was now too familiar with this position
of ours for it to be worth holding much longer, and a
working party was sent to prepare another position
out in the country near the Château des Trois Tours.
Before we moved, however, the big Messines attack
took place—on June 7th. Messines lies well to the
south of Ypres, but the batteries in Ypres had to fire
during the night to occupy the enemy's attention in
front of us. But we still had only one gun in use,
and that went out of action before the bombardment
was finished. It came as cheer to our hearts, worn
as we were, to hear the explosion of our mines on
Hill 60 (which, though five miles away, fairly rocked
our dug-outs), and to learn later of the thousands of
prisoners who had been captured. But the victory
led to no improvement in our situation ; rather, the
Boche appeared to be making reprisals for our success,
for he sent over more gas than ever. It seemed only
a matter of time and more of us were bound to be
caught, and the only question now on the lips of
perhaps most of us, the question asked petulantly,
eagerly, every hour of the day, was, " When is that
move coming off ? " At length the order came for
June 11th. Our exit from Ypres was not less harassed
than our entrance and our stay there. Fritz was
ranging as we moved off in the evening ; the parade
ordered was impossible, and we were instructed to
make off in couples, and at intervals of fifty yards.
Bricks were flying off the Prison, a little to our left,
and it was a hazardous proceeding crossing the
canal, for he was strafing the bridge. We had to
dash quickly across, and drop into a ditch on the

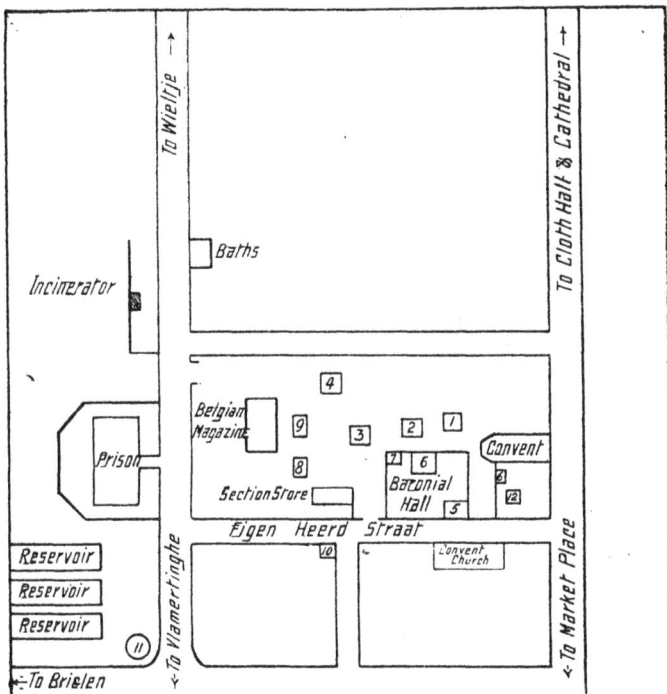

Map labels:
To Wieltje →
To Cloth Hall & Cathedral ↑
Baths
Incinerator
Belgian Magazine
Prison
Section Store
Reservoir
Reservoir
Reservoir
To Vlamertinghe
To Brielen
Eigen Heerd Straat
Baronial Hall
Convent
Convent Church
To Market Place

1. A Sub ⎫
2. B   ,,   ⎬ Gun-pits
3. C   ,,   ⎪
4. D   ,,   ⎭
5. A   ,, ⎫ Dug-outs
6. B   ,, ⎭
7. Cookhouse, First Site
8. C Sub ⎫ Dug-outs
9. D   ,,   ⎭
10. Divisional Canteen
11. Water Tower
12. Cookhouse, Second Site

PLAN OF THE BATTERY POSITION AT YPRES

other side ; and after that, with shells falling about the roads, it was a long run, an adventurous journey, before we got near the new position. But we were out of Ypres at last—thank heaven for it ! Our apprenticeship to warfare had been a rough one—it could be reckoned over now ! And, as it turned out, not too soon had we left, for, apparently in anticipation of another big British attack, the Boche from now on subjected Ypres to bombardments even heavier than those in the past, using 12- and 15-inch and armour-piercing shells, and the town became in literal truth untenable.

CHAPTER II

THE reports that had reached us from the
advance party at the new position had led
us to expect a pleasant change when at
length we should move from Ypres ; and such proved
to be the case. From that ruined city we went to
green fields and comparative peace. Subconsciously,
indeed, surprise took us now, as later on in France,
that war could be waged in such fair surroundings,
for essentially in our experience so far it had been
associated with ruin and waste. But here the warm
June sunlight lay on green, low-lying fields in hay,
spangled with buttercups ; Nature seemed lovely as
never before to us men from London town, late of
Ypres city ; and for days we moved about with a
constant sense of relief.

Out of the level and sparsely-wooded meadow-land
that lies between Vlamertinghe and Elverdinghe there
rises, some quarter of a mile to the left of the Vlamer-
tinghe-Brielen road, a distinctive dark-green mass—
lofty trees surrounding the fine modern château of
Trois Tours, and standing with it upon a low mound.
The front of the château looks away from the road,
and the trees are kept from closing in the view by a

CHÂTEAU DES TROIS TOURS

small lake, spring fed, of beautifully clear water. Our guns were to be placed between the château and the road, behind the narrowest of streams, which runs in shy obscurity beneath its pollarded willows across this stretch of country. Well behind stood two comfortable-looking Flemish farm buildings, the one, Marsh Farm, to the rear of the château, amidst tilled land; the other, Roan Farm, near the road. There were even a few civilians about at first, though farms and château had long been appropriated to the Army's use. Very little shelling had been done even on these known buildings, and the country as a whole was practically undamaged, for though Trois Tours was as near the front as Ypres, it was two miles to the north-west, and had not suffered from the fire concentrated on that unhappy city.

A fine, broad-gauge railway had been constructed, running past the château wood on our side, while 200 yards behind our position ran a good road.

All our guns, as has been mentioned, had been put out of action at Ypres, and when we came to Trois Tours we were for nearly three weeks without them. We spent this time in preparing the position. Camouflage, road-making, Decauville-laying, dug-out building—there was sufficient to do without those guns ever coming up! That, however, was " not to be thought of," and we had to make a road for their passage from the Brielen road to the position. For sixty yards or so the ground was level, though soft and muddy, but, after that, it sloped sharply, forming the bank of the little stream which here ran parallel with the high road. We had to cut our road through

the bank, therefore, and were not displeased with the
result.   When the guns eventually came up, at the
beginning of July, only two were brought in this way,
and, of course, with the long distance to be traversed,
a good deal of exertion was entailed.   Even more
laborious was it to bring in the other guns from the
rear road.   It was about eleven o'clock at night, and
they had to be man-handled into position, the ground
being judged too soft for the tractors to move on.
We put the drag-ropes on the wheels and pulled away
with a good heart at first, but as hour succeeded hour
through the night, and the hope of getting sleep gradually faded away from our dulled minds, we became too
tired to talk, became just dumbly, unreasonably resent-
ful, only the officers in charge and the N.C.O.s seeming
to retain any activity, with their " Fresh purchase,
lads! "   " Come, now, a good pull! "   We pulled with
slow, heavy action, until at last, as dawn broke, we
had got those infernal brutes up to their positions.
And then we could rest a bit.

This heavy labour was typical of our life at Trois
Tours.   At Ypres we were in an old position, and old
dug-outs ; but here we had to make everything, and
we were kept working from early morning, before
breakfast, till nine or ten at night, and, of course,
Sunday brought no change.   How we cursed the day-
light-saving bill just put into force !   It cost us an
hour's sleep daily, for whereas we ceased work at
dark, we rose by the clock !

For some days a squad of men was employed on
the spreading of the camouflage.   The Major was
rightly desirous that our *locale* should remain in its

present peaceful state as long as possible ; we meant
to fire a great deal, but there was no reason why the
Boche should disfigure the countryside if we could
help it, so camouflage was put up on a scale rarely
attempted : a strip four to six feet wide over the whole
length from the high road to the wood, broadening
out of course over the actual gun position. It was a
great sight, that almost interminable green awning,
under which men walked with dinners in hand or
shells on shoulders. The passing Tommy joked about
it, of course. " Wanter keep the sun off 'em, those
artillery chaps do ; cushy job theirs, ain't it ? " But
the concealment so afforded from inquisitive Boche
'planes was certainly of value. Moreover, was it
not enough to gratify any battery's pride to see
Corps Camouflage Officers bringing visitors over so
that they might learn how camouflage ought to be
put up ?

Shell-humping ! That, and almost that alone, is
what Trois Tours stands for in many men's memories.
The lorries left the shells by one or other of the roads,
and it was a question of carrying each 100-lb. beast
a distance of at least 200 yards. Multiply those
figures, and consider the enormous number of foot-
pounds of energy employed in shell-humping alone
at this position. They came up in huge numbers—
1,000 at the very beginning, then 600, then 1,000,
and so on. Very few men carried one shell the whole
distance ; usually teams of three split the task between
them. ". Toiling, rejoicing, sorrowing ! " No, toiling,
sweating, cursing, resting the shell now on one, now
on the other shoulder, carrying it for a change in one's

hands in front and finding oneself after a score of
yards bowed down with the weight—so the chains of
men passed across the grass for several hours each
night. Only one man had cause to bless this game—
the shell slipped from his shoulder, and he got to
Blighty with a crushed foot. There was one historic
shell, too, which was known to the officers to have
dropped into the stream, and they set Wheeler Hinch
to work to recover it ; two or three hours it occupied
him, but at length the shell came up. The officers
appeared to view it as a pearl from the depths of the
ocean ; but, if so, its value did not depend on its
uniqueness, as the men knew. The fatigue of shell-
humping was reduced after a time by the construction
of a Decauville (light railway) line from the Brielen
road to our gun position, a task which the battery
accomplished under the guidance of an architect
member. Another line, from the rear road to the
position, it was left to the R.E.s to construct.

There was a big shell-dump a little way from Trois
Tours, and often some of our men had to go to work
on it. On July 10th the Boche put a shell by the
dump, near a party of our men, and wounded
Brock, while A. S. Clark was blown right over a
hedge, and went down with shell-shock.

" Filled sandbags all morning, afternoon, and evening
till ten p.m." That is the entry, repeated day after
day, in diaries of this period. Yet, though the hours
were long, it really wasn't too bad out there in the
sunshine ; you watched with keen interest some of
the numerous air fights that took place now, or chatted
easily with your partner as you took it in turns to

hold and fill the bags, unless he was one of those ferocious workers, ruthless to himself and to others. But, thank goodness! most of the men knew the merits of leisureliness these summer days.

The dug-outs were at first in the open—two fairly big ones for C and D Subs. on the position, a still bigger one for the Right Section by the Brielen road. They were made of elephant iron, strengthened with sandbags. Old members of the Right Section still recall with mirth their dug-out—the " Pagoda," as it was termed—an abode of curves and beauty and discomfort; for an attempt was made to place a second story of elephant irons on those forming the side walls, and the result was not successful. This dug-out, moreover, was built on a slope, which drained down to the stream, and when it rained the water glided under the higher side and gently overflowed the floor. So it was necessary to bring in duck-boards to sleep on; but there were not too many of these, and if you went away from the dug-out for one night, on your return you might find your duck-board appropriated, and realise ruefully, as you looked at the moist floor, that your luck was out. Yet another drawback to this dug-out was its distance from the cookhouse in the wood; one's arms fairly ached, when one was mess-orderly, with carrying the food this three hundred yards. Better physical ache, though, than the execrations of one's comrades, which one man earned. With a flash of genius he deposited the dixie of stew and the dish of rice on a shallow barrow. He wheeled it over part of the undulating way, and then, going down a bank, the viands slipped off, and hardly anything was saved for twenty hungry men's dinner.

The immunity from shell-fire which the position enjoyed when the battery took it up continued for some days. Then, on June 17th, when our first reinforcing draft came up, some one was telling the new men what a cushy place they had come to, and forgot to touch wood, and within an hour or two Boche shells were falling about the position, and every one had to clear to a flank. It was seen now that it was unwise to have the Left Section dug-outs so near the guns, and billets were made in the wood, which was well to the left. And these were genuine dug-outs, the floor seven to eight feet below ground-level, for it was here possible to dig so deep without coming on water : long, comfortable places, with their curved iron roofs, and strong wooden pillars down the centre. You felt that you were descending into the fairy palace of Peter Pan as you clambered of an evening down amongst the roots of the trees into these habitations, bright with the light of many candles. There were three of these big dug-outs, besides an officers' mess and a cookhouse. So far it had been impossible to arrange any system of relief, but it was now endeavoured to secure that at least men should get one night's sleep out of two ; the two sections in turn did night-shoots, and the section on duty occupied the billet by the roadside while the other one slept in the wood. B Sub. for some time lived in a room in the château itself ; they thought they had three stories above them, and were safe ; but a shell that burst outside and broke what plate-glass was left in their windows caused them to look into the matter a little more closely ; then they discovered they had only the lead of the roof to protect them. Like wise men they descended and slept in the cellars, redolent of wine no longer there, and there they were unharmed when the building itself was hit more than once.

For the Boche had become fairly active over this rural stretch of land. Naturally, he often sent a few shells over on the railway near the wood, and in crossing it to get to the billets there, no man lingered. Some thought, indeed, that the strafe on June 17th, already referred to, was intended for the railway area. Some big guns had come up near us, a 12-inch railway-mounted, for a time, as well as another 6-inch battery, and these apparently were spotted by the Boche. The wood was subject to spasmodic bursts of fire all the time, some of the great trees were uprooted, and now and then a shell fell into the lake. Yet it was felt that that gunner was peculiarly unnerved who averred that one shell which went into the lake had come up the other side of his dug-out ; he had heard it and felt it, though his experience stopped short of seeing it. A working party from our 2A and 2B Horse Batteries had been attached to us, and they were living at Marsh Farm along with some other troops, when a shell caught the building and knocked out over a score of men. One big shoot, indeed, Fritz had on our guns. It was on July 15th, a day when, as our spotter [1] noticed, his balloons were particularly

[1] Man detailed for observing and reporting approach of enemy aeroplanes.

well placed for observing us, and he appears to have
seen our flashes, for after we had sent off a few rounds,
over his came.   He corrected his first shots, and got
well on to our position.   Our men cleared to the
wood, and from there observed the strafe.   It was
splendid shooting—not a burst on the wood side of
the railway.   Some 200 rounds Fritz put over ; he
knocked out D gun, and cut up the position ; then he
closed, as if he had finished with the battery, and he
never repeated the performance.

Four or five of our men had an unpleasant time on
June 25th, when they were sent up to the ruined
village of Brielen, a mile or so in front of our position,
to get rubble (bricks from the destroyed houses).
Working away in the sunshine, they had partly loaded
the lorry when a shell or two dropping near drove
them away for a bit.   They restarted, but apparently
under balloon observation, for, at once, more shells
came over, and they cleared again to a flank.   After
a little the A.S.C. driver who was with them went up
to get his lorry away ; he found the radiator smashed,
but enough water left for the journey back to the
position, and the party were just going to the lorry
when a shell burst right by them.   It blew them all
flat on the ground, and Heal and the driver were
badly wounded.   There were no stretchers, but they
could not wait in that exposed position, so the
wounded men were carried as well as might be, over
awful ground, entangled with wire and cut up with
shell-holes, to a dug-out away from the line of fire.   It
was none too comfortable there with Fritz dropping
them all about, but at length, after a couple of hours,

the stretchers arrived. And then Fritz was shrapnel-
ling the road to Roan Farm, where the dressing-station
was ! However, the party—Fitness, Brownsill, Bocking, Oulsnam, and Goodman—took the risk, and
managed to get through all right with their charges.

It was on the same day that Hyde was wounded,
by a shell bursting five yards from the Right Section
cookhouse. The wood and the château were sometimes very unhealthy now. One day, in a strafe
lasting some hours, Fritz had direct hits on two dug-
outs adjoining ours, killing and wounding ten men,
whom some of ours, well led by " Jimmy " Mordin,
the " Quarter-bloke," extricated from the débris.

At times life did seem as precarious at Trois Tours
as at Ypres. But there were undoubted alleviations.
There was the lake for bathing in—a great treat—
until too many dead fish forbade. The official bathing
hours were only five to six in the evening, but at
early morning, or any other time, men would drop
into the cool waters. And then the strenuous days
were seen to necessitate some relaxation, and at the
end of June the custom was commenced of a party
of a score or so of men going each day to Poperinghe.
Pop. is a drab little Flemish town, but, like Béthune,
it has stood for much to many thousands of British
soldiers—a glimpse of those comforts almost forgotten
in the primitive, earthy life up the line. To think of
getting a bath and a change of grub again ! Happy
as sandboys were we as we first went off early in the
morning to " Vlam.," and there, picking up some
lorry or other, rolled away along the avenued road
to Pop., leisurely filling our pipes as we sat there,

8

talking to and bantering one another. Inevitably we
recalled our march up this road on May 6th. That
was less than two months ago, yet so sternly had
this new life claimed entire possession of us, it seemed
a year. Unremitting toil, danger, violent death—we
knew now what these were, and we felt hardened even
in this short period in a way that we could never
have been by any other form of experience, however
long. But enough of these reflections. Shall we be
able to get a good bottle of wine at Pop. ? It is the
great hope of some of us.   First, however, to the
baths. These turned out to be the regulation Army
spray-baths, in crude enough surroundings, but we
had the good luck now, as nearly always afterwards,
to obtain a change of new underclothing. And
now where to feed ?   There were various little
shops about where Tommy was catered for, with
pork-chops, eggs, and chips ; but was there anywhere where one could get better fare ?   Cyril's
Restaurant was reserved for officers—ugh ! But the
" British Hostel "—oh ! we soon discovered that—a
place where we were always welcome, and where a
good, appetising dinner was always obtainable. Men
of our horse batteries used to come there too, and
either in the kitchen or the bare room upstairs (for
even here we must not trespass on officers' preserves),
we would sit and feed joyously, comparing notes,
telling yarns, what time the flowing cup went round.
Then to the pictures or to some pierrot performance,
or a visit to Talbot House, that most genuine of
soldiers' homes. Then a quest—generally fruitless,
except at Talbot House, where there was a great

crush—for a cup of tea, and so back again to sand-bagging, shell-humping, and clearing to a flank.

An episode that stands out in the memory of all that took part in it was a forward expedition on the night of July 16th. Thirty men were told to parade at half-past seven, and learned with natural disgust, at the end of a day on the guns, that they were to go up to help dig in a cable. In company with a party of R.G.A. men they were marched up to Bridge 4, spanning the Yser Canal, and had to wait there till dark. There seemed a spice of adventure about this—there was, indeed! for as soon as they had crossed the canal they found the Boche was shelling the road, and they had to jump into a communication trench, along which, feeling too much like infantrymen for their comfort, they proceeded for over a mile till they came to the spot where they had to dig. And pretty quickly they dug too, with machine-gun bullets and gas coming over; for a time they had to work in their gas-masks. A dark, nervy night for most! Sergeant Williams had volunteered for the party, and as ever at such times kept their spirits up, and kept them together when, returning at two in the morning, they lost their way. Eventually, however, they got back at four o'clock, and crawled, worn out, into the blankets.

What tremendous shoots they were at Trois Tours compared with those of later times! On numerous occasions four guns fired over 400 shells between them. Humping, fusing, firing of shells—there seemed nothing else done some days. Perhaps this seems natural enough to the lay reader, who imagines that

out at the front every man is playing a Hercules',
as well as a hero's, part the whole time. Not so ; and
that is one of the attractions of life up the line : that
though the work when it has to be done is intense,
and often done under circumstances of danger, yet
there is much slack time.   But it wasn't so for us at
Trois Tours ; the days were over-full, and though the
arrival of the draft of thirty men brought some relief,
the fatigue was undoubtedly responsible for the large
number of men who had to go to hospital in July and
August, as many as twenty-seven reporting sick on
one day.

And they were slow shoots, too, at the beginning at
any rate, for they were " aeroplane " shoots ; we had
to wait after each shot for the correction to be sig-
nalled.

We were now, as always henceforth, engaged
chiefly on counter-battery tasks, and some good work
was done.   The Boche cannot have enjoyed British
howitzer work in general.   Sometimes we were firing
on him at a slow rate of fire (about eight rounds per
hour for each gun) for twenty-four hours, and what
he suffered may be illustrated by one report that
came through—that at first the aerial photograph
showed one gun knocked out, but on further developing, it was found that the other three were also knocked
out (the range being over 7,000 yards).   With all the
hard work, there was always an element of interest
in a shoot ; to the end one rarely went at it mechani-
cally, as might perhaps have been expected.   Just
now there was one shoot in particular in which our
enthusiasm, as we worked on the gun, was roused to

a high pitch by " Eddy's " (if I may speak irreverently) calling out to us, with his ear to the telephone over which the report was coming, " Mostly O.K.'s." Sir Douglas Haig's report for these days puts such work in its proper perspective. " A definite aerial offensive," he says, " had been launched, and the effective work of our airmen once more enabled our batteries to carry out successfully a methodical and comprehensive artillery programme. So effective was our counter-battery work that the enemy commenced to withdraw his guns to places of greater security."

It may be mentioned that at night a practice was adopted here which was not employed at any other position. The guns were as usual laid on the S.O.S.[1] line, and, in addition, the cartridges were inserted and the lanyard hooked on. If therefore a call came through, the man on guard, on his way to arouse the sleeping gunners, would run rapidly along, pulling off all four guns—putting, on his own, the wind up those Boches thousands of yards away, who suddenly found four big bursts taking place amongst them.

It was after we had been three or four weeks at Trois Tours that particularly heavy firing was done, and this confirmed the rumour, now prevalent everywhere, that a big offensive was soon to start on our front. Before us lay Poelcapelle, and beyond that Passchendaele Ridge ; it was on and about the former that our own guns were firing, and if once, pushing past Poelcapelle, our men got the Ridge, they would be looking down on Roulers and the level

[1] Signal from infantry in the front line that they are needing artillery help.

plain of Flanders. We noticed a battery now behind nearly every hedge; no longer was this a haunt of rural peace as we had first known it. And, with the continuous bombardment maintained, Fritz, it was said, was getting disturbed, and on the 27th we were actually told to be ready to move off at a moment's notice. On this day, in fact, Fritz did withdraw from a section of his trenches, which our men, crossing the Yser canal, occupied and retained. But he was going to be driven well back, that was certain. There were all the preparations to be observed—Tanks, a prisoners' cage just by the wood, even, on the 30th, tents this side of Vlamertinghe (unsafe habitations unless a push was to be made at once); and as usual Fritz showed that he too had knowledge of what was impending by strafing our back areas pretty steadily for a couple of days before the 31st.

For July 31st, as every soldier knows, did see the great push started—the attack which was to have taken us so very far, and perhaps shortened the war, but which, ruined by the weather, gave us little more than three or four thousand yards of damnable shell-holes. It was at 3.50 a.m. that the great cannonade opened out ; all the noise that had assailed our ears before, seemed as nothing ; at the moment the atmosphere became noise, a roar that filled all space, and with it the dark sky became a mass as of blood with the flashes of innumerable guns. The boys were going over ! Theirs was the task of extremest danger ; with all our heart we wished them well, and we worked with eagerness, with alacrity, to help to keep the Boche guns out of action. By six o'clock prisoners were coming down the road, some of them helping our own walking wounded; and from the latter we heard satisfactory reports: "Yes, Jerry's running; we've got his first line, though he fought hard. Our artillery was jolly good." At a slower rate now, but continuously, we put the shells over till eleven o'clock. Fritz replied with only a couple of H. Vicks,[1] both into Roan Farm.

Now we were expecting to move off at any minute, and, heavy though the work would be, we were eager for it, eager to follow up the great advance. Major Edmondson went off at midday and chose a new position beyond the morning's front line. But the day went on, and no move was made. One gun indeed had been pulled out in the morning, ready for moving, but Group ordered it to be put back, and at ten in the evening we had to start firing again, for Fritz was counter-attacking. And the rain, which had begun in the afternoon, poured steadily down. Thunderstorms we had had in plenty of late, but this was a continuous heavy rain, coming at the end of a twenty hours' day of keen anticipation which had gradually passed into disappointment. Gloom took possession of us as we thought of the great effort being frustrated—for, however unfavourable weather conditions could be overcome in France, they could not be disregarded here; these clayey lowlands became bogged, and gripped the feet of infantrymen trying to advance; the heavy guns, essential for following up, sank deep into the ground, and could not be moved

[1] *I.e.* High-velocity shells, sent from guns with a range of 20,000 yards.

except by " caterpillars." In heaviness of heart we went
at midnight to our damp dug-outs. Each team went
out in turn during the night to fire off a dozen rounds
an hour, and always the rain was continuing. And
so it was all next day—that leaden, dismal day. Yet
at length in the evening there was a sigh of relief—we
were to move off : still raining, but anything was
better than this dull inaction. And now eight mortal
hours we were pulling and heaving at the guns
to get them out of their mud-baths to a spot where
the tractors could grip them ; and then at four in the
morning of August 2nd the men, carrying their kit,
marched up the dreary road to the new position,
Essex Farm. There was only one bright spot—this
was the night of the first rum issue !

CHAPTER III

" SCOTCHING-UP " AN ADVANCE

THE guns were left on the roadside at the new position, the caterpillars went away, and, wet and fed up, we tried in that sea of mud to find some shelter for a couple of hours' sleep. Crouched and crushed together under some elephant irons, we slept sitting, knees hunched up to chin, and woke up to find ourselves still dripping wet ! Essex Farm ! There was nothing of the farm left here—it was simply a dreary field by the side of the road. We drudged about in the rain, getting the stores out of the lorries, had breakfast (and these were the times when bully and tea seemed a feast of the gods), and then tried to move the guns to their positions in the field. Impossible—they sank deep in the mud ; we gave wastefully of our strength, but the tractors had to be sent for again, and at length the guns were brought in.

" A blurred memory—blurred by rain," that is how one man sums up his impressions of the eight days at Essex Farm. We had to be out for much of the day on shoots, some of them the usual long ones, though there was no great zero [1] strafe, and nearly

[1] Zero hour is the hour when the infantry attack, and the artillery begins the barrage and bombardment.

41

always it was out in the drizzling rain that we had to work, with wet fingers, screwing the fuses on, with muddy handspikes, and ropes greasy with mud, moving the trail deep-sunk in its muddy bed. We were wet on and off for a week, and in the rare intervals of bright weather our clothes dried on us. It was known that this position was only a temporary one, so our dug-outs were of the crudest—elephant irons resting on low sandbag walls, the ends open in some cases, so that the men sleeping there enjoyed an extra wetting when the rain drove in. What a life! One man's boots had shrunk so much with the wet that he was unable to wear them ; a big fellow all round, there were none—of his size—in the " Quarter's " Stores, and he had to spend five bootless, useless days in the damp dug-out. He wasn't happy. Nor were we.

Some men from 401 Siege Battery were at this time attached to us, so much had we fallen below strength. They were a set of good fellows, and, amongst other things, they brought us now an element of cheer by taking over our cookhouse (which was, in our hands, even less a success now than at other periods), and showing us what splendid meals could be produced from the unvaried army rations. Parcels now were even more welcome than usual. " Had a gooseberry tart to-day ; jolly good." " Supper of sardines and tinned fruit "—such are typical notes. But don't think, gentle reader, because we obtained these delicacies (many of them through the self-denial of our people at home, which, be sure, we appreciated) that therefore all was well with us. Suppose we had had a respectable supper, and even written up

our diary (" Pause," reads one entry, " while I move
into a fresh position, as the rain is dripping down my
neck "), and then got down to sleep : what fun was
it, do you think, to have to leave even these hovels
for a long shoot in the hopeless hours of the night, or,
as happened most nights, to have to clear to a flank
because Fritz was dropping shells all about them, and to
return half an hour later, wet and wretched, to our
blankets ? Happily our casualties here were few ;
Morris and one of the R.G.A. sergeants were wounded.
On one occasion when shrapnel was coming over,
men caught out in it found the queerest of shelters—
the front part of a Tank, which had stuck, crossing
the railway line.

At length on August 9th another move forward
was made, with two guns, and this time we did get
beyond the Yser Canal.   Fairly high banks lie on each
side of this terribly famous waterway, and the several
roads slope downwards to wooden bridges, narrow but
strong, constructed by our skilful engineers.   It was
tricky work, crossing for the first time Bridge 4 that
night, for the Boche made a point of intermittently
shelling the bridges ; but we got along without hurt,
and spent the makeshift kind of night—dossing down
anywhere—to which we were becoming accustomed in
new positions.   Happily the weather had turned finer,
though there had been sharp showers during the day.
We were not struck with this new position—Burnt Farm,
as it was called.   The guns were in a sloping field on
the right, 200 yards or so from the road (the tractors
having drawn them straight into this position, for we
had learnt so much from our experience at Essex Farm).

We were at a bend in the road ; a Decauville ran across it ; near by was a big R.E. dump, and a little way off was a cross-roads.   One of these alone was sufficient to attract Boche fire ; put all together, add that batteries were congregated thickly in this neighbourhood, and it will not seem surprising that shells were coming over at all hours, and that we suffered, in proportion, our heaviest losses here—which might well have been multiplied but for good luck.   We would hear shells dropping one or two hundred yards away, and find out afterwards that half-a-dozen poor fellows on the 8-inch gun behind us had been killed or wounded ; or, again, perhaps the Boche would put an H. Vick or two on the roads, and knock out, as we learned later, several men of a Labour Corps working there.   A good fellow, Oulsnam, of our battery, was mortally wounded,—Miller seriously, on the 12th ; they were in a queue by the cookhouse waiting for dinner when Fritz suddenly opened out.   Again, on the 17th, about four o'clock, he started a strafe on the 8-inch battery.   The early shells fell short of the target.   The first one sent our men off the position to the dug-outs, but a second shell came before one of them, Fogden, had got there, and killed him.   He was an exceptionally cool fellow, and as true a friend as a man could desire.   Another fatal burst of fire took place a day or two later in the evening.   Bannister and Emson, brothers-in-law, were sitting on a low dug-out talking, and were both hit by the first shell, Bannister seriously. He was put on a stretcher, and Bishop and Hayward were taking him down to the dressing-station when another shell, bursting near, knocked them down, and wounded Hayward. Bannister, a quiet, pleasant fellow, died of his wounds.

Our other two guns came up on the 12th. We were soon at our old task of changing billets, for the mere tarpaulin shelters at first put up by no means satisfied us when we discovered what an unhealthy spot this was ; so a number of dug-outs were made in a trench on the left of the road, where we companied with some of the men of 2A Battery, a number of whom were again attached to us as a working party. The officers, also, changed their dug-outs from one side of the road, which Fritz had been shelling, to the other. As soon as the transfer was made, he shelled the other side ! Those who remained in the original " bivvies " [1] above ground improved them with elephant irons and sandbags, to be at least splinter proof. It was in one of these that Dyer was wounded without his knowing it—for some time at least ; which, however, is a not uncommon experience in casualty cases. It was at night, and he and his comrades were trying in an interval of being shelled to get a little sleep, they lying side by side and he at their feet. He felt a big kick in the back, a not unlikely sensation in that position, especially if his chums had been sharing in a cucumber which one of the observers had brought back in triumph from Pop. A couple of hours later, at 4 a.m., they all went out on a shoot, and Corporal MacMillan, ever considerate, insisted on looking at the tender spot, found it bruised, and at the dressing-station it was discovered that Dyer had actually a fragment of shell in his back.

[1] *I.e.* bivouacs.

It was a dull, pedestrian life nowadays.   The novelty
that had stimulated us at Ypres had worn off ; there
was not the spaciousness and greenness which had made
Trois Tours, with all its strenuous work, attractive.
The hopes of July 31st had largely died down, and we
could not see the war ending yet.   All we saw in
prospect was a continuance of this hard, grinding
labour in this country repulsive to look at.   No
change from day to day ; the only excitement that
of avoiding death.   And one by one men were dropping out from our midst—killed, wounded, sick. Well,
well—it had to be stuck.

The day off at Pop., in fact, though highly enjoyable, did not really provide sufficient relaxation,
coming as it did only once in eight or nine days.   The
dug-outs at Trois Tours were still kept on as a rest-
billet for the men that had to be excused duty, but
the conditions were hardly perfect for invalids, since,
horse-lines being near, Fritz came over bombing
nearly every night ; one night John Simon was
wounded with a bomb-splinter.

Our most notable shoot from Burnt Farm was an
aeroplane shoot on the 12th.   We dropped on the target
almost at once—indeed, in ranging we got three
O.K.s and a dozen Y.s (next to O.K.s) ; and then,
the satisfied aeroplane leaving us, we proceeded to
put 300 rounds on the battery.   So successful was
this shoot that the Brigadier-General rang us up to
congratulate us.   Poelcapelle was a frequent target
of ours nowadays.   On the 16th there seemed to be
a push on our front, for at 4.45 a.m. we found ourselves opening out with all the other batteries in the

neighbourhood. As a matter of fact, this was the second stage of the great offensive, and gave us Lange-marck. And it was the British success this day, anticipated for some weeks, which enabled us at length to make the move forward which we had been led to expect.

Turco Farm had been chosen for our definite position forward, and an advance party was at work for some days there—as usual under that indefatigable man, Bishop ; but their reports were not favourable—" a rottener place still than this," they said, throwing down their spades in disgust, as they returned of an evening to Essex Farm. And when we saw the place ourselves we were almost inclined to agree. Going up past Hammond's Corner, with the long, low rise of Pilckem Ridge to our left, we were in the country which the one side and the other had contested for three years, and it seemed now not for a minute like an ordinary, cultivated countryside, not even like a tract of wild nature—it was nothing but the arena of war, with the litter of war all about it—old trenches, rusting iron, ugly shell-holes, and hovels, low and mis-shapen, of iron and timber ; a little patch of grass here and there, even a fragmentary hedge, but all torn about and bedraggled by shell-fire.

Here, near the old British front-line trenches, was to be our position. The guns, brought up on the night of August 20th, lay, amidst shell-holes, just to the left of the Ypres-Poelcapelle road, and the billets were well to the left of them, also amidst shell-holes now, but really on the site of the farm buildings, of which nothing remained but the brick foundations

and two great gate-posts. The dug-outs in time
became so numerous as quite to form a colony,
clustered around the big farm pond, a row of half-a-
dozen which bore away at right angles from the pond
rejoicing in the name of " Sea View."   On the further
side of the pond stood the ruined " Avenue "—a
dozen tall shattered trunks, clean shorn of branch
and twig.

From the beginning it seemed as if this was going
to be an unhealthy spot for us. The first night had
been calm, and we were working at the guns and dug-
outs the next morning when two or three shots, a
salvo, came roaring over and burst a little distance
in front. It seemed best to clear, and that quickly.
We moved back, and found Fritz was continuing, and
we had need to retreat further and further back until
we reached some trenches over half a mile away, and
let Fritz work his will on our position. Here, there,
and everywhere he put them, a vigorous pummelling
of the whole area for a couple of hours, during which
we, keeping well in the trenches, were standing in
nearly two feet of water. When at length he eased
off we actually found ourselves near Burnt Farm, and
picked up some dinner there. These " area-strafes "
were a favourite exercise of Fritz in these months ;
for he knew that the country was packed with artillery,
and that if he only covered generally the area, he was
bound to do some damage.

But there were particular causes too, here, as at
Burnt Farm, of our catching a good deal of Fritz's
fire. We were by an important road. A Decauville
railway ran between our billets and guns, and

crossed the road just by us ; near it there was a
big dump, and through the Avenue ran a duck-board
track, used by infantry, which the Boche had spotted.

However, there was plenty of work to be done to
keep us from troubling about Fritz's attentions,
except when they were forced on us.   There were as
large numbers of shells as ever to drag about and fire
off.   And a great deal of interest was taken in building
dug-outs, which were more in the nature of private
residences than at previous positions.   Three or four
chums would join together to erect one—something
fairly substantial, as the battery was likely to be
here some time.   This entailed, first, much scrounging ;
sandbags, perhaps, might be officially supplied, but
other things—elephant-irons, planks, duck-boards—
you had to " win " on your own, from various sources,
when there was nobody about.   And then you were
held up for cartridge-boxes for the sides ; everybody
else was wanting these, nearly everybody else had
taken some, and the cooks had collared the last !
Never mind, plenty of firing nowadays ; it wouldn't
be long before another thirty cartridges had been
used, and then we would certainly have those two
empty boxes.   So, bit by bit, a dug-out was put
together, and though to the civilian it would seem " only
a tumble-down nest," yet it was a little home, with
camaraderie, if not love, waiting there, a happy
sharing of parcels and puffing of pipes together, and
at times a good-humoured hand at cards.   Some
skilful builders put little fireplaces in their dug-outs,
and old stumps of trees were hacked about to provide
fuel.   Most of these little cabins stood four feet high

4

(not sunk into the ground at all), and were just long enough for a six-footer to lie in. Of course they were not like those at Ypres for strength ; shells would not bounce off them. But they were splinter-proof— a valuable consideration, since a shell bursts only on three or four feet of ground, but, with an instantaneous fuse, its splinters fly three hundred or more yards.

The daily programme, and the nightly too, was as before—strafing and being strafed. One day there would be seventy-five rounds sent off from each gun, interrupted twice by the Boche's dropping a few 5·9's and 8-inch about, and driving us, if circumstances permitted, to shelter; then the next day he might keep us off the guns for several hours. Perhaps we fired a couple of hundred rounds the day after, and only had a few shells anywhere near, and this might be followed by a regular strafe of the battery. Take, for instance, an account of September 3rd, as given in one man's diary :

"After dinner Fritz started shelling, and is still going on (4 p.m.). He has got on to the battery nicely, and has set all our cartridges alight. He is using 8-inch, 5·9 and 4·2 shells, and is very near here at times, so that nearly everybody has cleared out. Our fuses are popping away merrily, I can hear. I thought I would write it all up now as my thoughts are fresh, and in case anything does happen, I should like my diary to be up to date.

"The 8-inch have stopped just now. I expect counter-battery are on their track. Oh, no ! here they are again.

"4.45 p.m.—Have just had a shave. I thought I

need not waste time, even if Fritz is shelling. Wrote
a letter home ; Fritz has stopped, so have posted it.

" 5.45.—He has started again ; nothing much more
to relate. [Next day.] Fritz appears to have had a
direct hit on the observers' stores during his strafe
yesterday."

Fritz seemed particularly to disapprove of the
attempted beautifying of our position. We put up
a canteen, an elaborate affair ; he blew it to bits
in forty-eight hours. We were making a more spacious
cookhouse ; he ruined that, along with much good
provender, and we had to be content with our former
unhygienic wigwam.

Sometimes now we actually had a little free time
in the evening. Then, if it was fine, we could lie out
on the remnants of grass and read the Blighty papers,
or crawl into the dug-outs and improvise some high
supper—soup, perhaps, rabbit, or curried bully ;
borrow a gramophone and roar out a song or two, and
drink a good draught of rum. And then to sleep,
and be awakened by a gas-alarm. Yes, there they
were, falling somewhere near. "The Major has
ordered us to clear till it's all over " ; or perhaps we
were too sleepy to move, and then, resigned to whatever happened—but keeping our gas-masks handy—
we fell off to sleep again. After a big strafing with
gas one night, we saw many dead rats lying about in
the morning.

During this latter part of August there was a certain
lull in our great offensive, but various local attacks
were made round St. Julien, to our right. We co-
operated in these. Thus on August 27th we took part

in a great strafe which started at 1.55 p.m. and lasted till 8. Our target was VD1, a Boche battery near Spriet. The chart of the hostile battery map-square will show how their artillery was ranged on the Ypres front, and also illustrate over what long distances counter-battery work can be of use to infantry. (On

• SPRIET

1000 YARDS

1000 YARDS

C. 8000 YARDS

VD5 · VD2
VD3 ···
VD1 ··· VD7
·VD4 ··· VD6

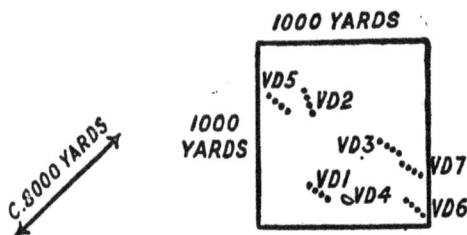

OUR POSITION ON
PILCKEM RIDGE

C. 4000 YARDS

• ST. JULIEN

some map-squares one would see six times as many batteries marked as these.)

On September 7th, in the course of a short strafe by the Boche, a shell dropped full on a dug-out in the Avenue, killed Heathcote and Upsdale, and mortally wounded Read. All three were good fellows; Heathcote's bright humour had often cheered his comrades, and their loss greatly distressed the battery.

Now, on the 12th, came a blessed relief—a four days'
rest at Millain.   No one but soldiers who have lived
in similar circumstances can conceive the lifting of our
spirits, the unspoken gratitude, not to the Army, but
to Providence, that we experienced as we emerged
from these terrible waste lands where death had been
ever our neighbour.   No wonder that when we arrived
at our destination, after a long ride in omnibuses,
we were " hoarse with much singing, but very pleased
with ourselves."   It was like a re-birth to be in
ordinary peaceful life again.   The sound of a cock
crowing, a little child crying—these were wonderfully
delightful to men so long out of the world of normal
human beings.   There were two big marquees for
the two sections, and rich, varied, and joyous was the
conversation in them each night.   It was nearly five
months since we had come out, raw men, from
Blighty.   Had we in our civilian career had one adventure or escape, such as we had had scores of in those five
months, it would have been an incident to relate for
life.   Up the line they had become a matter of course
—hardly calling for mention ; but here our tongues
were unloosed ; we looked back musingly, appreciatively, over these recent days.   It was delightful, too,
to wake up in the morning, and not know when you
had to go on the guns again : you were gloriously
free now.   There was a beautiful view if you walked
up on the hills—which it was a joy merely to see after
Ypres flatness ; or for the asking you could have a
pass and go into St. Omer, there to find out, not the
glories of G.H.Q., but the bounties of the estaminets.
(Alas for the dignitaries that overdid this pleasure,

and were C.B. for the remainder of the stay at Millain !)
On one day the lorries were chartered for a trip to
Calais—a splendid day that ! On the Sunday there
was a church parade, appreciated by many, for it was
only now and then, at Trois Tours, that services had
been held.

All too short was the rest, for on the 17th we had
to return in preparation for a big attack on the 20th.
I have altogether failed in my effort to depict existence
in the Ypres salient, if I need to say how we felt as we
left these pleasant pastures of Millain for a further
stay of indefinite length in that tormented land.

Two officers joined us now who remained with us
until the end of the war. Both had already had considerable experience. 2nd Lieut., afterwards Captain,
Chattey, had served with our 1A Horse Battery in
Egypt, on the Canal and against the Senoussi, and
coming out to France in 1916 as an R.F.A. officer,
had been wounded at Bernafay Wood in September ;
after his recovery he had spent some time at Prees
Heath with our reserve. 2nd Lieut. Coleman had
served in France since May 1916 with other siege
batteries ; he had been through the Somme battles,
and been wounded at Montauban.

The Boche gave us a royal greeting back to the
position, putting over about five hundred rounds of
5·9's and 8-inch, the day after our return. We had
a new gun on the road ready to be brought in ; Fritz
ruined that.

For nearly the whole of the next day, September
19th, we ourselves were on the guns, shelling the
Poelcapelle area. In the afternoon Fritz put over

two shells, one minus, one plus, and the men on the
guns were ordered to clear.   Just as they were by
the Decauville line, a third came over, killing Fitness,
and wounding Nicholls, Bull, and three men of the
Queen Victoria Rifles, of whom a party were at present
attached to us.   Fitness was a man whose sterling
character had approved him to all.   The same night
MacCarthy was badly wounded, a shell falling outside
his dug-out, and a splinter going through an empty
cartridge-box in the wall.   This Boche activity was
doubtless part of his usual attempt to minimise our
impending strafe ; but that duly came off on the
20th, when yet another push was made towards
Passchendaele.   It was a rainy, misty morning,
though from Box O.P. the men on duty could see
the smoke-stacks and débris pillars of the barrage
heavily rising from the ground.   Many prisoners
came down the road, and we learned that the attack
had been successful, though pill-boxes had given
much trouble.

But the advance on our front was not a big one,
and we got little relief from it.   The wearing life at
Turco continued.   Something of a novelty was provided by Gothas coming over in the daylight, and
dropping bombs round about ; but it was as before
when shells or gas came over at night, driving the
weary sleepers afield or into the ruined concrete
buildings in the neighbourhood.   The worst night for
gas was the 28th.   In a general strafe Fritz knocked
out one of our guns, and Galbraith and Hasler were
gassed.   Major Edmondson, going out to help, was
himself gassed, and so too was Heller, now a corporal in

the Orderly Room, but who, with the old instinct still
strong in him, had rushed out to help, unfortunately
without his gas-mask on.

Readers at home may remember how, in the autumn
of 1917, they followed with eagerness the frequent reports
of a further push towards Passchendaele ridge and of
fresh hundreds of prisoners being taken. They may
recall the name of Poelcapelle, a village at the base
of the ridge, the greater part of which was at length
captured on the morning of October 4th. Do they
realise how the circumstances robbed the victory of
any attractiveness it may have had ? That morning,
for instance—for we were turned out for the stunt at
5.30, to keep on firing till 3 p.m.—was a wretched,
rainy one, a drizzle that, one would have thought,
would have taken all the spirit out of our infantrymen
going over the top ; and when they went over, what
was it for ? Poelcapelle was long enough ago a wreck ;
what had held us up so far were some extraordinarily
thick and strong concrete dug-outs in the old brewery
and other places there. The land all round that was
captured was, as ever, ugly beyond description. It
was piecemeal gains in such a world that constituted
so much of the war in the Ypres salient. The Higher
Command indeed realised after this particular attack
that, almost certainly, it was now too late in the year
to effect the capture of the ridge. Yet much of the
German strength had been concentrated on this
sector, and circumstances rendered it most desirable
to keep it there. The great Austro-German onslaught
on the Italians, which resulted in the disaster of
Caporetto, was now taking place, and we were bound

to afford our Allies all the help we could. The French, for their part, attacked in October at Malmaison ; we were planning, for the end of November, the Cambrai attack, for which we could spare none too many troops. So, one morning after another, and nearly all wet—October 9th, 12th, 22nd, 26th, 30th, November 6th, 10th, 15th—advances were made towards this terrible Passchendaele Ridge, and many men gave up their lives on those dull mornings in the fall of the year.

Our battery was on the left of the British front of attack, and was in action on each of these occasions. One recalls with tragic interest those old orders that used to come to us : " Operations will be resumed on a date which has been made known to all concerned," or " Such and such a corps are making an attack to-morrow. Zero hour will be notified later." Then, amidst many other directions, would appear our target : " 309 will neutralise VD 23." And later came the note, " Zero is 5.35 a.m." When the action started, British aeroplanes would be up, if the weather per-mitted, acting in co-operation with our batteries, and immediately they observed the flashes of an enemy battery in the area allotted to them, they would send a wireless message down. This constituted an N.F. call ("now firing"), and took precedence over all other orders, and at once the battery that received the call would turn its attention to the Boche guns which were endeavouring to hold up our advance.

CHAPTER IV

NEWSOME'S HOUSE

THE progress of October 4th and 9th allowed of two of our guns going forward on the 10th, and a few days later they were followed by the other two. Our new position was some 1,200 yards in front of Turco. The country, level and open, showed a face of verdure still, and isolated trees were still standing, though hacked by shell-fire; yet here too one seemed lost in a howling wilderness of war and the scars of war. The road went forward amidst gaping shell-holes and torn-up earth, timber oddments and furtive-looking little dug-outs; you looked hopelessly at it, and hopelessly then at the guns firing away there on the right, in what had once been a meadow; and yet more hopelessly you withdrew into your hole of a habitation. For B and C Subs. at least did reach the limit in the way of accommodation here. There was an old pill-box—" Newsome's House "—standing away from the left of the road, and affording a natural billet for the officers on duty; sadly confined quarters, of course, which they had to creep into, so low was the entrance. Under the hither side of this were the " Tin Hut," where B Sub. lived, and the " Chicken Run," where C Sub. lived.

The Tin Hut was a comfortless enough structure, but
it had a uniform arched roof of elephant-iron, and a
man could lie straight in it ; but the Chicken Run—
heaven grant that I may inhabit a dog-kennel before
I spend another couple of nights in such a place I
Diogenes in his tub was more comfortable, and had
less motive for misanthropy. It was a lean-to hovel ;
you crawled in through a three-foot-high doorway,
the sodden blanket which formed the door flapping
in your face as a welcome ; then you unwarily rose
and caught your head on the sloping roof, which, however, gently impelled you to the further side—only
five feet away—where you could just stand up. You
thought with dismay of sleeping here. How in the
world was it to be done ? How were eight or nine
men, six-footers several of them, to " get down to
it " in this place, sixteen feet by five ? Well, it was
done by lying slantwise, but much skill was necessary,
and much good nature too in allowing one another
the requisite space. It was a memorable night when
one man in particular first slept here—an exceptionally long fellow. His dismay was tragic ; his opinions,
freely vented as he woke up every ten minutes during
the night, survive in one's memory still. The flooring
was duck-boards ; fragments of cheese, bacon, mouldy
cigarettes soon slipped beneath, until one slept only
by covering one's nose in the blanket. Yet the Wireless men were at least as badly off, sleeping in a rat-
hole, amidst little streams of water, at the foot of the
Chicken Run. But there was one great set-off to all
this discomfort—we were on the lee-side of the pill-
box, and so were sheltered in the frequent area

strafes to which the Boche treated us here. A and
D Subs. had dug-outs on the other side of the road
near the guns ; they were in the open country, and
not too comfortable when the Boche was strafing ; it
was then a question of clearing off into the wild out
of the scope of his activity, or into an old concrete
dug-out fairly near. To D Sub. dug-out a little
annexe had been built ; Doyle was in this once when
a shell landed into the original portion, blowing nearly
everything west except the gunner.

Very soon after we had come to this new position
we lost some good men. On October 15th Fritz
shelled the area heavily for two or three hours in
the late afternoon, driving all of us to shelter, both
gun-teams and a working party of ten men who had
come up for the day from Turco. We sat in the
dug-outs and listened to the shells coming over and
bursting in one place and another. At length, about
six o'clock, he slackened off, and permission was
given to those who wished, to return to Turco. It
was no pleasant journey ; the area had been full of
activity just when Fritz opened out, and dead horses
now lay strewn along the roadside, and continually
the fresh earth flung across the road called one's
hurried attention to the shell-holes burst open but a
few minutes before. Men indeed thought themselves lucky not to catch one or two odd shells that
were still coming over. Alas ! two men, fast friends,
Cherry and Maylam, were hit. When they failed to
appear at Turco, inquiries were quickly sent through
to Newsome's House, and it appeared that they had
set off from Newsome's with two other men, who,

however, had fallen behind them, but who had now arrived safely at Turco. Search parties were sent out during all the evening, and at length Fulford Brown and Woodcock found the bodies near Kempton Park Corner. A party of men at once proceeded to this spot to fetch the bodies ; they have described the oppression of their feelings as they went at midnight up the deadly silent road, so sinister a place, on their sad errand. Cherry and Maylam were buried in the cemetery by Bridge 4, where lie the bodies of other members of the battery killed at Turco. It was on this same day, October 15th, that we heard of the death of Behar, who had gone to hospital a week before, suffering from gas-poisoning and overstrain.

Minor operations against Passchendaele Ridge were, as has been mentioned, continued by our army during October and November, and we were generally called on to take our part in the " zero " strafes. Particularly does the attack of October 26th stand out. It had been preceded by a day or two's heavy bombardment, and on the day itself—the inevitable wet, gloomy day—we were firing from 5.45 a.m. until the evening. We heard very good reports of the stunt, though it appeared later that in front of us the water-logged ground had held up our men ; on our right the Canadians advanced along the Ravebeek. Fritz sent over plenty of H. Vicks during the day, and one of our officers, Mr. Sheppard, was wounded in the leg. Unhappily, he succumbed in hospital to the effects of the wound and shock.

Apart from zero strafes, which were naturally

infrequent at this time of the year, we were set to fire, systematically and persistently, on battery positions, and, during the night, on roads. There was always work to be done indeed at Newsome's, but life was monotonous there ; day succeeded day, all more or less dismal ; we kept cheerful, but that was the triumph of man over circumstances. Take a typical day, or rather, start it at night, to show how the day was prepared for. A good tot of rum before we got down among the blankets—that certainly was cheering, and enabled us, cramped as we were, to get quickly and warmly off to sleep. But after a couple of hours there would come the rough cry, " Turn out, you fellows ! Action for B and C Subs. ! " and, rubbing our eyes, and slightly " terse," we would pull our boots on, and roll out into the darkness. Across the road—with a sudden exclamation, " Hullo, he's dropping them about ! But " (as another fell) " not too near "—we trailed after the sergeant or corporal, and so into the field, he flashing his torchlight upon the track, and the rear-most man cursing at the haste of the party as, far away from the light, he slipped off the duck-board and got well muddied. Then ten or twenty rounds are sent off, with perhaps the gun working badly—for in this sodden soil the spade could not grip well, and the gun consequently moved about on the platform a great deal. At length, " That makes the twenty, surely, sergeant," says some one (who hasn't been counting), longing to be done with the dull game ; it is allowed that it **does,** and we trail back to the dug-outs again. It **was** twelve when we went out ; it is nearly two now. We are quickly asleep, and happy if we're not called out for another hour or two's shooting during the night. At half-past eight in the morning we are rudely aroused : " Come on there, breakfast up ! " and we open our heavy eyes, " Oh, good heavens, raining again ! " So we make a rush across to the cook-house, and get our porridge and bacon, and entreat that we, being honourable and well-deserving soldiers, may have our bread dipped in the bacon-fat. We munch away in our dug-outs, put a pipe on, and then, soon after nine, go out on to the guns. Many men have lately had strong mackintoshes and gum-boots sent out to them ; indeed, the " Quarter's " Stores have issued twelve pairs of " boots, gum, thigh," intended, so the signallers say, for their sole use, but which the gunners, and particularly the Numbers 1, have been glad to find, are more generally distributed. Such equipment is certainly needed as we squelch about the position, pushing shells along the little Decauville line which somehow manages to run through the quagmire, or cleaning the muddy shells with a bucket of water from a neighbouring shell-hole—this latter a stationary occupation, which permits one to muse mournfully on this life in comparison with what we have been used to, until suddenly there is the old sound " -s-s-sh, crash ! " and a few bits of mud come flying about. " Any one hurt ? No ? Then clear," shouts the officer on duty, and off we clear into a dug-out or out into the wilds on a flank. When the strafe is over we return to the gun, perhaps to give Fritz a taste of what he has just given us.

Let us hope by this time the weather has cleared up, and we can eat our dinner comfortably, standing around the cook-house. The dinner is practically always stew and rice, but these are appetising enough nowadays, with Lillicrap and Higgins in the cook-house. Perhaps this is the day when, over dinner, we are proud to hear of a plucky deed done in the strafe of the morning. Some Labour Company men working on the road were caught by a shell, three killed and two wounded. MacMillan and Smart ran up to them, followed by Mr. Edmondson, Challis, and Woodcock, and carried the wounded men to Minty Farm dressing-station up the road. Shells dropped about them as they went, blowing them once flat on the ground, but they achieved their journey without any damage beyond a severe scratch to one of them. Or it may be a week later, and now we are hearing that through this incident the first decorations have come to the battery, the Military Cross for Mr. Edmondson and the Military Medal for Woodcock. Anyhow, after a chat and a smoke, it's out to the guns or shell-humping again—another dull afternoon until at length dusk comes on, and we thankfully retire for tea. By now, perhaps, the mail has come up ; eagerly we read our letters, and doubtless amongst the set of us there's a parcel or several parcels to supplement the bread and jam for tea, or to furnish cake, sausage-rolls, or bacon for supper. So, perhaps with clothes drying on us, we sit, crowded together, for the three or four hours of an evening, pleased even with " Chicken Run " accommodation after the cheerlessness of the outer world. We sharpen our tongues on one another with rough invective, and welcome the rum issue as heartily as we did twenty-four hours ago.

A frequent topic of our conversation was—breeches ! Alone, I think, amongst siege batteries we had the privilege of wearing breeches instead of trousers. Unfortunately, it was difficult to avail ourselves of the privilege. The breeches we were issued with at Headquarters or the Base were wearing out, and our " Quarter's " Stores could obtain for us only trousers. We wanted to preserve our high estate and distinctive nether garments, and we made many a journey to one part and another of the district where we thought we might obtain breeches. Sometimes we were successful, often not. Men clung to their original attire for months until it became thoroughly disreputable, and needs must they take to the pedestrian garb which their minds abhorred. By the summer of 1918 we had become a composite crowd in this respect— many in smart breeches, others in trousers worn in an ordinary infantry fashion, but yet others with their trousers pulled long over their knees in base imitation of the style of Guards' officers. However, it was not these gentlemen, but rather those that wore Burberries and very " posh " caps, or had a grave, impressive step and a swagger oilskin, who used always to receive— and, like Field Marshals, return—salutes.

I have described above a comparatively comfortable kind of night ; I must not omit mention of the way in which the gas-guard spent his night, performing a duty which came to each gunner about once a week. By the most pernicious of arrangements— from the point of view of those who lost the toss—

5

two men were on guard from six till midnight, and
then two others had the six hours of the night. Sup-
posing you were one of the unfortunates, you started
your spell of guard by ensconcing yourself in a little
iron erection just behind the guns, where you and
your partner were cheerful for the first hour or two,
eating some grub, then became cold and intolerably
sleepy, and thought with bitterness of another four
hours of this painful trying to keep awake. However,
a shell or two would probably come over to arouse
you. Fritz put a fair amount of gas over at night
here; it might even be, as happened to one man,
that you cleared from the shed because one shell
came near, and so escaped the second, which blew it
up. Anyhow, a gun-team was almost certain to
appear in the small hours of the morning for a shoot;
then it was, " Gas-guard! Gas-guard! What about
the picket-lamp!"¹ Oh, that wicked lamp! It
hung on a stick fifty yards to the rear of the gun;
out into the murky darkness to light it the gas-guard
had to go, and slithered, ere he knew it, down the
side of a shell-hole, picked himself out, and tumbled
forward into another; then, horribly muddy and
cursing sinfully, he went with more caution round
other shell-holes, great and small, while over the
waste came to him the shouts of the indignant gun-
team, urging him to more haste, more slithering.
Well, that lamp was lit at last, and then, when the
gas-guard had scrambled back to his shelter, perhaps
it had gone out, and all was to do again. It was

¹ Used at night as an " aiming-point," by relation to which the
gun is laid on the target.

MAJOR A. J. EDMONDSON

MAJOR J. H. KNOX, M.C.

MAJOR J. C. G. SPOONER.

CAPTAIN A. S. C. CHATTEY

generally two men in a very evil temper who were relieved by the other gas-guards at six in the morning.

A risk to be avoided in gun-work is that of " prematures "—that is, of the shell's bursting before it reaches the enemy's lines. If due care, particularly in cleaning and ramming home the shell, is not taken, it may burst among the infantry in front, or among the gun-team themselves. The worst form of " premature " is that in which the gun-piece bursts at the moment of explosion. We only had two " prematures " during all our time in action, and, curiously enough, both took place at Newsome's. In the first case, the shell, for a cause not ascertained, burst when only a few feet from the gun, and wounded Lane, Elphick, and Kirk. The second accident was quite explicable. D Sub. were about to leave the gun, and were leaving it just ready for firing, the " pulling-off " lanyard hanging down by the side ; it was exceptional to leave it thus, and one man, not noticing the lanyard, trod on it, and the gun went off. This was not really a " premature " ; the shell travelled far enough, of course, and probably troubled some Boche, as it was meant to, but the unexpected shock troubled some of our men a bit too.

It was while we were at Newsome's that Major Edmondson left the battery, his eyes being affected by gas. The memory of his cool leadership, invaluable for any body of men whatsoever during its initiation into active service, ever remained with the battery he had so ably commanded. Captain Knox succeeded him as O.C. On October 31st the Earl of Denbigh, Colonel of the H.A.C., accompanied by Sir Lucas

Tooth, visited Turco, and addressed the men there.
Here too it may be mentioned that at the same time
as the decorations above referred to were awarded,
Captain Knox received the Military Cross and Sergeant
Tansley the Military Medal for having extinguished,
under shell-fire, camouflage that had caught alight.

Another attack in this area was now being planned,
and in order that we might help effectively in it, we
were ordered early in November to secure a new
position. One was accordingly chosen about a mile
forward, and working parties went up there daily.
It was not the most cheerful of experiences. The
way lay along a road that showed every morning
fresh O.K.'s ; then, past a German cemetery, you
followed a duck-board track, on one side or the other
of which Fritz was nearly always dropping his shells ;
often enough, you had, yourself, to dive into a shell-
hole because he was dropping them too close. The
position itself lay in country so vile that it almost
drove you mad to look around, and nearly every day,
as you worked, the Boche shells crept in closer and
closer, and finally forced you and your party well
away. One day, when a G.S. wagon was up there,
unloading stores, a shell came almost on top of it,
wounding two men, Hornsby and the A.S.C. driver,
and killing the horses. No guns were brought up,
for the Boche appeared to have direct observation
of the position, and after a time it was abandoned.

CHAPTER V

IT became necessary once again to find a new forward position, and soon a spot was selected beyond the Steenbeck, and indeed beyond the Langemarck-St. Julien road, a move which resulted in our being again the most forward siege battery on this sector of the salient ; there was, in fact, a 4·5 battery behind us, and a 60-pounder to our left rear. Hannix-beek Farm, from which our position took one of its names, was the term applied to a small heap of bricks that we passed on the hither side of the Langemarck road as we went up the duck-board track to the position. Dog's Body was another name we used—the origin apparently being the quite valid idea that even a dog could only live here as a corpse. Drear and desolate, indeed, beyond words did the scene appear even to eyes accustomed to Turco and New-some's. A wide plain stretched before us—a plain of shell-holes joined by greasy, yellow mud. No sign of kindly Nature anywhere—no grass, no hedges ; nothing of man's useful labours, only the earth torn, ruined, degraded, as the fell work of man's destructive powers. On our left stood a long line of shattered

skeletons of trees; they marked where ran, in a
somewhat deep gully, the little stream of the Lekke-
boterbekke, dismal and encumbered with débris.
Beyond the stream the ground rose slightly, while,
limiting the dreariness in front of us, could be dimly
seen the higher land around Westroosebeke, the exten-
sion of the Passchendaele Ridge.

It will perhaps be no wonder, then, that when
Captain Chattey halted the first digging party amidst
this scene, and said, " Here is the new position,"
involuntarily we questioned, " Where ? " He pointed
it out, and we did indeed perceive a couple of tolerably
large squares of ground amongst the shell-holes. The
weather had been persistently wet, and our first duty
was to try to drain the water away from the selected
sites. Oh, that clinging, viscous Flanders mud !
We tried to dig little channels between one hole and
another ; the spade could hardly be withdrawn from
the octopus-like grip of the mud, and then, immediately one had withdrawn it, with the smallest
quantity of mud on it, the mud closed in again on the
hole, like a foul, slimy quicksand. Happily, in a few
days, the weather set in frosty, and our labours were
better repaid. Had it not been so, indeed, we could
never have placed the guns in position.

So clayey and soft was the soil here that we had
to lay down gun-platforms of a special kind. It
would not have been sufficient to place, as usual,
strong planks on the ground ; we had first to sink
fascines in it, throw road-metal on the intervening
spaces, and on this surface rest a double-deck platform, well nailed together, of beech-slabs. Similarly,

AERIAL PHOTOGRAPH, SHOWING THE HANNIXBEEK POSITION AND POEL-
CAPELLE AREA WHEN IN GERMAN OCCUPATION, JULY 28TH, 1917

To Langemarck

Rat House

To
Langemarck

Hannixbeke
Farm

Suspected
German
Bty

3og Pos.ᴺ Dec 1917

German
Bty

Bulow Farm

Lekkeboterbeek

TRENCHES

To Langemarck

Pheasant Farm

Cemetery

To Poelcapelle

N
E
W
S

To St. Julien

To Zonnebeke

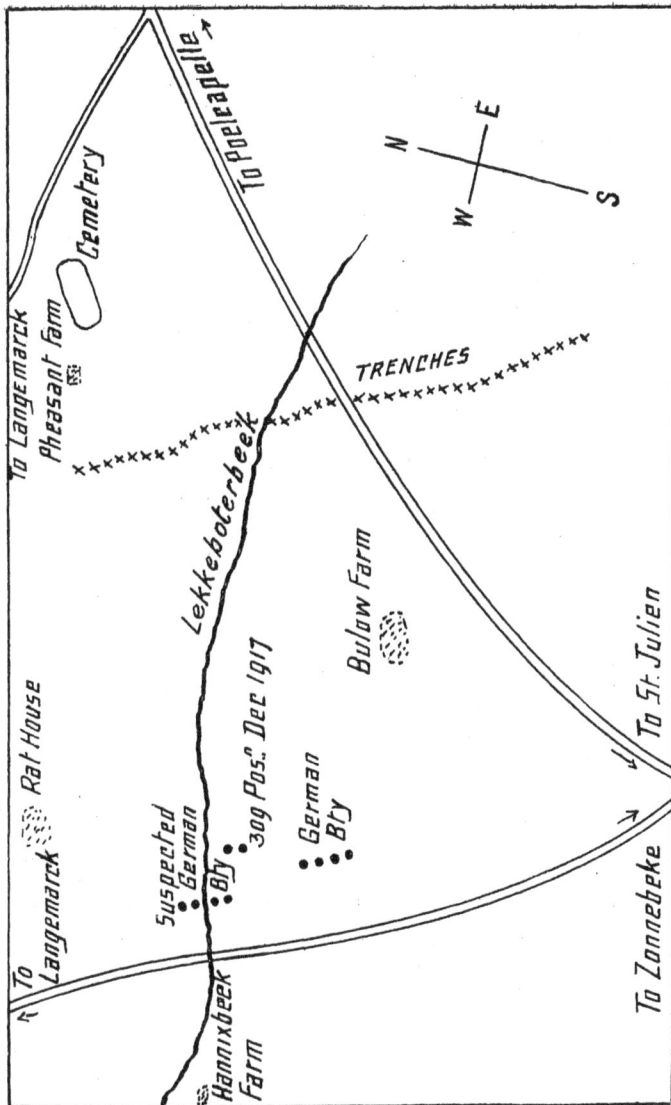

KEY TO AERIAL PHOTOGRAPH OF THE HANNIXBEEK POSITION ON JULY 28TH, 1917

for trail supports, we had to drive in a quarter-circle of seven-foot stakes, in which we interwove some more fascines. Then, on November 25th, the two guns were brought up by gallant teams of eight horses, this being the only occasion on which horses did us this service. It was, too, the first time the guns had travelled to a position by daylight ; but, in this dull weather, it was judged that the risk of Boche 'planes observing us was very slight, and could be taken. A couple of days' hard work now lay before us, for we had to man-handle the guns from the roadside to the position, a distance of at least two hundred yards, over ground pitted with big shell-holes, and along the middle of which ran a Decauville railway whose raised track presented a tremendous obstacle. Three and a half tons is the weight of a six-inch howitzer —and we had reason to know it. A temporary plank road had to be made over part of the ground to be traversed, while over the latter half, strong wooden troughs, specially constructed for this occasion, were used. It was as continuous a piece of pulling on a gun as the battery ever did, and by six o'clock in the evening, when in the darkness we were still straining our muscles on the rope, the " Together heave, lads," and " Fresh purchase," had become very tedious. A Labour Company was assisting us, but they, lucky fellows, went off at two each day. However, the guns lay at last on their platforms, " pointing at the foe," and when our Brigade Colonel came up he congratulated Major Knox and the Numbers 1, Sergeant Bishop and Corporal MacMillan, on the achievement, saying he had never seen guns

in such a position before. While we were at work
there was a figure standing by whom we did not yet
know, a sturdily-built man in a ranker's tunic, who
now and then gave us sound, practical hints. Soon
we came to learn how characteristic these were of our
new officer, Mr. Baugh, a blunt, friendly man, whose
pluck and capacity had just won him a commission in
the field.

Meanwhile, where were the gun-teams to sleep?
There was an old Boche pill-box to the right rear of
the position, and behind this a party of R.E.s rapidly
built us a long dug-out of elephant-iron, with sandbags at the base. It was quite a palatial erection for
that front—one could actually stand up in it, walk
along it! For safety the floor was a couple of
feet beneath the ground; the disadvantage of this
it was left to our successors, in wet weather, to
find out.

Our first shoot was on November 28th, when we
proposed to register on Spriet Mill, Major Knox
directing from Maison du Hibou. Proposed indeed!
We went little further! The gun-platforms were
good, the dug-out was comfortable, the Boche seemed
to have no particular hostility to our area, and Mr.
P. H. Edmondson remarkèd, with his usual gaiety,
about 1.30 p.m., " You know, I like this position. I
think I shall ask the skipper to let me have permanent
charge of it." A few minutes after came the call,
" Both guns, action!" Out we ran across the hard
ground, laid and loaded the guns, and to inaugurate
the proceedings fired a salvo. Another round or two
from each gun, when—crash! a hundred yards to

our left rear ; almost before we had caught sight of
the smoke and débris arising from that shell, another
had burst much nearer to us, and simultaneously
came another, twenty yards from our left gun.   It
was a Boche salvo !   He was retaliating with a vengeance.   " Clear ! " shouted Mr. Edmondson.   Hurriedly we put the camouflage on, and doubled back
to the dug-out.   The concert had started.   Crash !
in all directions round about they fell.   Mr. Edmondson
went more than once to the door of the dug-out to
see where they were dropping, only to be driven back
by a shower of mud from bursts forty or fifty yards
off.   We sat and tried to enjoy it.   " I don't think I
like this position quite so much now," remarked Mr.
Edmondson after a time.   Crash ! crash ! ! they continued to fall, and to keep our minds occupied, he
suggested a sweepstake on the number of shells that
came over.   The successful, because the average,
number was 182, but actually it was computed that
near three hundred fell in the fifty minutes the bombardment lasted.   Gradually the bursts became less
frequent, and died off altogether.   It was a general
area-strafe, not directed on us particularly, yet we
had cause for deep thankfulness that no shell had
landed on our dug-out.   After that, we set to work
to make a false roof of lengths of railway-line, and
eventually were able to delude ourselves into the
belief that a 5·9 O.K. on the dug-out would not
harm us.

Our occupation of Hannixbeek lasted for over three
weeks.   The opening experience, it will be agreed,
had not been a pleasant one, but on the whole this

position ranks among our best from the point of view
of personal feeling. The desolateness of the country,
of course, did not diminish, but one became accustomed to it. The weather was healthy almost the
whole time, hard and frosty ; one felt invigorated as
one came out into the keen air in the morning, even
though one looked but on gaunt tree-trunks and ice-
bound shell-holes. There was the usual hard work
on shells to keep us fit, and then of course guns and
platforms needed frequent attention. We of C Sub.
were lucky with our platform, and the gun moved
easily. But B gun seemed very frequently to drift

"From the strict centre and the angelic line."

Then there was a cry, " Help us pull out, C Sub."
" Oh, hang it ! there they are again," some of us
would say ; or others, " Delighted, I'm sure." A
rampart had to be thrown up in front of each gun
to keep off splinters as far as possible. And once or
twice, tired towards the end of the afternoon, we
were quite glad when a shell dropped not too far
away. " Come on, let's clear "—if the sergeant didn't
say it to us, we said it to him.

And then the long evenings in the dug-out ! We
were a larger number living together than had been
the case at any of our former positions, and perhaps
were correspondingly merrier. There we sat on our
bundles of kit in that long dug-out, ten men a side—
two rows of figures, animated or reposing, shown up
by the light of a candle here and there ; we chatted,
chaffed, unceasingly smoked, played cards or chess,

passed the rum round, even on one occasion com-
plimented Schollar, the cook (always a worthy man
in that department), on a wonderful variant he had
provided us in dinners—steak and onions, rice and
figs. So close was the atmosphere that, even though
it was a cold December, we were always warm in there,
without any artificial heating arrangement ; indeed,
the condensed moisture dropped off the iron arches,
under which we were sitting, upon our hair. Sometimes we discussed the probable length of the war,
its rights and wrongs. There was at this time a strong
disposition, natural enough amongst men living the
life to which soldiers were condemned, to criticise our
Government for having failed in the past year to
make peace. Yet we knew where guilt lay, and we
agreed heartily with the indictment of Germany
which one of us read out aloud from Mr. Gerard's
recent book, while we commiserated with ourselves
on the vivid picture drawn there of our position. " Is
it not a shame," he wrote, " that the world should
have been so disturbed ? That peaceful men are
compelled to lie out in the mud and filth in the depth
of raw winter, shot at and stormed and shelled, waiting
for a chance to murder some other inoffensive fellow-
creature ? "

From the beginning, however, every second or
third evening heard song and mirth arising from our
midst. Corporal Cundell, of C Sub., suggested these
informal concerts, and was generally the chairman—
and a jovial one too. Greenhow was our principal
vocalist, his store of musical-comedy songs being, as
frequently, a great asset to his comrades. And how

the chorus would surge upward as we sang with
Schollar about

> " The little black girl who sat upon a stile,"

or echoed Morris's inspiring ditty :

> " O de ham-bone am sweet, an' de bacon am good,
>   An' de 'possum fat an' berry, berry fine ;
>   But give me, ah give me—*ah*, how I wish you would !—
>   Dat water-melon hanging on de vine."

H. J. Jones's songs, Skilbeck's recitations, Mr. Glover's
" Moya, my girl," all helped to make the evenings
enjoyable ; and sometimes Mr. Baugh would describe
his earlier experiences in the war.   I can never hear
now those hackneyed songs, " If you were the only
girl in the world," " Let this great big world keep
turning," and the like, without being carried in
memory back to that low, arched structure behind
the old pill-box, which stood out lonely in that ruined
stretch of country, and feeling myself again with the
score of companionable men who cheered themselves
there against discomfort, danger, and the thoughts,
enervating in their sweetness, their remoteness, of home.

The good luck we had experienced in our first
strafing continued throughout our stay at Hannixbeek. No shell touched our dug-out. Had it been
otherwise——! For bombardments to the full as
severe as that opening one took place on at least
three other occasions, and there was no clearing to a
flank at this position ; we had to stick it in our dug-
out in the midst of it all. Once, as at Turco, there
was a direct hit on the cookhouse which adjoined the
dug-out, and the scattered porridge whitened the roof

of the pill-box.   Well, too, do men recall the supposed
consequences of a shoot we undertook one day on a
Boche pill-box near Westroosebeke.   This was visible
to us, even with the naked eye, and we had the almost
unique experience of seeing each of our twelve rounds
burst.   Several seemed to be O.K.'s, but the pill-box
was still there at the end of the shoot !   The Boche's
eyes were not less good than ours, and about 9.30 that
evening he " let it rip."   We had had a sing-song as
merry as usual, and were laying our blankets down,
when the ground rocked with a sudden burst near us.
Our minds flew from laughter and song to the thought
of danger.   The shells fell heavy, violent, all around
us.   One sat on one's kit and waited ; waited for one
knew not what ;   mentally pictured the roof rent
asunder, and Death descending amongst us all; yet,
with an effort, smiled and chatted with one's companions.   Time after time the earth swayed beneath
us ; twice, so close was the burst, the blast blew out
the candles in the dug-out.   Yet when the strafe
ceased, about 10.5, all were yet alive, though with
nerves jangled by the strain.   A few minutes after
we had ourselves to turn out for a shoot.   Clear,
peaceful, the cool air seemed, which so lately had been
a crashing hurricane of death.   There was a duck-
board track from the dug-out to the guns, a distance
of perhaps thirty yards.   Walking along it as usual
that night we were brought to a halt half-way—the
duck-boards unexpectedly ceased—across the path lay
a great freshly-made shell-hole.   There were at least
two others, as we noticed next morning, equally near
to the dug-out.

Another day there was a stirring incident. The
Boche was seen strafing the 60-pounders on the slope
to our left. Our men had seen the shelling, and had
kept in the dug-out, when a 'phone message came
through from the 60-pounders for stretchers; there
had been a hit on one of their dug-outs, and several
casualties. Captain Chattey dashed straight out with
a stretcher; shells fell by him as he ran, and those
watching from the doorway of our dug-out feared
that he must be struck; but he was not, nor were
Fulford Brown and Challis, who had quickly followed
him, and who, with him, moved the wounded men to
the dressing-station.

The Boche reminded us while at Hannixbeek what
a methodical fellow he was—a characteristic more
marked in the earlier than in these later stages of the
war. For between 8.30 and 8.45 every morning, for
a week or two, he sent us over half a dozen shells, so
that, after a couple of days, we were forbidden to
leave the dug-out during that period. I might even
add here that on one occasion we were not without
danger from our friends. The 4·5's behind us were
one day about to start a shoot, and our officers
mounted on the top of our pill-box to observe it. A
suggestion reached them that they should come down,
as they were right in the line of the 4·5 shells! A
feature of life at Hannixbeek, as we lay at night in
our blankets, used to be the sharp order to those 4·5's,
" Half-minute, battery fire ! " Crack—crack—crack—
crack—crack—crack, they rang out through the frosty
air. It was beautiful gun-work.

As for our own shooting, we had taken up so ad-

vanced a position as Hannixbeek in anticipation of
an attack to be made on the night of December 1st–
2nd.   This was duly made, and we fired in it, but
unfortunately it met with but little success.   We
retained the position, however, and fired (but not too
frequently, as we could often be observed) on batteries,
and at night on roads, our " arc of fire " extending
from Stadendreef almost to Passchendaele itself, but
our chief activity centring round Westroosebeke.

Signallers speak naughtily about Hannixbeek.   Their
'phone lines ran by the duck-board track, a couple of
miles long, which we used in coming up from Newsome's, and this the Boche rarely left alone for more
than an hour or two.   Nearly every night the lines
would be broken, and out into the darkness the
signallers on duty had to go, and grope their way
down the track.   There were thirty or forty lines all
bunched together by the duck-boards, and when you
had come to the break, it was a long job finding the
other end of your own wire among all these.   And
perhaps in the middle a shell or two would come near,
and " awkward knobs " would fly about.   Now and
then, indeed, signallers from other batteries took shelter
in our dug-out, having been caught, when out " on
lines," in a sudden burst of fire.

It was at Hannixbeek that it was first found possible
in our battery for gun-teams to work in two reliefs—
forty-eight hours on and off in turn for each man.
We did not mind now or in future how hard we had
to work or how often we were called out in the night
during our spell of duty, so long as we had the alternate
two days and nights perfectly free.   Down the duck-

boards (assuming they weren't being shelled) in high
spirits we went on the morning we were relieved, picked
up our mail at Newsome's, then on to the repose of
our little dug-outs at Turco, and next day on to Pop.,
where a bath and a change of clothing made us respect
ourselves again, and a good lunch at that friendly
"British Hostel" put us at peace with the world.

CHAPTER VI

" REST . . . DOTH GREATLY PLEASE "

FOR weeks past rumours had circulated that the battery was going out on a long rest, and these seemed to have some foundation when, on December 21st, we did withdraw from the Hannix-beek position. That was a cold, grey day, and the hopelessness of life out here sank into one's heart as one carted gun-stores to a Decauville trolley, and then had nothing to do for ten minutes but look round on that forlorn country

" Where all the face of nature seems a monstrous septic sore ;
  Where the bowels of earth hang open, like the guts of something
    slain,
  And the rot and wreck of everything are churned and churned
    again ! "
                                        " I never saw
      Such starved, ignoble nature ; nothing throve :
      For flowers—as well expect a cedar grove."

A few H. Vicks coming over drove us to the flank, and ended such musing. At 12.30 p.m. we handed over this position to 5 Siege Battery. We had apparently seen the best of it, for a few days after, the dug-out, which had been so comfortable for us, was flooded with a couple of feet of water, and there was some heavy strafing for our successors to endure.

We spent Christmas week scattered about our three old positions, the great majority of the battery being at Turco. Dull days these ! Lucky chaps got into Pop. for a day, but most men were working all the time at Turco, putting up new big dug-outs, though it was very doubtful whether we should need them for long. C. Sub. dug-out was designed with meticulous care, and then, unfortunately, the elephant-irons didn't adapt themselves to the measurements. The two architects were confounded and sad, and the heathen raged. However, the dug-out was erected and then the architects made a rampart of model sandbagging at a very slow rate. The heathen made another with splendid rapidity—it collapsed in a week.

Just now we were gratified to hear that Fulford Brown had been awarded the Belgian " Croix de Guerre " for his coolness on many trying occasions during the recent months.

The weather on Christmas Day was about the worst of the year—a driving snowstorm nearly all day. In the morning we paraded on the Decauville line, and went to a church service in a Nissen hut near by. (This was the occasion when our worthy sergeant-major, endeavouring to hurry up a comparatively new man for the parade, seemed extremely wroth when he got the innocent answer, " All right, I won't be a minute, old man." " Old man be d——d," came his stunning reply, and he took the offender's name, apparently for disciplinary measures ; but of course nothing came of it.) Then we searched for wood. I see still the figure of one Ben, laden with duck-boarding from an

old trench, and slipping down twice with it as we
passed over other trenches, treacherous with frost
and ice, so that in great ire he at length cursed and
left his burden. The issue beef and plum-pudding
were very good, and were supplemented by delicacies
from Blighty, and we had wine in from Pop. ; and in
the evening there were sing-songs at the various positions. We looked cheerful, but the cramped, comfortless conditions on that day of all days made our
minds dwell sadly on home. However, a couple of
days after, the outlook improved ; we were really
going on rest. And any soldier will agree that after
eight months of practically continuous action on the
Ypres front we had some claim to a rest. We were
indeed about to get our share now.

On December 28th then, in army style, we were
aroused unnecessarily early, and spent the morning
hanging about, for the lorries didn't arrive till after
dinner. Then they were packed up, and, in a manner
we were to be familiarised with later on, we ensconced
ourselves amongst the stores in them, and so, hopefully, away. We went through Pop. and out along
the Proven road, and came with delight on pleasant,
cultivated country again ; little copses of ash and
elder, and a beautiful château set amidst shrubs and
fair trees, where multitudinous rooks filled the air
with their noise. What blessed peace, what blessed
calm and cheer for the eyes after that horrible salient !
Here were Belgian farm-carts with their teams of
three horses, the horse in the middle rising above the
two weaker ones ; here men and women driving in
traps, and even girls cycling along ; well, they may

have been the most ordinary of civilians, but it was strange and refreshing to see such again. Three kilos along the road we turned to the left down a hard, knobbly lane, the rich rays of the setting sun shining peacefully on us as we made our way between woods and open fields. So we came to Clifford Camp, a genuine home of rest for most of the battery for the next five weeks.

It was a pleasant little camp, and its ways were pleasant. A double row of Nissen huts had been put up in a big orchard; 109 S.B. occupied the one side, and we the other. Facing the nearer end was the farmhouse, where, having squelched one's way over the farm midden, one could get eggs and sometimes milk at 4 o'clock in the afternoon. Work was very light here. There was a parade at some time in the morning; we had got out of the way of these, and the considerate men in charge didn't require any marked rigidity of posture, and the parades became less and less formal, the rifle inspection, at first a thing of solemnity, being at the end forgotten. After parade we did the ordinary fatigues, and took a hand in improving the camp—some put up matchboarding, some put down duck-boards, some camouflaged the huts; amidst the weird lines of paint on one hut, the initiated can still discern the mystic letters " H.A.C." Sometimes N.C.O.s not of our battery, who were temporarily in charge of us, professed themselves nonplussed. " There's a party given me for a fatigue," said one of them, " I set 'em to work, an' before I can turn round they're all gone but two." No work was done, even nominally, in the afternoon. For the

guard a picket, or policeman, was soon substituted ;
he had to walk round the camp with a stick, and avoid
reporting offenders.

" You are thought here," says Dogberry to his
subordinate, " to be the most senseless and fit man
for the constable of the watch. You are to bid any
man stand, in the prince's name."

" How if a' will not stand ? "

" Why, then, take no note of him, but let him go ;
and presently call the rest of the watch together, and
thank God you are rid of a knave."

One or two men, indeed, who happened to have
committed some light crime (such as crossing Bridge 4
without carrying a gas-mask) were immediately made
camp policemen for the day.

A free, jolly life again—what a treat to enjoy that !
You rushed across the grass in the morning to get
some of the freezing cold water from the dirty well
(partly fed by the water already used for ablutions),
and it was fine to see turf and hedges and no shell-
holes ; you joked about at work (if you had not disappeared)—how different from humping muddy shells
up the line ; and then, after dinner, off you walked
with your pals laughing and roistering into Proven or
Watou. There you could see the pictures, or go
into some comfortable house or café and obtain pork
chops (no meat but pork in this country) and *pommes
de terre frites* and omelettes and wine, and you came
home feeling that it was a good war after all. We
found out an excellent café at Proven, where Sub-
section dinners were arranged—very fine affairs !

There were one or two entertaining mysteries during

our stay here. Twice a hayrick was set on fire, and the culprit not discovered ; one or two wiseacres professed to have inner knowledge, and were urged by their comrades to impart it, but, in whatever condition, they gave no other answer than, " Never you mind." There was something strange, too, about that motor-cycle, as to which, even after this lapse of time, I can say no more than that—it disappeared ! But, talking of strange phenomena, ought we not to mention the fate of that pig which had been bought as Christmas fare for us with money kindly sent from the Court of Assistants ? It lay in our cookhouse at Proven, too big for our cooks to handle, yet night by night it grew mysteriously less in bulk. Had ever substantial beast before so evanescent a body? Rumour had it that the sergeants' mess took one good joint, and whoever wanted a chop went and cut one off. At length we found a friend in the person of 109 cook, who roasted the remainder for us. So ignobly passed poor pig.

We re-started the canteen at Clifford Camp with a big barrel of beer and some tinned fruit, over the sale of which " Jumbo " Symes, an old Gallipoli warrior, presided ; the ease of the post suited him, and he held it against all comers, with a fighting spirit that later found higher scope. A game of football was played now and then, and a match against 109 resulted in a win, 4-0, Lauder scoring most of the goals.

All this time there was a guard left behind at the old positions, and faring very differently. Some had thought that this would prove the real rest, rather than Proven, and so had volunteered to remain at

Turco—they soon found out their mistake. The very first day after the battery had left, it was breakfast at 8 for the men at Turco and Newsome's, and then off on a long tramp of several kilos along the snowy ground to Salvation Corner, where two gun-pits had to be dug. Dug? that seemed impossible! The ground was hard as iron—frozen to a depth of three inches. Depressed at the unexpected demand made on them, even more than by the ineffectiveness of their toil, the men picked and chipped disconsolately for an hour or two until—a brain wave! one man drove a pick right under the frozen surface and levered up a great slab of it. That turned the task into a game, and we went on for days, levering up the biggest slabs we could. We worked morning and afternoon. It wasn't too cheerful in that dull weather, sitting on the floor in a cold Nissen hut, eating a tin of cold bully for dinner, especially when reports came through of the fine goings-on at Proven. However, after a fortnight, all the party on guard were relieved by men who came back from Proven—all, that is, except one unfortunate fellow who, for supposed offences, had been penalised by a high authority one day, and " admonished " by the same two days later. Two gun-pits were now made on Canal Bank. They were splendid pits, more elaborate by far than those we used ourselves ; there were revetment walls around them, fascines and rubble were sunk for backing, and pit-props were driven in. We wondered always why we and other batteries were making gun-positions so many miles behind the line. Nobody seemed to know. The positions at Salvation Corner were amidst the Nissen huts of an R.E.s' camp. "A fine time you'll have here if these gun-pits ever are used," we used to tell them. "Your tin roofs won't stand many 5·9's." But our questions were answered when in March the Boche attacked on the Ypres front as well as on the Somme, Passchendaele was evacuated, and a rear line, in which lay Salvation Corner, was taken up.

We made other gun-positions on Admirals' Road, near to our own settlements at Turco and Newsome's. We went along the first morning under an N.C.O., and were within a hundred or two yards of the place at which we were to work when we suddenly saw there a spit, a burst, and a pillar of smoke rising. It was our old friend, H. Vicks. Fritz dropped them all the morning, and Mr. Glover, approaching from another direction, came coolly over the low rise which he was shelling. Naturally we deferred our start. It was more cheerful this last fortnight on Admirals' Road than the earlier at Salvation Corner. The weather was milder, and there were more of us working together ; indeed, some had been glad to return to Turco, for they had not found Proven, with all its ease, a thoroughly healthy place. We pulled two guns in here on January 22nd, and fired, but only for registration purposes.

The weeks slipped on, and on February 1st the score or two of men still left at Clifford Camp packed up stores and rejoined the rest up in the old positions. But the stay here was not to be for long, and labour such as F Sub. spent in fitting up a hot-water spray bath (a Government issue, but not to them) was but

POSITIONS ON THE YPRES FRONT

poorly repaid. The huge barrel of beer belonging to the canteen had not been drained dry at Proven ; it was now set up in state outside the cookhouse at Turco, and Schollar disposed of the beverage at the wicked price of ninepence a pint. Little did he think this was going to rise up against him in print one day ! There was nothing in the way of work now beyond the necessary fatigues, and a few minutes' rifle drill or gas-drill each day ; and a route march that was attempted one morning was not sufficiently approved of to be repeated, Turco being still within the battle area. I remember wangling three days in Pop. that week on one pretext or other (and cleverer chaps, I am sure, did themselves still better)—happy days, with a good meal, and a comfortable lounge and read in Talbot House, and one most enjoyable evening listening to the " Jesmond Jesters."

February 8th was a day spent in packing all the stores on the lorries, and February 9th saw us early astir and riding down to Pop. So, after nine months' stay here, we left the Ypres front, that land of stark desolation and brooding sorrow, which yet had not failed of appeal to what there was of manliest in us.

CHAPTER VII

A FAIR CORNER OF FRANCE

O Hephaistos, graver-of-silver, make for me no panoply of war—
what have I to do with battles ?—but carve out for me a hollow
wine-cup.
And fashion upon it for me no stars, neither the wagon nor
gloomy Orion.
But carve vines upon it for me and grape-clusters and the Mænads
plucking them ; grave upon it a wine-press and those that tread out
the grapes, and laughing Pans, and the golden Loves.—ANACREON.

WE were arrived at Pop. then. Whither now ?
None of us gunners knew ; we never did
know. On these moves rankers travelled
for days over the slow French railways, and never
learned until they got out where they had been making
for. And on this occasion the R.T.O. at Pop. himself had little use for us. We had arrived before
9 a.m. ; he could not get us away until 9 p.m. at
earliest. With rare common sense—for generally bodies
of soldiers in our position were confined within narrow
bounds and had to spend hours kicking their heels—
our officers allowed us to go out into the town, and
we spent a merry day there. We spent the night,
too, at Pop. station—some in the rest camp, most in
the cattle-trucks. Eventually we left Pop. at 11 the
next morning. We were grouped in our sub-sections
in the cattle-trucks, sets of chums together, so that

we had the cheerfullest of journeys—taking it in turns
to sit at the open door and look out at the fields and
villages en route, passing round to one another papers,
books and the contents of opportunely-arrived parcels,
and snuggling close up to one another in our blankets
during the cold night.   Our train halted at Calais
late in the evening, and we remember gratefully the
helpers at the Salvation Army Hut there ; we knocked
them up about ten o'clock, and they soon had fine
platefuls of bacon and eggs ready for us—a splendid
change after a day of bully beef.

Our train rolled tediously along the next day, with
us still wondering, " Where are we going to ? " Further
south than the Arras sector, anyhow, we seemed to
be making for.   And when in the evening (Monday,
the 11th) we arrived at Abbeville and detrained, a
rumour lately prevalent became fact—we were not
going to another front at all yet !   Where then ?   To
Sailly-Flibeaucourt, to the Fifth Army Artillery School
there, a place which few of us knew had existed
before, but which we were to know thoroughly well
and with considerable pleasure during the next six
weeks.   Sailly is some twelve kilos from Abbeville,
and we mounted the lorries—which, of course, had
come from Pop. by road—for the journey.   But a
bitter experience befell at least two of us here.   We
had to act as brakesmen on C gun, and I can only
hope the brakesmen on the other guns managed better
than we did.   Being told there was a big hill ahead,
we ran behind the gun from the start, instead of
sitting on it and saving our legs.   The guns rattled
off at a good speed, and we were in no condition for

running. A hundred yards saw us panting, a hundred
and fifty desperate, our feet fell uncertainly on the
cobbles, our life seemed escaping from us in anguished
panting as we struggled madly to keep pace with
that tyrannous gun—and then, when at the verge of
collapse, mercy—it was slowing down ; yes, heaven
was kind ! There rose the long hill in front of us, we
could walk !

However, it was better than we had ever hoped
for to be rolling along the fine avenue of the great
Route Nationale that evening. The country was for
the most part open and cultivated. The camp itself
was like Clifford Camp, but on a larger scale. A long
line of Nissen huts, parallel with the shorter series of
officers' quarters, stretched across the upper part of
a great, sloping field. Behind, fumigated with the
smoke from two incinerators, lay tilled land, meadows,
and copses. In the lower part of the field were a
fine football ground, stables for R.F.A. batteries,
and an excellent Y.M.C.A. hut. A noble wood
bordered the field at the bottom-end, and along its
whole length—over a kilometre—ran a grassy way,
undulating but direct, and standing at any point in
it you could look along it to the village end, and see
there the façade of the stately château.

We quickly settled down to the life here, and much
did we appreciate it. Quite a number of the amenities of life were ours here : plank beds, though no
straw, so that it was draughtier to sleep on them than
on the floor ; ablution sheds for decently washing in,
though water was very scarce ; actually there was a
dining-hall, at which we could once more sit down at

table, and even eat, on alternate days, roast joints
(of a sort) again ; and at the Y.M.C.A. we found con-
veniences for reading and writing. And then, outside
the camp, what creature comforts ! Ah, that corner
estaminet, my comrades ! how I used to find you
there by the dozen ! How you used to enjoy the
company there, not less than the wine ! How full of
kindly pugnacity you were as you strolled into camp,
even after lights were out ! And I, my comrades,
how could I advocate the true Prohibitionist doctrine
when I had first eased my throat with a glass of wine
at your expense ! Do you remember how, late one
evening, under the influence, was it ? of the silvery
moon, you projected a boar-hunt (with bayonets) in
famous Creçy's forest ?   It didn't come off, but the
valorous proposal shall never be forgotten. And
who may ever forget the severity shown by our regi-
mental policemen, Wenham and Lowe, under the
inspiration of their sergeant, Woodcock ? They were
as implacable as Dogberry himself, and their methods
were his.

" You are," said Dogberry, " to call at all ale-
houses, and bid those that are drunk get them to bed."

" How if they will not ? "

" Why, then, let them alone till they are sober ;
if they make you not then the better answer, you
may say they are not the men you took them for."

Perhaps it was to avoid our police-friends' strict-
ness, perhaps to get a change from that universal
soldiers' feast—eggs and chips—which alone was
obtainable in Sailly, that often of an evening some of
us used to walk a mile or two across the fields or

through the woods to such pleasant little villages as
Nouvion and Le Titre. When training in London,
little parties of us had always lunched together at
some familiar City house : now we renewed those
early days of friendship round a luscious joint of
pork and a big omelette in a hospitable French estaminet. Rare as such delicacies were, not all of us
had lost our civilian fastidiousness (some indeed never
did, and actually up the line waxed healthy by refusing ever to touch bacon and stew). Once one of
my chums, feeling qualms in his stomach, begged
sadly as we ordered the omelette : " Ask them not
to put too much fat with it." It came on, substantial
and not too oily, but his nerve failed him. " Ask
them," he said hopelessly, " ask them if they've got
an apple." Generally, however, we fell to work with
the appetites of men sick of long months of stew and
rice. And then what merry walks homewards, with
talk flowing high and free, or robustiousness so great
that we must perforce rush at and overwhelm one
another on the soft grass ! In turn, too, everybody
was able to get to Abbeville for a day, and pleasant
it was to wander round the narrow streets of the
historic little town, and taste the repasts of the Tête
de Bœuf or Pomme d'Or. Never, surely, did a unit
enjoy rests better than 309 S.B. ! Never, surely, did
one deserve to !

For let us not overlook our steady work at Sailly.
We did work, and with energy, morning and afternoon,
every day, with the exception of Sunday. The arrangement under which we were living at the camp was,
in fact, that our guns should be at the disposal of the

school (where officers and N.C.O.s took a four months'
course), while the personnel should be available for
fatigues and the work necessary for finishing the
camp. Thus it happens that the concrete flooring
of the stabling in the camp shows still—I hope—what
business men and bankers can do ; and the roads at
the school what practical sense stockbrokers, and even
schoolmasters, have. The figures cut after a day at
coal fatigue demonstrated, too, that in point of black-
ness there need be no difference between musical
artistes, pipe manufacturers, and chimney sweeps.
On the more technical side a layers' class was held,
mainly under the direction of Mr. Coleman ; there
were some excellent lectures given by Mr. Edmondson
and Mr. Glover, and a night or two were spent in
digging practice gun-pits in the grassy track (alas, it
was hard chalk beneath the grass !) through the wood.
A Lewis Gun course was attended by many men ;
when the guard's turn-out seemed too bad, genial
William Stokes, the sergeant-major, used to take us
in rifle drill ; and " Jumbo," *ipse solus*, took a course
in physical jerks, sported the drawn-swords, and
claimed the extra pay. The latter, too, was much
interested in the Chinese labourers who came over
from Noyelles to work at the camp and amuse us with
their antics.

On February 6th we became a 6-gun battery,
being reinforced by the arrival of a new section, the
Centre (who ranked now as C and D Subs., while the
old Left Section were known in future as E and F).
Our new comrades worthily took their share in the
work, and not less in the recreation, described.

Two other batteries beside ourselves were living
in the camp—C/95 R.F.A. and 109 Heavies—and
there was a vigorous social life. We had many keen
football matches, particularly against the school staff,
whom we beat by 5—1 and 3—2, though when they
called to their aid the officers attending the course,
we only managed to draw, 1—1. In Jimmy Wells,
Bert Turney, Lauder, Lockett, Edmonds, Webb, and
others we had some skilful players. Once our XI.
went to Abbeville to play the Australian C.C.S. there.
Some of the " Aussies " had only played Rugger
before, and it was all in the game to push our men
away with their hands. Good sportsmen as they
are, we allowed them considerable latitude, and beat
them, 2—0. 109 we beat and lost to in turn, and we
beat C/95 by 4—2. We turned out a Rugger team
too, and in Major Knox, Denby, and the "Quarter's"
Stores staff, Jimmy Mordin and MacFarlane, we had
some shining lights; but several men in the scrum
could well have exchanged places with the Aussies
mentioned above, for their respective knowledge of
the two games, so we lost to the school, 20 points to
nil. Mr. Edmondson, a fine player, was very energetic
over hockey, " the game of the gods," and our team
beat 109 by 3—1. Yes, there was great athletic
activity at Sailly, nor was all of it displayed outside
the huts. For instance, in one hut lived, amongst
others, a guileless, slim young Anglo-Indian, yclept
" Birdie," and a hefty East Anglian, who had lately
assumed the pomp of orderly bombardier. His duties
kept him away from the hut till long after " lights
out " ; and when he at length used to come in, it

THE CENTRE SECTION

was his custom, either out of affection, or because his
great muscles called for exercise, to drag the un-
offending "Birdie" out of his blankets. He had
done this twice one night, and gone forth again to
discharge his duties. It was certain that, on his
return, he would once more assault his young friend.
So he did ; bent over him in the dark, gently murmur-
ing, "Think I'd better have you out once again,
Birdie," but this time Birdie wasn't such an easy
prey ; indeed, the attacker found himself gripped
with unexpected force—gripped, nay, ignominiously
thrust on the floor, and sat on. "Ha, wilt thou eat
the leek now, my brave bully ? " For, indeed, it
was a Welshman, notable for strength, who had
exchanged places a few minutes before with "Birdie."
Another frequent theatre of operations was an A Sub.
hut, especially when "Jimmy" was trying to find his
washing.

Then there was the artistic side of camp life. On
the lowest level of this we put two or three grama-
phones that wandered round the huts till finally they
became incorporated in one depressed instrument.
Perhaps we rise, as we speak of the periodical cinema
shows at the Y.M.C.A. Well above these, anyhow,
come some excellent concerts given by the Y.M.C.A.
Concert Party from Abbeville, and a performance of
Cousin Kate by their Dramatic Party, which, cleverly
acted, kept us interested from start to finish. And
as climax of all, a partial judgment will place the
concert given on February 27th by our own Pierrot
troupe. There had seemed many practices for this,
especially to us who toiled on fatigues outside the hall,

7

and heard the efforts of our comrades within, privileged
to escape fatigues ; but the result certainly was
excellent. The hall was crowded with men from
camp and School, full of appreciation for items rendered by McNeill, Fry, and the others, and enthu-
siastic over Greenhow's dashing rendering of what
one wit termed " entirely new songs which were so
famous twenty years ago." In the hour preceding
the concert we had cause to admire the ability as a
pianist of C. E. Smith, whose loss we were afterwards
to lament.

It seemed like the ordered ways of peace to have
at Sailly the opportunity of again attending a religious
service every Sunday. The school chaplain was in
charge of the Church of England parades, while one
week-evening a fine address was given by the Rev.
Neville Talbot. Our Roman Catholic members attended services in the village church, and our Noncon-
formists were ministered to by visiting chaplains, and
on one Sunday by Professor George Hare Leonard,
of Bristol.

CHAPTER VIII

THE RETREAT OF MARCH 1918

SAILLY had been a home of peace for us. The war was now to reassert, in the most peremptory manner, its sway over our lives. No need to remind the reader that throughout the winter of 1917-8 the whole world was anticipating a great and desperate onslaught by the Germans, relieved now of all concern from Russia, on the Allied lines. " When, where would it come ? " The question was asked continually, even by us at Sailly. Yet March 21st, that stern day for the British army, came and went ; we gunners at least knew nothing of what had commenced in the mists of dawn far away beyond Péronne, and of the bloody struggle that had followed throughout the day as our out-numbered men fell, fighting, back. But immediately we met one another on the morning of Friday, the 22nd, the air seemed full of rumours. " The Boche attacked yesterday ; thousands of our fellows were captured ; he's pushing on." So far, however, there had been no time for definite news, and when we passed from the parade-ground, trivial chat about the fatigues we were doing and about camp life hardly gave place now and then to a surmise as to what

events were really happening up the line, and as to
how our own position would be affected.

We were soon to know. I remember how some of
us who were making up a gravel path in the School-
grounds at the end nearest the camp had—unofficially
—broken off at 11 for a cup of coffee, when, ere we
had drunk it, there came the sudden order, " Leave
your tools, everything—back to camp at once ! The
battery's moving off in four hours' time." It was
true then ! Back to the war again ! With sobered,
but not depressed, minds—for we had had a splendid
rest, we knew it : the call to the life of danger again
did not irk us—we made our way for the last time by
the path down the sloping fields, and up through the
gateway of the big trees into the camp.

Personal kits were quickly overhauled and packed ;
books hurriedly returned to the Y.M.C.A. library ;
that spare shirt, those extra socks, where were they ?
Oh, at the washerwoman's in the village. Well, there
they must be left. If one's water-bottle had no cork,
a champagne-bottle cork was easily to be obtained
from the officers' mess. Next the shells and cartridges,
fifty for each gun, had to be loaded, and then the
stores. Down the field we carried these to the waiting
lorries at the gate. And here took place a truly
deplorable incident. Two crates of oranges—issue—
were deposited by the lorries to be packed when
convenient. They were left there too long. You
carried your burden of spades, handspikes, or what
not to the lorries, and, turning round, swept up a
couple of oranges. They were eaten before you had
come down with another load, and now you saw how

small the stock was growing. " Good heavens, those fellows will have cleared them all up in a minute ! " So you clutched another two, or three, while a friendly, complaisant officer looked elsewhere. Soon the empty crates bore mute witness to the shameful deed.

At length, about half-past six in the evening, we left the camp. The flag was flying in the School-grounds as we passed, and the School-band played us a farewell. (Alas ! a few days after, the School sergeant-major was dead—killed by a bomb—and the commandant, Major Davidson, wounded.) It was a fine evening, pure, light clouds above us in the blue sky, the wide expanse of fields and meadows clearly seen around us, and we marched away with cheerful hearts. We boarded the lorries on the high-road, a mile or so away from Sailly. That ride along the beautiful avenue of the Route Nationale, past the places with such pleasant associations for us—Hautvillars, Le Titre, Abbeville—seemed but little like the entrance into a great conflict.

Soon we were out of the area we had come to know these last few weeks. Steadily we kept on through the evening hours. Every vehicle seemed almost choked with stores of one sort or another, ten-foot planks, handspikes, spades, tins of grease, great rolls of camouflage ; but among these, at all levels and in all sorts of niches, the men were perched. Perhaps they were best off, though cold, who sat on the limber, or on the trail of the gun to act as brakesmen. About eleven we halted near an estaminet outside the village of Ailly le Haut Clocher. The gunners feared at first that the delights of the estaminet were to be

barred to them, but they vociferated their need of
these, and in the end all of us who wanted, obtained
a great hunch of good French bread and cheese and
a draught of excellent wine. Tea, too, was made by
our cooks. Then into the lorries again, and so on
through the hours of the night, snatching what little
sleep we could in our cramped positions.

Early in the morning, the 23rd, we found ourselves
jolting over the cobbles of a big town, and our heavy
eyes lighted up with interest as we looked on Amiens.
There was a short halt near the railway station, but
before we could find the local Y.M.C.A. hut, back into
the lorries we had to clamber. Soon, however, we
stopped again, this time at the village of Longueau.
Here all was nervousness and trepidation. The
Boche, it was certain, had advanced considerably.
Perhaps he might be quite near. His objective was
undoubtedly Amiens. Our objective, at any rate,
was breakfast, and from the low slope where the
lorries were standing, we walked quickly back to the
village, went into a promising-looking estaminet, and
found ourselves amongst twenty or thirty other men
all on the same errand ; yet it was not long before
those harassed, indulgent Frenchwomen had provided
all of us with the " beaucoup " eggs and coffee we
were demanding. When we came back to the lorries
an official breakfast—and a good one—was supplied.
Alas that our appetites were already sated ! But
there were three or four who had little appetite for
any kind of food, for, the fumes of petrol-waste
acting on bodies tired by the hard night, Massingham, Seton, and even " long Jonah " collapsed on

getting out of the lorries, and took some time to come round.

We had now to dump our spare kits, so that the lorries containing them could be utilised for more ammunition. They were left at Villers-Bretonneux, a name that sounds sadly yet in our ears. For long weeks we hoped to regain the kits, but " Aussies," Germans, " Aussies " in turn held the village ; in the end there was hardly a wall left standing there, and spare shirts, our rubber boots, waterproofs, as well as our souvenirs gathered in nearly twelve months of war, all went west !

On we rumble once more with our long column, six guns attached to their special lorries (F.W.D.s) [1] and thirteen other lorries. A rather impressive sight one always found them, especially if seen against the sky-line—this series of animated, cumbrous vehicles passing across the open plain, coerced invisibly to follow in their due station one behind another ; they seemed indeed out of place, these ugly mechanical monsters striding between the quiet meadows and cornfields of Nature's effortless realm.

It was a beautiful day, this March 23rd ; there was sunshine on the broad fields of France, but the little country-places that we went through seemed full of tremor. People stood at their doors to watch the soldiers going up to face the Boche, craved for the latest rumours of the terrible advance, and now, as the afternoon drew on, refugees passed us in their

[1] Four-wheel drives, constructed specially for hauling guns, in such a way that the rear-wheels as well as the front exert a direct pull on the guns.

carts, laden with chairs, mattresses, pictures, or themselves, though over-old or over-young, pushing their
goods before them on hand-carts ; touching sights,
all of them. About four o'clock we halted, and,
wearied and cramped, were glad to stretch our limbs
on the beautiful grass by the roadside, while we
munched our tea.

And so on once more, and now we understand we
are getting well within the battle area. The fine road
on which we are travelling is indeed used by many
vehicles, but all are moving in the opposite direction—
we seem the only people going eastwards. Those that
put the wind up their brethren call out to us as they
pass that if we go forward another thousand, two
thousand, or what not number of yards we shall fall
into the hands of the Boche. Where indeed are we
going ? The road before us, passing out of sight
through a low ridge, is ominously silent. The Boche—
how near is he behind that ridge ? Artillerymen as
we are, we begin to think of getting ready our rifles.

The onward march of the Boche had indeed led
here, as in many other cases, to a temporary loss of
contact. On the morning of the 22nd—before the
battery left Sailly, that is—Major Knox had gone
forward to receive orders from 47th Brigade. Brigade
had been lodged at Villers-Faucon, but on the 21st
and 22nd had hurriedly retreated to Bussu, and again
to Cléry. At Bussu the Major found them then, and
it was decided that our battery should be brought up
there to aid in stemming the Boche advance. The
Major came back to us at Longueau on the Saturday
morning with these instructions, then disappeared,

as it were, into the blue again, in a determined effort
to maintain communications with Brigade. He soon
sent back, however, a dispatch rider, who reached
us at Villers-Bretonneux with the message that we
should now proceed to Cléry. But what the people
we passed that afternoon were saying, was more or
less true. The Boche was in Cléry now. To go
forward was to run into his hands. We could not
remain on the high road—that had to be kept clear
for retreating field artillery, and the battery therefore,
under Captain Chattey, turned towards Cappy, in a
direction roughly parallel with our line.

We gunners didn't know all about this at the time,
though we felt there was a certain perplexity. It
was striking, however, to turn and take the narrow
cross-country road, through the rolling stretches of
grass-land, with still that low ridge, beyond which so
much might be taking place, on our right. This evening, like the last, was beautifully clear. At a particularly bad part of the road one lorry got " ditched,"
and the whole column was held up while we worked
strenuously for an hour with levers and jacks until
she could move again. We were not in the best of
moods for delays like this. Soon after, however, we
came to Cappy; the lorries were parked down the
long, sloping road which leads to the cross-roads, and
some tea was prepared. (And we weren't so fatigued
that we failed to grumble because no jam was served
out.) Trouble seemed very near as we hung about the
lorries that night (for we had orders to sleep in them, if
we could, but not to go away). The ordinary routine
of life of course had stopped ; estaminets there were,

but selling nothing ; the inhabitants were moving away even at that late hour.   Many soldiers were straggling through the village, some so exhausted with the privations of the last three days that they were seized now with epileptic fits.   We spoke to more than one group of R.F.A. men :

"What's happened, chum ? "

"What's happened ! Why, Jerry's through ; he's got all our guns ; we had to cut off to save our skins "— and comrades were dead behind them.   It was plain enough that our line had been overwhelmed, and our army was retreating.   And now White ran across us, one of a group of H.A.C. men who had been attached to 109 Siege Battery, and from him we learned how this sister-battery had been assailed on the morning of the 21st, and our own friends had suffered.[1]

Meanwhile, our officers were trying to solve their perplexity.   The Major had lost them, and they had lost him.   Captain Chattey went out in quest of him, but returned unsuccessful, having hardly evaded the urgent solicitations of a brigadier-general that he should temporarily loan him the services of the battery. Mr. Edmondson then went out, apparently at a venture ; but, to his colleagues' surprise, he returned with news.   Light at last !   He had found the Major on the road near Hem Wood, and had received instructions that the battery should go along to take up a position there.   So, nearing midnight, we set off again, being probably the last siege battery to cross the Somme at Cappy before the bridge was blown up, rumbled along the country roads, and about 2 o'clock

[1] See Appendix II.

on the morning of Sunday, the 24th, finally took up a position, not at Hem, but at Curlu Corner, for, half an hour before, we had been transferred from the 47th to the 6th Brigade, with a corresponding change of location.

Here it was then that we first took part in resisting the terrific German push which in one phase or another was to tax our country's strength for nearly three months. We were not sorry to join battle in these circumstances. As we unlimbered the guns and pulled them on the grass by the roadside in those still hours, we wondered what might come at any time down that road—whether Uhlans, or the field-grey infantry, or perhaps our more familiar enemy, 5·9 salvos ; but we worked steadily, cheerfully enough. Yet we were dog-tired, after spending thirty hours or more cramped up in the lorries, with hardly any sleep and not too much food. One could have fainted with exhaustion any minute. Carrying a shell seemed a nightmare's task ; fetching a few spadefuls of chalk from near by was a job that I, at least, was glad to leave almost wholly to that strong and willing chum, "Hughie." A situation pregnant with suggestion indeed ! these little groups of men working on the grass by the deserted road, solitary under the stars, with night enshrouding us, and deepening the sense of danger.

Slowly dawn came, and showed us our position. But for the road, which drove, a line of white, straight ahead on our left, our world was an expanse of green, grassy ground, sloping very gently downwards on our right to the little stream of the Ancre, continuous in front of us till closed in, some eight hundred yards away, by a low ridge. On the other side of the road the ground was higher, and a bank a few feet high faced us. We had brought only four guns into action ; they were in two sections a little way off the road, C and F some fifty yards in front of D and E. Both in front of and behind us were field artillery batteries.

About 3 o'clock our attention had been called from our work on the guns by the sounds of heavy machinery clanking down the road. It was the Tanks in retreat ! They rolled past in dozens, an almost unceasing procession ; light came, and it did our spirits no good to realise that these monsters were withdrawing from facing the enemy in front of us. At 6 o'clock, however, we started firing, with great goodwill, for, phlegmatic as British people are, we did detest the Boche who was causing all this trouble. He was known to be advancing from Cléry, and we helped to keep up a curtain of fire about that village. This was the first time our new section, the Centre, had been in action, and for part of them, C Sub., it proved very disappointing. Several months' training, a brand-new gun, a great conflict ; they made ready, and pulled off the first shot with eager spirits. It was the first and the last of that day's war, for something went wrong with the gun, it could not be fired again, and it was ignominiously pulled out to the side of the road.

As the morning-hours came and went, we began to settle down at this position. A hearty breakfast, for which we went back in relays to the lorries, parked by a chalk-pit at the elbow of the road behind us, renewed our strength and our spirits. It was a beautiful, sunny day ; it did not hurt one to think of the silvery church-bells ringing over the countryside at home this Sunday morning. Our front again appeared to be becoming stabilised, for long columns of infantrymen marched past us up the road. In a pause in our own firing some of us went seeking water for a wash. It was strange, after Ypres, to have to search so long before one came across a shell-hole, and equally strange then to find hardly any water in it.

But our quietude was rudely disturbed. About half-past ten there suddenly came the order, " Fire off all fused shells as quickly as possible, and get everything ready for pulling out."

" Hasn't the Boche been held up after all ? " we queried.

" No, he's broken through again ; we must clear, and pretty quickly." Enough said. Those guns were man-handled out into the road as if they were children's perambulators, the combined teams pulling like so many Hercules. One man was actually seen carrying a ten-foot plank, which usually engaged the strength of four men. We understood what the proverbial excitement of battle was as we struggled to flee ! It seemed good fortune now that C Sub.'s gun was already on the roadside. As it was, the last gun (F) was not yet limbered up when the Boche shells began coming over the ridge. Fritz was getting on the road. An early one fell by the 18-pounder battery in front of us, and, as we heard afterwards, killed Colonel Sinclair, a former adjutant of the H.A.C. Fritz lengthened out, and dropped a shell or two half-way between the ridge and us ; then another, near where that mass of

men were still tugging away at F gun.   It was limbered
up at last !   If we were not to shoot, it seemed little
fun to stay and be shot at, and we were glad when
at length the lorries, whose engines had for some time
been throbbing to get away, set off, and we passed
round the corner to our rear.

Soon we found ourselves in a big stream of traffic
of all descriptions—lorries, guns, staff-cars trying to
make their way in front of everything, caterpillars,
G.S. waggons—it seemed as if some huge, loosely-
articulated serpent were crawling down the chalky
road that warm spring afternoon.   It was not a
disordered retreat, for doubtless each unit knew its
destination as well as we did, and, as for us, about
half-past three we turned to the left off the main road
near Maricourt, and put the three guns in action on
a narrow country road.   Then we started shooting
again, helping this time, too, to maintain a curtain of
fire before Cléry.   Now and then we had to check
ourselves in firing for a minute while some cavalry-
man, with despatches, dashed past.   We were fright-
fully hungry, for we had had no dinner, and a slice of
bread and jam and some tea that were now served out
seemed very good to us as we lay about on the ragged
grass.   We kept on firing, but it was in quite a leisurely
way, and so far removed from one another are many
of the combatants in modern warfare, it was almost
difficult to believe in the quiet country lane, that
sunny afternoon, that we were actually taking part in
a momentous struggle.   Yet we were vitally concerned in what was occurring beyond our sight ; a
fact of which we were sharply reminded about five

o'clock, when another peremptory order came to retire. The guns were easy enough to pull out this time, and soon we were travelling down the high road again. Our third position was near the Plateau rail-head in a field by a wood. It was hard work pulling the guns over the grass, and then we waited some little time. Fanciful people thought they could see the Boche cavalry on the skyline a considerable distance off. Certain it is that we did not stay to fire a round here, but, limbering up, moved off once again to draw in this time at what was known as Bronfay Farm.

We were now by the side of the Maricourt-Bray road, which here runs across a fairly high stretch of country. The view was wide enough, but our particular spot was not a beautiful one—a square of waste ground, with an old cowshed in front of us, and to our rear an old brick building, used previously as a dressing-station. We did hope at length to stay a few hours here, and E Sub. detailed a man to secure the least draughty corner of the shed for its billets. F Sub., wandering further afield, scrounged from another deserted dressing-station mattresses and palliasses, and slept that night in princely ease. All the time, as we worked on the gun, we were hoping for a good sound meal, and great was our disgust when we heard that only bully and bread were available. Our protests, however, sympathised with by Mr. Coleman, led to these edibles being supplemented by porridge, and, about midnight, by stew. And then, joy of joys, to stretch ourselves at last in our blankets for a few hours' sleep ! The firing from the guns shook us every time, for each team had in turn to go out to

help in maintaining a barrage near Maricourt, but
the very closing our eyes brought ease, after our two
days and nights without rest. And then what a
happy surprise in the morning, when relief gun-teams
came up ! We had thought the exigencies of the
retreat would not allow of our former system being
adopted. A nondescript team E Sub. called their
relief ; there was the non-combatant trumpeter on it,
one or two semi-invalids, a man from another Sub. :
but they seemed a set of genuine benefactors that
Monday morning.

A word should here be said about the rest of the
battery. When we were suddenly called away from
Sailly, only one gun-team was selected in each Sub.,
and naturally the strongest men were put on it. Most
of the remainder were detailed to collect ammunition
for the battery. At this time specialists—that is,
men with special, and supposed " cushy " jobs—were
employed on these fatigues, and the gunners relate an
unkind story about two of them, both sedate men,
who knew one another's weakness ; how, as the
100-lb. shells lay calling to be handled, the one would
innocently stand aside, his attention attracted by
distant bursts of shells, as he remarked, " Oh, look
there, look there," and how the other would insist
to him politely but firmly, " Come, your shell, C——.
Thank you, I'm *after* you." The " ammo." fatigue,
indeed, was almost as tiring a job as being on the
guns. With the continued retreat it was difficult to
find the ammunition dumps ; one after the other they
were falling into the hands of the Boche. It was
sometimes a long journey by night as well as day on

which our party blindly went in quest of them. At
some dumps that were found, confusion prevailed ;
there seemed no responsible authority, and—great
shock to our soldiers' sense of fitness—men could take
stores without producing a " chit." Then, when sup-
plies had been obtained, it was a problem to find the
battery. Indeed, when the guns were at Cappy on
Saturday evening, a couple of ammunition lorries
under Mr. Glover were travelling for some time, in
the supposed track of the battery, along the eastern
bank of the Somme, and they were undoubtedly very
lucky to find a bridge and make their way back
before the Boche reached the river-bank.

Let us keep away from the guns a little longer, and
turn to the experiences of the teams that had been
relieved that Monday morning. We trudged and
" lorry-jumped " three or four kilos on the road to
Bray, and then found the so-called " rest-billet "—a
dirty tin-shed, its floor littered with stores, paper, and
old tins. There was a cold wind blowing, and that
comfortless, draughty shed, set in a dull, chalky
compound, made our yesterday's position on the guns
at Curlu Corner seem quite attractive. However, we
tried to make the best of things. Two or three of us
brought up a huge old door from a chalk-pit near by,
and carrying it into the shed to the momentary dismay
of the rest, made quite a good floor for the corner where
we hoped to sleep. Most settled down to write the
home-letters. Plainly visible from our shed was Bray,
a pretty village nestling in its trees in the dip behind
us. In front of us could be seen a line of trenches
cutting the chalky hillside, and we were drawn to this

8

old battle-line ; we walked along it, peered down into the old dug-outs, and settled ourselves down in sheltered nooks for a nap.

Towards evening the rumour passed about that we should not spend the night at this shed after all, and we were very fed-up, for, no matter how comfortless the place, we wanted a night's sleep there. Some of our number were called out to return to the guns, which led the remainder of us, in no unselfish spirit, to hope that the sacrifice of these might propitiate the God of Unrest. But it was not to be. About ten o'clock there came that horrid cry : " Pack up your kits at once ! The lorries are waiting." And off we cut once again, through that foul Boche's continuing pressure.

So we spent two or three hours more cramped up in the lorries, already full of stores. It was horribly cold ; one dozed for a few minutes to wake up half-frozen. When we looked out, we saw roads congested with transport of every description, and the scene lit up for miles around by the glare of burning huts, camps, and aerodromes. When we stopped at about two o'clock we found ourselves at Corbie, where we went wearily searching for any kind of billet, and quite lucky three of us deemed ourselves who dis-covered one of the great French farm-wagons, clam-bered into it, and, sheltered under its canvas cover, slept the sleep of the just.

For myself, I left my companions still slumbering at eight the next morning, and went to see what this town of Corbie was like. Rear-guards were just leaving the big square in the centre of the town ; we had had a poor enough night, but it was distressing to think of thousands of our infantrymen who had had to spend the bitter night without blankets out here in the open. Nearly all the civilians had evacuated the place, but one, a baker, who was on the point of departing, was disposing of his stock, and it was a treat to be able to buy a couple of great round French loaves for a franc. There was a little shop, too, selling hard-boiled eggs, and with a dozen or so of these I went back to breakfast with my chums. But they were soon on the track of still greater delicacies, and during the rest of the day they returned to the lorries laden with bottles of wine, champagne, and a barrel of cider, all presumably purchased at a cheap rate ! Some of this was appreciated by troops who passed us on their way up the line. One of our number even obtained useful equipment for war— some china egg-cups and two or three golf-balls, yellow with age. Poorer loot was surely never treasured by a soldier.

Hundreds of stragglers came through Corbie in ones and twos, though, indeed, many skirted the town, having no wish to get into the Stragglers' Camp, and be immediately sent into the fight again. They were tired and incommunicative, but we gathered that, while the Boche by the continuous onrush of masses of men had forced our troops back, he had paid terribly for his gain of ground.

During the day we found a barn of fine straw near the lorries, and in this, early in the evening, we settled down comfortably. There was a little dissension between four members of A Sub., two of whom, being in high spirits, seemed to want to appropriate the space and straw already bespoke by the other two, and there was a stern clamour, " Steady with that light, you fool," when another fellow came in waving a candle about. But we were nearly all well asleep when again, about ten o'clock, came that odious, loathsome cry, " Pack up kits at once, and into the lorries ! " Oh, damn that Boche ! A plague upon his epileptic visage !

How those lorries revolved that night ! Some sense of direction must have been lacking or clouded, for we went twice round the square ere we could make our exit from the town (the R.E.s who were waiting to blow up the bridge inquiring of us, as we passed over it, if we were the last out of the town, for the Boche, they said, was expected there at one o'clock). Then, when we had gone a mile or so along a road, it abruptly ended, and we had to turn round a dozen or more lorries and a gun which had—horrible, unnecessary labour !—to be unlimbered ere it could be brought round on the soft, grassy earth. At length we found the proper road, rumbled on for an hour or two, and about midnight stopped in a village which we afterwards came to know well—Pont Noyelles. We preferred any home to those lorries, with all their lumber, but all barns and empty houses were crowded with infantrymen, and in the lorries most had to spend the night. We of E Sub., however, were attracted by a long, low house, locked-up, but with a glass vestibule, unlocked, at one end. I describe this place so particularly to show how in war one appreciates the most rudimentary forms of comfort, for often afterwards we recalled our pleasure at being enabled to stretch ourselves, and go cosily off to sleep, on the brick floor of that snug little apartment. Alas ! that Elysium was rudely broken into ! Again at 4 o'clock came the cry, " Pack your kits and into the lorries at once ! " In wicked tempers we turned out again. What was up ? Some said the Boche was nearing us ; others merely that we had been ordered out of the village so as not to impede the passage of other troops. So off again, only a thousand yards from the village along the high road. There the lorries were parked. We tried no more to obtain billets ; there was, in fact, nothing but field and road there, and settling down to doze or freeze in the lorries, we wished, like the Apostle, " for the day." It was a wretched night for us ; breakfast, delayed while we went about to scrounge wood for the fire, made no great amends for it ; even the sight of the Orderly Room oracle, striding, a Napoleonic figure, up and down the road, did not inspire us, and it was even with pleasure that at about 10 o'clock in the morning we went up again to the guns at Laviéville.

During these two days the relief gun-teams had had fully as much variety and strain as we had had in the first period on the guns. They had indeed no strafing, except that which a smith-gunner inflicted on his chief, when, in excitement and, presumably, error, he smote him on the forehead with a heavy maul; a tin hat and a strong skull saved " Knackers " from absolute extinction, but not from temporary disfigurement.

From Bronfay Farm they fired fairly continuously throughout Monday, the 25th. As is shown in Sir

Douglas Haig's dispatch, the district around Bray
was evacuated through a mistake. In fact, our men
were preparing their beds for this, the second night,
at this position, when at 10 o'clock, like us in our tin-
shed further down the road, they received sudden
orders to retire. Fused shells were rapidly fired off ;
others left ; cartridges were destroyed. Need there
was of haste, for within an hour, as we learned afterwards, a Tank was in action on the spot where our
guns, with their range of ten thousand yards, had
been. As the guns came back through Bray they
picked up half-a-dozen men of the resting gun-teams
who, having been left behind in the confusion of the
hurried flight from the tin-shed, were trudging along
on foot ; and these give vivid descriptions of their
ride on the gun-trails during the freezing night. The
guns now wandered about in much the same manner
as two nights previously, and through much the
same cause, the rapid changing of plans necessitated
by the enemy's advance. It was Major Knox's
intention that a position should be occupied at St.
Etenheim. He had gone on in advance, but after a
while, changing his mind, decided that the guns should
be placed at Morlancourt. A message to this effect
reached Mr. Edmondson, who took two guns off to
this village ; through a strenuous night the teams
toiled here. But the other two guns had dropped
behind ; Mr. Glover, who was with them, did not
receive the message, nor during these night-hours
could the route taken by the guns in front be observed.
Once they found themselves certainly on the wrong
road, and it was necessary to turn round in a field ;

F.W.D.s and guns, however, sank deeply in the soft grass and would not move, so " Out with the spades and drag-ropes ! Throw straw, bits of wood, anything under the wheels to make them grip," and partly digging, partly hauling at the ropes, with all the time some anxiety as to whether the Boche might not be getting unpleasantly near, after an hour's toil the great vehicles were persuaded to move out and round. These two guns went now on to the main Bray-Corbie road, and halted there for the rest of the night.   An early breakfast was served, the hot tea being a god-send after the night's cold, and a fresh message from the Major having now arrived, the guns moved on again to Laviéville.   On the journey the battery sustained its first casualty in the retreat.   Most of the men, exhausted with the strain of recent days and nights, were asleep as the lorries jolted along, but the attention of those who were awake was attracted by what appeared to be three British 'planes manœuvring overhead.   However, one at least was a German, for it suddenly swooped down till only fifty yards from the lorries, and poured a stream of machine-gun bullets on them.   The men awake ducked, came up in a second, laughing a little nervously perhaps, as that danger was past ; a well-known voice ordered, " Put on your tin hats, boys."   And it was then that the lorry-driver, looking back through his little opening, called out, " Why, there's one of your men hit." It was poor young Pollack.   He had been fast asleep, and the bullet, entering his spine, as was found out a little later, killed him instantaneously, for he made not a murmur.   He was a high-spirited, good-natured

lad of nineteen, a Rumanian, who had made his way
to England to fight with us against the enemy who
had overrun his native land.

The two guns with Mr. Edmondson at Morlancourt
received orders early this morning to move on to
Laviéville. They had not fired a shot.

CHAPTER IX

HOLDING UP THE BOCHE : LAVIÉVILLE AND BONNAY

IT was on March 26th that the battery took up the position by Laviéville. There were many civilians still about the village, but with nervous haste they were preparing for flight ; and more suitable occupants of what was now to become a war-zone were the infantrymen bivouacked in a hollow near the village, and the cavalry whom we saw in the dip to our rear. For we were on high ground here, and there was a pronounced slope down towards the great Amiens-Albert road, half a mile or so to our right. We came up from it by a narrow road, and placed some of our guns on each side of this, the nearest one being a hundred yards from the village. The retreat in our sector had now definitely stopped ; an order had been issued on the night of March 27th that, at all costs, the line of the Ancre was to be held, and, as one consequence, a concentration of artillery had taken place on our side of Laviéville. There were 4·5 and 18-pounder batteries all around us, continually changing their positions, one or two almost on the skyline a couple of hundred yards to our right front ; and near the village of Bresle, which lay between us and the Amiens-Albert road, were our brigade friends, 146 and 109 S.B. During

the first days the noise of the British fire was almost
continuous. Some diabolical spite, venting itself in
all kinds of shrieking, booming rage, we seemed to
have against our unseen enemy.

Unseen, but not alas, unfelt ! The village, the
cross-roads at which it stood, and the wood behind
it, quickly attracted Fritz's attention. At any time
of the day or night he would open out on it with his
heaviest guns, and for perhaps an hour one would
hear the shells come roaring over in a continuous
series, and see the great columns of smoke and débris
constantly rising from amidst the shaken houses.
On more than one evening, so wild had seemed his
anger, men remarked as they turned into their dug-
outs, " Fritz will knock the village to hell to-night."
Battered and broken, indeed, it appeared as one went
to seek wood or straw in it—bricks lying along its
quiet little streets, thin fingers of lath and rafter
sticking forth from the side of some ruined house.
And through those terrible times three aged people
refused to leave their homes. Jumbo Symes one day
was wandering about the village, and called to me,
cautiously approaching the place, to talk to an old
lady whom he had just seen in the garden. She
invited us inside her house. The glass of the windows
had already been shattered, and the loose tiles shaken
off the roof. By the stove sat her husband, a weak
old man, whom the ever-threatening danger seemed
to have practically paralysed, for he sat quite speech-
less. He was a tailor, and on a counter lay his cloth
and scissors ; the room was well kept, and madame
was tidying it up while we were there. These little

articles of peaceful life, this feminine clinging to the
care and orderliness of the home, how infinitely
pathetic they seemed in their futility now, when a
shell might at any moment sweep all to oblivion!
We asked madame why they would not flee. " Non,
non, m'sieu', nous sommes trop vieux pour partir :
il nous faut rester ici." Even while we were drinking
coffee with them there came that terrible roar through
the air, that earth-shaking explosion. The poor little
lady clutched convulsively at us. The window-
shutters, which had been fastened up, were thrown
open by the burst. Yet before the débris had well
finished falling on the house, madame was outside,
fixing up the shutters again. We looked at the great
eight-inch shell-hole less than thirty yards away, and
left the tragic old couple, sadly wondering whether
Providence would so marvellously preserve them
through following days. They were eventually evacuated, so we heard, but the third old person was found
dead in a cellar.

Proximity to the village was indeed so dangerous
that our guns nearest to it were shifted, one by one,
to our right flank. But the whole area itself soon
became suspect to Fritz, and from time to time he
would indulge us with an area-strafe. Happily, it
was generally light, field artillery stuff that he threw
over at us, though it must have been a heavy shell
that, on one occasion, blew F Sub. limber right over
the gun. When a strafe was on, we found shelter in
the big holes which the French dig in the side of their
roads for drainage purposes.

There were a number of casualties at this position.

On the 28th poor Parkinson was hit as he was crouching behind the low bank of the road, and the shock and loss of blood proved fatal. He had been a fine, spirited worker on the gun, a good comrade. Another day three signallers from another battery working near us were hit ; our men carried them for temporary shelter into a drainage-hole, and a minute after all were covered with earth from a burst on the edge of the hole ! We lost two good men on April 1st, two quiet, reliable fellows. The lorry containing the teams who had just been relieved had left the position, and was at the meeting of the Bresle road with the main Albert-Amiens road, when a stray shell burst just behind it. Four men were sitting on the tail-board. E. A. M. Jones was killed instantaneously, Leech was so badly wounded that he died a few days after. The other two escaped with scratches and shock. Our dispatch rider, W. W. Green, was riding behind the lorry, and the shell burst between him and the lorry, but he was lucky enough to receive no hurt. On March 29th Major Knox was wounded. He and his batman, Pink, had just come up to ground-level from the officers' mess—the cellar of a farm at the crossroads—when a shell burst in the farmyard, and splinters caught the Major in the ankle, and Pink in the arm. Happily, neither wound was a grave one, but Major Knox had to go to England. His departure was felt by all to be a great loss, so much confidence had we in his ability and judgment. Captain Chattey temporarily took command of the battery.

Of course we ourselves were not idle, so far as this artillery game was concerned ; we fired at all times of the day and night. Now and in future, however, we rarely engaged in the long, long shoots of Ypres days ; only zero strafes and a rare 'plane shoot reminded us of those " unhappy, far-off days." It was " bursts of fire " that we generally sent over now— one to a dozen shots, mainly on roads, and quite as effective in harassing his communications would these be as a longer shoot, for the first shot or two would give the Boche warning, or lay him out, and the shelled area would be quickly cleared. Our targets lay in the zone south of Albert, particularly round by Dernancourt and Morlancourt, which the Boche now occupied. These days were still critical. It was not clear. that the Boche had relaxed his effort, and certainly his artillery activity was almost continuous, and might well presage a further attack. One day, an aeroplane flying over dropped us a message that hostile artillery fire was slackening. This was the only time that we received these messages from the skies, and, interesting as the method was, our personal experience at the time led us to attach as little value to the news thus transmitted as to the rumours now industriously circulated that we had captured Ostend and Zeebrugge. Another day an artillery colonel, meeting us in Bresle, said he knew we were having a hard time up by Laviéville, but we must hang on for another twenty-four hours, for it was hoped in that time that we should get the Boche on the run. We hung on for a good many twenty-four hours without learning that that was happening. Quite the contrary, indeed ; the Boche was planning a renewal of the attack on our lines. The authorities became aware of this, and were aware too that the Villers-Bretonneux sector was the threatened area, and it was accordingly ordered that several artillery brigades should contribute one battery each for work in that area. Ours was the battery selected in the 6th Brigade, and as a consequence we were transferred to the 27th Brigade, and moved on April 5th from Laviéville, across the Albert-Amiens road, to a position near Bonnay.

Three Military Medals were awarded for conduct during the last strenuous fortnight. The mention of them conjures up different pictures of the retreat : of " Bish," toiling with might and main to drag a gun into position, and, no sooner than that is done, setting himself and his panting men on another job ; of Dicky Bird, sitting in a grassy ditch at Curlu Corner, calmly working out the shoots ; and of W. W. Green, coming up with dispatches to Laviéville, begrimed, exhausted, after nearly thirty-six hours' continuous work on his motor-cycle ; he stays but for a few minutes' chat in a voice hoarse with fatigue, then off he journeys once again.

Those of us who were on rest at the time the battery moved to Bonnay heard not too encouraging a report of the new conditions. " Raining cats and dogs all the time we pulled out last night," said our chums ; " most of us had missed tea, so had nothing but a spoonful of rum from dinner till dawn ; the new position is in a narrow side-road, not a billet to be seen except an old cattle-shed." Exhausted and wet, indeed, the men, and the officers too, had practically given up the attempt to pull the guns into their position up a low bank when Mr. Edmondson came along with a frank appeal, " Come, you must help us pull these guns in, gentlemen,"—and the task was done. But once established in this position, we found it as pleasant a one as could be wished for, a fair tract of country, and—" healthy." The guns lay on a quiet country road running between Corbie and Bonnay. The Ancre—to which this road is parallel—runs here through a shallow, broad valley, and is hidden amongst marshy, well-wooded pasture and reedy ponds. On the further side of the valley there is a long ridge, and behind us also the ground, here carefully culti-vated corn and grass-land, rose in a gradual slope, which reached, towards La Houssoye, to our left rear, a height of fifty to a hundred metres. The houses of Bonnay, a little, now deserted village, could be seen through the trees half a mile to our left. Corbie, on our right, was further away, but over the trees we could see the roof of its big church, where, during our stay, two great shell-holes appeared.

Corbie, indeed, was the object of steady fire on the part of the Boche, but for nearly three weeks not a shell hurtled in the valley where we were—a grateful change from conditions at Laviéville. We realised that the trees and ridge in front of us screened us from Boche observation, but, even so, it was difficult to explain our complete immunity from hostile fire—until that immunity was roughly ended ; then we saw how the new Boche practice had been illustrated in our case, of lulling a threatened sector to sleep before breaking out on it with sudden violence. We took thankfully the peace that the gods gave us, and

quickly fell into a comfortable mode of life. It was
May, lovely, sunny weather for the most part. Some
of the Subs. lived under canvas along the roadside ;
E Sub.'s abode was the cattle-shed already referred
to, where also slept the signallers and dignitaries such
as the sergeant-major and medical orderly, while part
of it was used as a cookhouse. One walked from the
guns to the cookhouse along pleasant, green meadows.
There was brightness, merriment about. We fired,
but not too much ; most nights we had to do an hour
or two's " harassing fire " (an epithet which we considered applied to the effects of the fire on us as much
as on the enemy) ; but most days we had several hours
of leisure on the gun, when we sat and read, smoked,
bantered. Some men (particularly Jumbo and his
faithful attendant and cook) even preferred to remain
continuously with the guns instead of going down in
their turn to the rest-billets at Pont Noyelles, which
was, indeed, a rather unattractive village. Since the
end of March the Australians had come on this front,
and we were on friendly terms with these free sons of
earth. I remember once we were sending off a few
rounds at dawn, when a couple of Aussies came
toddling along the country road from Corbie. They
would not be content until they had pulled off a
round or two on our gun ; then they strolled home in
time for their reveillé, leaving us the richer by a bottle
of whisky. Yes, it was a " good war " at Bonnay—
until one day.

Of course we had our trials. Once we in E Sub.
had to turn out for a " strafe " just before dawn. We
had induced our sergeant to bear these sorrows of

early-rising with equanimity, but, to our distress, it
was the most amiable of men, a Welsh bombardier,
who showed an inclination to be terse this morning.
Two or three of us were having a few quips and cranks
with one another, and, though we were sure our work
was being efficiently done at the same time, this
" Nen C.O." upbraided us roundly. After a day or
two, however, it became safe to ask him about his
"four o'clock in the morning" mood. In the night-
shoots, again, there was bound to be a little confusion,
and it was with no more than reasonable bitterness
that the sergeant-major, on one occasion, was heard
begging Allen, as he moved across in the dark, not to
loiter on his face.

Five hours put a totally different complexion on
our rustic life. On the evening of April 23rd we were
getting into our blankets about ten o'clock as usual,
and we were not surprised at the cry, " Lights out,"
for, night after night, we had heard the rhythmic
hum of the Gothas flying overhead, and now, as on
previous nights, we thought, " The beasts are off to
Amiens and Abbeville again." Suddenly, instead of
the hum, came two terrific crashes near by, and an
outburst of flame to our rear. The very unexpected-
ness of the blow stunned us. We crouched low for a
moment, then cried out, " Any one hurt ? " " Yes,"
came the reply, and we found to our sorrow that
MacFarlane was losing blood freely from a wound in
the upper arm, and Downs, one of the cooks, had a
splinter embedded near the base of the vertebræ.
None could have been cooler than these two were,
" Mac " preserving strength of will to direct us even

9

though he was growing weak in body, while Downs stood by, almost with a laugh, waiting until Coston could dress his wound. Mac recovered; Downs, alas! died—a fine, humorous, good-natured man.

On returning from placing these two in the ambulance car, we looked at the bomb-holes—curiously small, half-spherical holes, but with great lines radiating from them and cutting the ground, the design being obviously to secure low flights for the splinters. What had led the raiders on this sole occasion to assail us? The moon cast a wonderfully intense light that night, and we actually wondered whether the roof of our shed, standing out bright as silver against the grass, had been visible to the Boche. But the probable reason was that he had perceived the flashes of the Australian 4·5's firing behind us. By the bomb which dropped near them, a small cartridge-dump was fired and three men knocked out.

Again we settled ourselves down in our blankets, and for some hours slept, when—was it a nightmare? could it be a fact?—the neighbourhood was resounding with enemy shell-fire. Hardly believing our ears, we sat up, and crash! crash! they fell, and mud and splinters spattered the roof of the cookhouse. This place offered no protection—we must go elsewhere—and steering as far as possible away from the line of fire, we made towards some trenches beyond the gun-position. " Gas! "—the exclamation came to our lips as the pungent smell assailed our nostrils; and hurriedly we thrust on our gas-masks. It was an unpleasant experience, wandering about in the half-light, with shells dropping here and there. Two of our men, sleeping by the roadside, were wounded right at the start, but happily not gravely. Dawn soon came, and revealed the whole valley under fire, pillars of smoke arising from Bonnay, hitherto immune, and troops of horses of the Australian artillery being led out from the village to the higher ground behind us, though shells bursting there, particularly gas-shells, with their long, heavy, smoke-clouds blown along by the wind, made that slope an unsatisfactory retreat. A shell that burst just by our officers' dug-out mortally wounded Mr. Rawe. He died as he was being carried down the road to Bonnay Field Hospital. He was a very quiet, retiring man, well liked by us, and in his death, as much as in any man's, one felt the horrible crime of war. Mr. Twine, who was one of those who undertook the unhealthy journey to the hospital, was gassed, not too seriously, coming back ; he was our gas-instructor, as we should not have failed to remind him had he reappeared in our midst.

Throughout this steady bombardment our guns kept on firing, the men having for much of the time to work in gas-masks. Mr. P. H. Edmondson worked on the guns with the men. It was in recognition of the merits of E Sub. team, as well as of his own, on this occasion, that Sergeant Seton received the Military Medal. But how variously persons regard their experiences ! One man, not on the gun-team that morning, inquired anxiously, as soon as he met a certain famous " George," how things had gone with the team during that hot three hours. " Oh, well enough," replied " George," " and here, you ought to have been with us ! Louie brought out a ripping cake ; it was a winner ! "

The strafe died down about six o'clock, and during
the rest of the day there was practically nothing over
on our position.   At intervals, however, we saw fine,
if disagreeable, effects on the Ancre in front of us.
Here the Aussies watered their horses, and here, too,
field-artillery teams were standing by, ready to return
to their position forward up the ridge.   Twice during
this day the Boche put a barrage along the river,

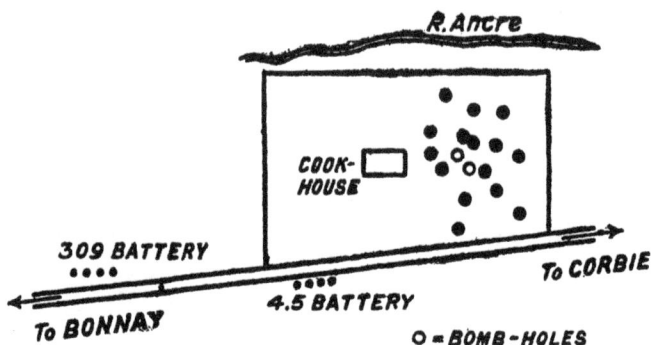

which threw up a broken curtain of fire and water
amongst the foliage of the riverside.

A remarkably interesting illustration of artillery
work was also afforded by the shell-holes in the field
where the cookhouse was.   Clustered thickly in the
one half of the field, they lay along definite lines, from
which one could at a glance perceive, roughly, the
area in which the Boche battery was situated.
Happily for us its " extreme traverse " [1] evidently just
failed to touch the cookhouse, for not a shell fell,

---

[1] The direction in which a gun is firing can be easily altered
several degrees right or left by the use of the " traversing gear."

from this particular battery at any rate, in the other half of the field.

Behind a hill, a mile to our right rear, were our Centre Section, a " silent section," placed there with a view to breaking forth into activity if ever the Boche neutralised our other guns.   On the 24th, and indeed the 25th as well, they underwent, like us, a heavy bombardment, happily without any serious casualties resulting.

It was a renewal of the great Boche push to Amiens that had been attempted this day of April 24th.   Our commanders knew that this was in prospect, and, as has been mentioned, had strengthened the artillery in the threatened area ; and on the fateful morning, British counter-preparations actually started twenty minutes before the Boche attacked at 3 (our own fire being directed on three woods, Vaire, Hamel, and Bois de l'Accroche, in which he was massing his troops).   However, the vigour of the enemy assault, aided by his employment of Tanks, which moved up unobserved under cover of mist, carried Villers-Bretonneux. There he remained during the day, unable to advance further, and subjected to heavy artillery fire, and at ten in the evening British and Australian troops, advancing from both flanks, brilliantly recaptured the village.

The official account of this action, issued on the 25th, contained a paragraph of considerable interest to us. " Our infantry are full of praise for the work of the Heavy Artillery yesterday. They state on several occasions the Heavy Artillery barrage was their sole protection, and a very substantial pro-

portion of their success is due to the work of the
' Heavies.' Prisoners testify to the deadly effect
of the Heavy Artillery barrages and the counter-
preparation."

So the Boche was frustrated once again. How
threatening, however, had been his advance may be
judged from the fact that during this morning of the
24th our Major received instructions to select another
rear position, to be occupied in case Corbie was taken
and our valley enfiladed. The Boche appears to have
brought up heavy guns particularly for this attack,
and to have withdrawn them when it failed. Certainly
our later days at Bonnay were as peaceful as our
earlier, except for one evening when at 6 o'clock a
queer, solitary shell knocked a tree over, fifty yards
to our left, and at nine o'clock a misguided trio came
over. On April 30th we returned to our old brigade,
the 47th, and pulled out from Bonnay and its valley
of broken peace.

While we were at Bonnay Major Spooner had
joined us as O.C.—on April 9th, a fortunate day for
the battery. Some details as to his career will be
of interest to those who served under him. Since
coming home from the East to join the Army he had
had a varied experience as an artillery officer, having
served in France with a field battery (37th Division,
A/125) from July 1915 to August 1916, worked with
4·5's at Forest Row, and returned to France in May
1917 as second in command of 353 Siege Battery. In
March 1918 he took a B.C. course in England, and
then rejoined his battery (210 S.B., to which he
had been transferred) at Henencourt, from which

he was posted to us. He remained with our
battery until long after the Armistice was signed,
and won the esteem of all, for while a strong,
decisive commander, he was ever considerate of his
men.

A word may here be said on the manner in which
our communications with Brigade were kept up during
the retreat. The systems developed by the British
Army did not break down even in those first days
of pressure ; thus in our case, even on March 24th,
when we changed positions so rapidly, a beginning
was made with laying telephone lines, though it was
not until we were at our last position that day, Bronfay
Farm, that these were completed, an " earth-return "
wire being laid to Brigade. Lamp and flag-communi-
cation also was established, for from the slope in front
of Bray on which the battery was, it was possible to
signal visibly to Brigade at the foot of the slope
behind Bray. This method, however, was not actually
needed, as the line kept O.K., and the only position
at which lamp and flag-signalling was employed was
at Bonnay. Here the O.P. was on the ridge in front of
us, the finest O.P. we ever had, for it looked on a wide
stretch of rolling grass and corn-land, with the beautiful Somme lagoons beneath, the thick green masses
of Vaire and Hamel woods on the slopes over to
the right, and here and there faint indications of the
Boche front-trenches. It was in accord with the
general character of our stay at Bonnay that the lines
were only broken once, and that of course was in the
big strafe of April 24th. Yet we maintained communications with Brigade that day (and were the only

battery to do so), for Moss in particular was out on
the lines, taking all sorts of risks—following up the
shells, it almost seemed, as they lighted by the wire,
and at once repairing the damage. He well earned
the Military Medal that was awarded him.

CHAPTER X

WE were due now for a fairly long rest ; so, on April 30th, leaving Bonnay, we passed well beyond Amiens to Bourdon, and, four days after, went on to Gorenflos, where for nearly three weeks we had a royal time. The village, a pleasant little one, with a massive grove of horse-chestnut trees shading the green, slopes downwards towards some pretty country, which, with its lanes and hedges and thickets, reminded us poignantly of England—poignantly, for as the thought of loved ones and the sweet home-life came to our minds, we felt but the more that the war held us in its grip ; we knew not when, if ever, we should see our own again ; and sadness, for a moment, overcame us.

We were billeted comfortably in barns and disused houses. Practically no work was invented for us—conduct on the part of the authorities which we highly appreciated, knowing, as every soldier does, how often in the army so-called " rests," urgently needed by the men, have been made the occasion for useless, wearying toil. So then we could spend the days as we liked—sitting out reading and writing in the orchards, then brightly green, and with a bird's nest

here and there ; sipping and smoking in the pleasant
estaminets of the place ; walking to neighbouring
villages. Those fresh, clean days !

> " Bliss was it to be alive,
> But to be young was very heaven."

Not quite, for still war, and the uncertainty of the
future, could not be wholly forgotten. We used to
walk to Domart, five or six kilos away, where one
could get what was unobtainable at Gorenflos, steaks
and eggs and *pommes de terre frites*. We went one
day to a house for these delicacies ; returned two
days after to find it destroyed by a bomb ! Happily
the inhabitants were unhurt, except for shock, but
we knew not whether to appreciate it, as considerate-
ness overriding their own troubles, or smile at the
estimate implied of the materialistic British soldier,
when they rejoined, immediately we had congratulated
them on their escape, " Mais vous avez besoin de
pommes de terre frites ! Hélas, m'sieu' ! Mais, si
vous revenez dans trois jours, vous en aurez."

It was at Gorenflos that we first came across the
Yanks—Engineers these, who had been working
during the winter up by Péronne. They were good
fellows, and it was of much interest to us to meet
them now, at a time when on America's solid help so
much was depending. Two day-trips were made
to St. Valéry, and most of the battery endured the
seven or eight hours' lorry riding for the sake of seeing
a town and the sea again. Now, too, the canteen
was restarted, on as democratic a basis as is possible
in the Army, and Batt commenced his eminently

successful career in this sphere, in which—so strong
is the power of affinity—he was later joined by Bombardier "Whaler." An expedition of three days up
forward was arranged for a limited company. The
reason why the six men of E Sub. were sent was never
disclosed by the officers ; the reason why the three
of A Sub. went was never disclosed by the men. The
nine, however, had a merry time together, not least
when they tried to explain to one another, and to
Mr. Edmondson, why they were being penalised.

Ask any Centre Section man about Gorenflos, and
he will make a wry face. The fact is, through having
had twelve days at Bonnay on a "silent position"—
days of severe work, and, at one period, heavy shelling—they had now, after eight days' rest, to represent the battery in action again. On May 8th, accordingly, they moved up to the Amiens-Albert road, an
area with which the whole battery was to be well
acquainted for the next three months.

On May 19th the remainder of us left Gorenflos.
It was a long, interesting journey back to the line :
first, through the pleasant little villages of Picardy
and the well-cultivated country ; then, from the crest
of a slope, Amiens comes in sight. Queen of the
plain the wide-spreading city with its great cathedral
looks. But nowadays the name is ominous. Since
the end of March, Amiens has been a target for the
Boche's shells and bombs—hardly any of its inhabitants are left, houses are smashed, the streets are a
tangle of broken telegraph-wires. Yes, we are nearing
the war area once again. The pleasant times of
peace are over ; again we know not what an hour

may bring to us.   Amiens has to be skirted by lorries ;
even as we pass we see the familiar cloud of smoke
and débris arise from the further quarter of the city.
The villages have no longer an attractive aspect, and
in the fields the growing crops are in many places
damaged by the tracks of Tanks, horses, and the like
across them.   One sees for the present, however, no
more shelling—that was concentrated on Amiens.

We spent four uneventful days in action near our
precursors of the Centre Section, and then the whole
battery retired a few kilos to Querrieu, where for
three weeks we occupied a reserve position ; the guns,
that is to say, were kept fully ready for action, but
there would be no action unless the Boche advanced
considerably.   As a matter of fact, it was thought possible that he might attempt to do so, and the battery
were given orders, in case he did break through, to
be ready to move to positions at St. Gratien, and
further back still to Rainneville.   We were instructed
that our guns might have to be pulled out of their
pits so as to cover any part of the Corps area in the
event of a temporary success by the enemy, and—this
indeed would have been a critical moment for us
wretched gunners !—arrangements had to be made
for the Lewis gun to be turned on any enemy, if they
got through our lines.

The Boche, however, attempted no further push on
this front, and we were enabled to pursue a life which
was, with modifications, a continuation of our life at
Gorenflos.   There was a little more work on the guns,
and an N.C.O.s' class was formed to run its usual
brief and chequered existence.   And every day a

score or so of men had to go as a fatigue party to
Cardinette, a few kilos away ; they used to come back
describing the expedition as the greatest " mike "
discovered, even in the Army. After a pleasant ride
there was perhaps an hour's digging to be done, and
the rest of the day one could lounge happily away in
the beautiful woods of the place. This stunt, too,
was reckoned a very good one, for the reason that
at Cardinette wine could be procured, long since
disappeared from the estaminets of Querrieu.

Querrieu is a village lying across the Amiens-Albert
road, and sloping down from it towards three small
lakes. The officers were billeted in the " Villa des
Roses," on the higher side of the main road ; the men
in empty cottages at the lower end of the village,
near the guns, which lay in an orchard by the lakes.
Two things stand out most in men's recollections of
Querrieu—the lakes and the H. Vicks. Immediately
the short morning parade, with its gas-mask or rifle
inspection, was over, or the unostentatious cleaning
of the gun had been done, " Are you coming for a
swim ? " was the question, and down we went to the
water. It was lovely soft water ; how we that had
known bodily discomfort during the winter revelled
in the daily bliss of its soft, cleansing touch ! On the
one side of the lakes, the ground, trodden down by
horses and men, was muddy or sun-baked on the
different days ; but on the other, where a château was
embosomed in a wood, beautiful firs and elms fringed
the bank, and coming to the lake from the dusty
village, or, as it happened later on, from a time
of stress up forward, one felt the cares of war, the

thought of its dangers as well as of its minor annoy-
ances, pass away as one went through the clean, cool
waters, and looked into the dark depths of the trees
or up at the skies where the fleecy clouds rioted with
one another across a heaven of infinite blue.

Except for the lakes Querrieu, as was but natural,
compared poorly with Gorenflos. Most of the inhabitants had fled, and the village looked neglected
and unkempt ; whitewashed walls, now splashed and
dirty, houses bare and open to any passer-by, weedy
or trampled-down gardens. Happily, the gross things
of earth—milk, eggs, and butter—were fairly easy to
obtain from the inhabitants who remained, and the
gardens afforded us new potatoes, cabbages, rasp-
berries, gooseberries, and flowers.

They were brave people, those few score inhabitants who remained. It was not, of course, nearly so
dangerous here as at Laviéville, which had been
within range of any kind of Boche gun ; but villages,
behind the lines, such as Querrieu—back-areas as
they were called—were subjected at this time to a
good deal of strafing with high-velocity guns. It was
not over-accurate shooting, but casualties sometimes
resulted. One day a shell burst among some Labour
men standing in a street near the lake, and killed
several ; while at Allonville, a village near by, two
H. Vicks, falling in crowded billets, killed or wounded
sixty men. The civilians, therefore, were facing
death as much as soldiers. Once or twice, when we
were drinking milk in one of the farm-kitchens in the
village, we heard two or three sudden bursts—not too
near, though they shook the building slightly. Two

aged ladies slowly moved down into the cellar ; our
host, a middle-aged " Poilu," temporarily released
for farm-work, ejaculated, " Brigand, le Boche !
Brigand ! " and stolidly went on with his supper. All
the inhabitants were served out with gas-masks by
the French authorities, and the little children carried
them about, proud of their sinister plaything. Once
a shell came unexpectedly over in a garden where
some of our men were sitting and playing cards.
Madly they ducked—one of them, literally, into a
bucket of water ! Another shell that came over was
approved of by the Aussies for it provided them with
some ready-killed hens. It was for some time a
custom of the Boche to send over three or four shells
about half-past seven in the morning. We would
hear them as we lay in bed, wait till we had counted
three, then, if there was a pause, that effort was
evidently finished ; so up, and down to the lake, to
learn perhaps that one of these recent shells had just
dropped into it.

On June 16th a great blow befell us, felt the more
keenly because, with all this intermittent shelling,
life at Querrieu followed generally such a peaceful
course. The Germans started shelling in the evening
near the lower end of the village, and, before the bombardment was finished, Mr. Glover and Mr. Baugh
left the officers' mess to see if the men were all right.
They had not gone two hundred yards when, as they
were crossing the high-road, a 5˙9 shell burst almost at
their feet, and both were instantaneously killed. They
were men of very different types and experiences, but
alike in a steady coolness and in an energy and keen-

ness that never flagged.   It was a hard fate that took
them from our midst.

Besides shelling, the Boche was very active bombing
in the neighbourhood of Querrieu.   The château, which
was used as a Staff headquarters, and the horse lines
by the lakes and elsewhere, were chiefly aimed at.
How frequently have we settled down in our blankets
for half an hour's comfortable read, when, " Lights
out ; there's a Boche about ! " some one suggests.
" No, no ! " the readers protest ; " that's one of ours
you can hear."   " No, it isn't, you mug ! Can't you
tell a Gotha yet ?   Besides, can't you hear the Ack-
Acks ? " [1] Grumbling, the readers put down their
Oppenheim or Anthony Hope.   Woof ! Woof ! come
the horrid sounds, putting all doubts at rest.   A
minute's pause.   " He seems to have passed over,"
remarks a literary one, anxious to get back to his
romance.   " No, he's not ; he's only shut off his
engines.   You wait a——"   Woof ! Woof ! six times
straight off.

" Heavens ! he's shovelling them out now, isn't
he ? "   And we lie without further remonstrance in
the darkness, or perhaps go to sleep while that bumping sound continues in the distance.

We didn't flatter ourselves that we were the direct
object of the Boche's attentions, though he gave the
cookhouse a rude shaking one night.   Now and then
we had spectacular compensation for our disturbance
Some one would report that "they'd got him in the
searchlights."   Out the less lethargic of us would
jump from our blankets ; yes, there in the apex of

---

[1] Anti-aircraft guns (Ack in signalling code = A).

the searchlights was a black object steadily mounting higher. Bursts of Ack-Ack fire clustered around him. "Go it, you devil!" encouraged some men. "He's a plucky fellow, that Boche! He's shooting at the Ack-Ack men," for down the beams of light the red tracer-bullets could be seen going, even as others were flying upwards, sent both to guide the aim of the machine-gunners and to fire the airman's petrol tank. With keen interest we watched for two or three minutes: "Ah! he's got away," and in truth the moving object was not to be seen in the long beams of light now groping, as it were blindly, across the dark ceiling of the skies.

With so much shelling and bombing about the village, many men thought it advisable to leave the houses at night, and sleep in the trenches near by. One set of men who did this placed a big door across the trench for a roof. Then they camouflaged it with gravel, and apparently too successfully, for, in the early morning, a horse walked heavily over it, and, a panel breaking, one of the sleepers awoke with a great iron-shod hoof and ugly fetlock just by his head. He had a fright!

One night three fires broke out in the village, and we wondered whether Boche agents had been at work. At any rate, a couple of nights after, occurred the longest H. Vick shoot that we ever experienced. A bombardment with ordinary guns may, of course, last any length of time, but an H. Vick shoot, on a place behind the line, is generally restricted to a few rounds. Such we hoped that this would be when we heard the first one or two come over. But plunk!

10

plunk ! they continued to come, and, as some struck
the ground with the soft thud as of an orange, " That's
gas ! " we agreed.   In all a couple of hundred came
over, at a slow rate, so that we could listen to them,
if we preferred that to sleeping, for three or four
hours.   Nearly all were plus, but in the morning we
found that three had fallen in the village between us
and the officers' mess ; the Mayor's good lady was
gassed, but not too seriously.   It was no wonder that
Colonel Andrewes, inspecting us next day, sympathised
with us on the fact that our stay at Querrieu, nominally a kind of rest, had not been altogether of that
nature.   These gas-shells came, it was suspected,
from captured 60-pounders of ours in Hamel Wood ;
anyhow, no more came over at Querrieu after the
Aussies took this wood on July 4th.

Although our guns were in this " reserve " position
at Querrieu for only three weeks, our rest-billets
remained there for another couple of months.   Very
familiar, therefore, did the place become to us.   It
was there that the Spanish 'flu found us, and laid
nearly half the battery low.   Nor was this the only
one of the amenities of civilisation that we now
enjoyed.   A strapping young French woman rode
daily into the village to sell us—*inter alios*—the
English newspapers ; concert parties, the " Gunners,"
" Cheerios," and others treated us to the latest London
melodies ; and out on the cool lawn of the " Villa des
Roses," we had ourselves a cheerful concert one night,
at which Mr. Edmondson and Mr. Glover, both soon
to be lost to us, rendered their amusing duet on " The
Very Best Battery."   We played much cricket too.

We possessed a crack bowler in Batt (weighed down
as he was with the cares of his canteen, and the hard
duty of refusing to let other troops have more than
our own men had), a good wicket-keeper in Fulford
Brown, and excellent all-round men in Clarkson and
Coulter. We beat our sister battery, 146, by an
innings and fifty runs, but an Aussie team, in which
appeared Parks, the Test Match player, and Victor
Trumper's brother, " put it across " us badly. Playing on the bumpy ground was rather more dangerous
than being strafed by the Boche, and a wicket matting
was sent for by a Yorkshire enthusiast and proved of
much value.

Religious services were held on Sunday mornings
in the deserted village schoolroom, where still old
maps hung on the walls, and the exercise-books of the
poor little kiddies were scattered about on the desks.
Some of us in the evenings attended (some did not)
the services at the Y.M.C.A.—quiet, restful times,
presided over by Australian padres, active in thought,
and gratefully unconventional in phrasing.

Towards the end of June a G.R.O. was issued, as
a result of the Boche's back-area strafing propensities,
that no troops were to be billeted in villages, and we
accordingly had to move into a field on the other side
of the road from the orchard in which our guns had
lain. This field, big and square-shaped, and sloping
gently up from the road, seemed to have been chiselled
out of the earth, for except at the road-end it was
lower by some feet than the surrounding land. A
bank, ten feet high in parts, was thus provided, and
in it, with considerable labour, we carved out our

habitations—comfortable, roomy dug-outs ; we roofed
them with tarpaulin and corrugated iron, fixed clothes-
pegs, shelves, a clock here and there in them, scrounged
a few chairs, and were not at all badly off. Living in
these cool earthen cells, indeed, almost seemed the
proper mode of existence that hot summer time. It
was a merry life. I wish I could describe the constant
chaff and banter that went on in our midst ! To the
outsider it would appear very small beer, no doubt.
He wouldn't understand our ironical references to
one another's failings and lapses—to one man's supposed ambition to get a " stripe," or to another's
prolonged stay at the base or a " Con. Camp," conduct
for which there was perfectly legitimate explanation,
but which, we must sadly believe, indicated some vice
—indolence, or what not—on the part of the man in
question. He wouldn't understand the lively attacks
of the gunners " sans phrases " on the " observers,"
" spotters," and " limber-gunners," nor the fierceness
with which these specialists defended their right to
be excused fatigues. Only the soldier, or any man
similarly circumstanced, would understand, and give
us credit for the fact that, living as we were in the
rudest of styles, and day in, day out, with the same
men, where monotony might have bred boredom, and
intimacy irritableness, we stayed these tendencies,
and preferred the lighter, cheerier outlook.

CHAPTER XI

IT will be recalled that the months of June and
July were a period of comparative quiet on the
British front, set in between the turbulent experiences of the March retreat and the ordered haste
of our final offensive. That our battery profited by
this quiet will have been evident from the last few
pages, for even when the guns were several kilos in
front of Querrieu we had not too hard a time. The
Centre and Right sections, both before and after our
stay in reserve at Querrieu, occupied positions along
the Amiens-Albert road some nine kilos from the latter
town, now of course in German hands; the Left
Section were a couple of kilos further back along the
same road, near the village of Franvillers. The
country round here is undulating chalk land. Along
many of the grassy slopes there are terraces, with
tracks broad enough for cart-traffic, and with a chalk
wall on the inner side several feet high. For years
to come the attention of the traveller passing along
the great roads of these districts will be attracted by
the whiteness of freshly-made cuttings along these
terraces; they occur, he will notice, in groups, so
that the level of some hillsides seems a regular alter-

nation of white chalk and green grass. These mark
the old British and German dug-outs and gun positions. The particular position occupied by the
Centre Section was on a broad track, running to the
right off the road, and the cup-like gun-pits we used
had been carved out of the terrace side by our predecessors. The ground in front of the guns sloped
very gently up, a field of grass ; very gently down,
behind, a great field of standing corn, neglected, and
partly spoiled by tracks, telephone-wires, shell-holes.
On the right, a couple of hundred yards away, rose
a long ridge, from the crest of which we could look
across to the shelled village of Morlancourt. The
Albert road on our left is adorned with the usual fine
avenue of trees, and the coolness of their shade was
very attractive to men working out in the hot whiteness of the chalky gun position. In lower-lying fields
on the left of the road were a 60-pounder and an
8-inch battery ; aligned with us in the terrace, but
further away from the road, was an Australian 4·5
battery, while the ridge on our right was used as an
infantry Brigade Headquarters.

The Centre Section, as has been mentioned, took up
this position on May 8th, and were kept busy improving the gun-pits and dug-outs ; they harassed
Boche roads pretty regularly, and at times engaged
in destructive shoots on his batteries. The Boche at
first was not greatly troubled about our area, but he
often shelled a little road that ran well to our rear
at the bottom of the cornfield ; and the ground that
sloped upwards on the other side of this road showed
on its grassy surface a pattern of darker, circular

patches—shell-holes new and old. On May 19th the Right Section came up, A gun being placed with the others in the terrace, B in a pit along the high road. It was only here four days, the whole position being then handed over temporarily to 200 S.B., but on June 13th their former positions were reoccupied by both sections along the Albert road. It was beautiful, sunny weather now ; the growing corn, the long line of dark trees, the grassy slopes made up a fine landscape ; there was sufficient, but not too much work ; and, considering it was war, men felt that they might have been far worse off.

The O.P. from here was Bir O.P., situated on the highest point of the ridge to our right. It commanded a wide view of the Ancre valley, particularly of the long slope and high ground on which Morlancourt stood, while on the far horizon one saw a fringe of trees marking where a high road ran. Signallers and officers spent pleasant days up here, with a large element of picnicking in them. Once two signallers found a nearly full bottle of whisky in the sap up here. " Once," says the author of *Peter and Wendy*, " a little boy, playing in St. James's Park, lost a halfpenny in the grass, and digging about for it, found a penny. There has been a lot of digging there since." Even the shooting—for if the officers saw enemy movement they would ring up the battery for a burst of fire—was conducted in a pleasant spirit. Thus an entry in a diary for one of these June days reads : " I had a pot at some dug-outs during the afternoon, with fair success," and on another, " Saw some Boches moving once in a hedge, so chucked

a few shells among them to show there was no ill-
feeling." Perhaps it was with the same kindly intention
that the Boche in turn shelled the O.P. from time to
time Thus on Whit-Monday, for example, an officer
had gone to the O.P. with no evil purpose, and was
mildly enjoying the fresh morning and the sunshine,
when at 7.30 a shell dropped, about six yards away.
He was behind a bank, and, with friendly curiosity,
waited to see what was going to happen, when another
dropped, a couple of yards away. This induced him,
with the telephonist, to clear into the sap, and just as
they were entering one dropped very near, happily
without hurting them. A continuous bombardment
confined them to the sap for two hours, and provided
them, when at length they were able to emerge, with
plenty of work, mending wires and sorting out kits.

Fritz was livelier now about the gun position too.
He seemed to have the 8-inch battery to our left rear
" taped," and at times we witnessed some splendid
shooting on it, the shells dropping right amidst the
camouflage. Now and then they fell short, or came a
little left, which irritated us. Thus on June 22nd
splinters from a shell that burst near the road caught
a cartridge-box, one of several which formed part of
the wall of A Sub. dug-out. It blazed up, a terrific
flame, for these boxes were full, and not of earth as
is usual with such cases ; the two men in the dug-out,
Barnes and Edwards, were severely burned. The
other boxes were bound to catch fire if left a minute,
but Captain Chattey and George Bastow rushed on
them and pulled them away. Boche shells were
dropping about too closely for comfort, and blew up

some trees by the roadside, but the same two turned
on to another piece of work, extinguishing some camouflage which had been set on fire on a limber. Later
they were mentioned in dispatches for their coolness
this day. On the 25th Fritz was again troublesome,
and some men who were being relieved at the time
had to clear off down the road as quickly as possible,
leaving their kits behind them. The modest ones
did not make their wants known when they arrived
at Querrieu, and spent the night but coldly, stamping
for hours up and down the field to keep their blood
in circulation. And when they returned to the position on the 27th Fritz evinced just as much hatred
of them. Their lorry had reached the point where
the Albert road crosses the little road to the rear of
our position when Fritz dropped one shell behind,
another in front of it. People fell, rather than climbed,
out of that lorry, and well to one flank or the other
everybody cleared with that horrid stimulus behind
them.

But it was on Friday, June 28th, that the tragedy
of our stay at this position took place. The day
opened clear and beautiful, with the sunshine dwelling
on the grass and corn amidst which men lived up
there. Suddenly, soon after nine o'clock, there came
the well-known roar through the air, and two shells—
a salvo, though of duds—fell behind the position. It
was a warning to our men, and many cleared, either to
the fine sap on the 4·5 position or to an unfinished sap
of our own. Another salvo came over ; this time the
shells burst, and our wireless operator could now
detect something ominous—a Boche aviator correct-

ing the shooting, apparently with the battery as
target.   Another shell, and one more came over,
right on the position ; then all ceased.   With splendid
gunnery the Boche had ranged on our position, and
he knew now exactly how to lay his guns for a destructive bombardment.   It was his habit, however, to
let two or three hours intervene between a ranging
shoot and a destructive shoot, and during the rest of
the morning, he sent no more shells over.   The gun-
teams, however, were not too happy ; they knew a
bombardment of some kind was impending, and they
kept in shelter as far as possible.   A working party
from the Franvillers section, which came up about
ten o'clock, was at once sent back by Captain Chattey,
with the exception of one man, who did not feel himself fortune's favourite.   Dinner at midday relieved
the tension, and after it men had settled down for a
smoke or a nap when, at 2.5, that roar came again
through the summer air, and the earth rocked—rocked,
for it was again with the impact of two duds.   Off
everybody cleared to the saps again, and for some
twenty-five minutes the Boche continued shelling the
position, sending over some forty rounds in all.   That
finished with all our men still unharmed.   But nobody
thought that the Boche was yet satisfied ; still that
anxiety brooded over the position, though, a 'plane
shoot on our part being in prospect, men had to stand
by for the present.

   This time the wait was not long.   Just after half-
past three a bombardment again started on the position, with yet another salvo of duds.   The two officers,
the Captain and Mr. Edmondson, were in the officers'

mess, a dug-out in the middle of the position. They came out now—the Captain first, in order to get to the telephone, report to Brigade that the shelling had recommenced, and ask that a big gun to our rear might try to neutralise the enemy. Mr. Edmondson followed on his way towards the sap. In the few yards he had to traverse he met one of our men dashing blindly across the position to the 4·5 sap at the other end, in which he had taken refuge during the previous strafe. But, as it happened, in this present strafe the first Boche shells had fallen at the 4·5 end of our position, and had the man gone on, he might well have run straight into one ; as it was, he was in the smoke and débris of the first salvo when Mr. Edmondson caught him by the arm, saying, " Where are you going, man ? Come this way," and turned him towards our sap. " He saved others. . . ." Both reached the sap-head, but Mr. Edmondson did not enter, but walked a few paces outside. Then the Captain came hurrying back from sending his message. They had hardly exchanged a few words before they heard another shell coming through the air. The sap was but a few yards away, but Mr. Edmondson, always a very cool man, was slow in getting there, the shell burst near by, and a splinter struck him. Crying out, " I'm hit," and conscious, as he must have been, of the gravity of the wound, he ran off the position in the direction of a dressing-station higher up the Albert road. Pollard, Ring, and the Captain dashed out at once, but Mr. Edmondson had already gone some fifty yards, become insensible, and had fallen when they came up with him. Ring bore him on his back to the dressing-station, where he died within a few minutes. He was a " white " man.

In this strafe only ten rounds came over, but they were well on the position, three holes appearing just behind the guns, and the spotter's machine-gun being knocked out.

Yet once more, between eight and nine o'clock, did the saddened men have to stand another bombardment ; it was of about the same number of shells, and started with the usual salvos of duds. Happily no loss was sustained on this occasion, though there were some trying moments after one shell had set on fire an 8-inch dump on the other side of the road. It flared up, and now Boche bombing 'planes came over, and there was the prospect of being bombed, as well as shelled, before the 8-inch men and our men, working desperately to smother the flame. When this strafe was over, those of the men who could not sleep in the sap went down to the Franvillers position for the night, as it was impossible to know whether the Boche would not shell the position again.

Mr. Edmondson was buried the next day in Querrieu Military Cemetery by the side of his two brother-officers. All of us who were free attended, mourning the loss of a bright, courageous man.

The original position was now condemned, as it was obviously known to the Boche, and the guns were moved on to the high road, with the exception of C gun, which, being on the left flank of the old position, was supposed to be more or less away from the enemy's line of fire. There was still fairly frequent shelling on the batteries near us, but the Boche was

apparently satisfied that he had destroyed our position, and, the new position being partly camouflaged
by the great trees along the road, as well as by art,
we suffered now but little from his attentions. This
was the period of "active defence" on the British
front. The Boche had for long desisted from attempt-
ing further advance, and our men were making various
local attacks preliminary to the great offensive of
August. From time to time the old familiar orders
were coming through to the battery: "On a date and
at a zero hour to be notified later, a minor operation
will be carried out by such-and-such a division. The
points of bombardment will be registered by batteries
in an unobtrusive manner." As early as May 19th
we were shooting from two to four in the early morning, assisting in the capture by the 2nd Australian
Division of Ville-sur-Ancre, with 400 prisoners. On
July 3rd the order was received for a hundred gas-
shells to be got ready on each gun. This was a big
number, and it was followed by a long shoot from
half-past three to nine in the early morning of July 4th.
Soon, however, we were gratified to hear that the
Australians, with four companies of Americans and
sixty Tanks, had captured Hamel and Vaire Woods,
places which we had from time to time shelled since
first we went to Laviéville.

It was judged advisable to move still further back,
and accordingly, on July 12th the Right Section guns
were placed in the low road to the rear of the original
position, while the Centre Section remained on the
high road, but were now on a downward slope three
hundred yards or so behind where they had been

before. They took over here two excellently camouflaged gun-pits, and good, if small, dug-outs, and the
working party from the Franvillers position dug a
sap here. Two days after this move had been made,
the Boche obtained O.K.'s on one of the vacated gun-
pits and on an adjoining dug-out. But life in the
new position was not without its incidents. Rickard
and Morris, for instance, the spotters, tell a tale how
on July 15th, a gloriously hot day, a shoot being just
over, they were lying on their backs in the cornfield
behind the Right Section guns (Morris doubtless with
his ancient nigger straw hat on), when suddenly a
salvo of two shells fell between them and the guns.
Snatching up tin hats and gas-masks they dashed up
the slope towards their dug-out, which was in the
middle of the field; but as they went, that old uncomfortable feeling came over them that Jerry was following them, for salvos of 4·2's kept falling about them.
There were shell-holes about into which they dived
time after time, and eventually they worked their
way to the sap by the roadside now under construction. They *were* hot, they say. However, when
they had rested a bit, and the firing seemed to have
ceased, they went back to fetch the mugs and plates
that they had left behind, and nearly ran into Jerry's
last shot, which he placed just behind the guns again.
It fell five to six yards away ; they threw themselves
flat down in the corn, and escaped damage. Nor did
any casualties occur amongst the Right Section, who
had had a rather warm time, the shoot being apparently on the road in which their guns were.

THE AMIENS-ALBERT ROAD

CHAPTER XII

URING all this time the Left Section were having what they describe as the finest time of the war. Franvillers ! The name calls up memories of sunny, green slopes, cool dug-outs, and a leisurely existence close to kindly Mother Earth. We built the dug-outs, it is true, largely as a protection against man's evil designs, but Nature did what she could in horrid times of war to win us to her love. The soft warmth of days in June, "when, if ever, come perfect days," the march of the silent stars across the heavens, the freshness of morning, the peace of evening—these we could enjoy, if we pleased, disturbed by hardly any cares, whether of work, of food, even of war.

Our two guns formed a " silent section," and during the whole time were only once used for a shoot (and, good luck to them ! the " Wabbits " had to do that, not we of the " senior " team). Of the dug-outs, some were by the roadside, but the majority were a little away from it, in a dell formed by an old chalk-pit, part of which was occupied by 312 Battery. They were carefully made, well roofed, and improved as time went on. Each held two or three men, parti-

cular chums ; thus " Uppy " and Greenhow were one
pair of troglodytes; Billy, " Baby," and their sergeant
of course hung together, wondering each morning
which of the others would fetch the breakfast ; while
the Welsh " Nen C.O." (at that time engaged on
writing his book, *Mugs I have Known*) allowed H. Vick
and Gibbs to live with him, so that they could detail
him for fatigues.

There was no need to rise early in the morning ;
after a leisurely breakfast, and perhaps a touch to
the guns, we jumped on to a passing lorry, towel in
hand (gas-mask also over our shoulder to remind us
we were at war), and so through La Houssoye and
Pont Noyelles to the cool waters of the lake at Querrieu. Reading, letter-writing, card- and chess-playing
—so the days passed. Any anxiety concerning us on
the part of our people at home was well out of place
then. And in the evening a short walk across the
cornfields brought us to the village of Franvillers.
Our billets had for a few days been in some houses
here ; but this, like other villages, attracted enemy
fire ; we well remember one great 8-inch that burst
in a garden near by while we were drawing water in
the village street, and there was another, a big knob
from which, coming through the window, rent the
wall of the room in which some of our men were
sleeping. Most of the inhabitants had therefore fled,
but here, as in worse-shelled villages, a number
remained. We asked them why.

" M'sieu', si nous partons, nous ne pourrons pas
revenir pendant la guerre. Notre mobilier sera brisé
ou volé ; il ne faut pas partir d'ici."

"But surely," we said, "it isn't worth the risk."

"Si, si, m'sieu'," rejoined madame firmly, "nous restons." Brave women they! They fitted up the cellar as a refuge, and sometimes they were glad to retreat to it. And materialists that we were, we had occasion to appreciate their courage, for from them we were able to get fresh milk and eggs daily, besides having the pleasure of a chat with some one outside the Army. Pretty, demure little M——! I wonder, and not I alone, whether that marriage will come off with the Aussie whose heart she had won. Grandma, a dear, benevolent dame, was learning English, studying her book with an air of great wisdom out in the farmyard of an evening, so that she could accompany the young couple to that wonderful country whence came these stalwart men. For me it was sufficient to get the little young lady to tot up her figures, and hopelessly entangle herself in them: "Ecoutez, m'sieu'! Vous avez douze œufs à dix sous. Ça fait cinq francs. Et vous avez encore. . . . Ça fait . . ." "Ça fait"—it was queerly pleasant to hear those words from the pretty face with the ringlets of dark hair.

On our right the land sloped away from the high road towards the village of Heilly, which was well shelled by the Boche. Beyond Heilly and the Somme valley the ground rose again in a long ridge, where several of our batteries were stationed, and on it I remember once seeing a particularly fine exhibition by the Boche of "searching and sweeping": the smoke (followed in a second or two by the sound of

11

the burst) rising at one spot, then, half a minute after,
a hundred yards to the right, then another hundred
yards to the right, and so on. But round us none
ever fell ; our guns, besides being silent, were too
well camouflaged both with the ordinary draping
and with a high curtain put up for us by Aussie
Engineers.

Gothas were about on most nights, and interrupted
often enough our reading by candle-light, but their
targets were horse-lines and batteries some distance
from us. Of course we were not sorry each night
when they had passed well away, and the thwack of
their missiles no longer resounded in our ears. One
night we thought wè had had a narrow escape—the
earth shaking with the bursts ; but it was two hundred
yards up the road that we later discovered the bomb-
holes, two great holes nearly opposite one another on
the two sides of the road, the corn flattened out for
ten yards round by the violence of the explosion.
The Boche airmen were very daring in their attacks
on our observation balloons. One evening, in particular, the rattle of machine-guns—a frequent sound—
broke out by us. We looked up ; our Ack-Ack guns,
also, were firing now, and near their bursts, unfortunately not too near, we saw a Boche 'plane heading
straight for one of our balloons. The observers
jumped overboard in their parachutes, and two small
swaying figures in the clear air slowly descended
earthwards. Meanwhile, undeterred by the barrage
put about—mostly behind—him, the Boche flew past
the balloon, and rose again. Had he missed it ?
They never did, when they flew so close. In a minute,

flames burst out from the huge mass, and it sank, a
slow, trailing pillar of smoke, to the earth. But
Fritz had not finished. " Why, he's after that other
one," came the cry, and in truth he had turned, and
was making straight for another balloon in an opposite
quarter of the sky, and this one too he had.   There
were obvious signs of " wind up " in the other balloons
visible to us ; they were slowly being hauled down.
But all too slowly ! Off to those further quarters of
the skies Fritz dashed, and, while we could hardly
believe our eyes, that same man had destroyed
yet two more balloons.   Then high aloft, leaving
those black pillars of smoke beneath him, he
soared, well pleased with himself, and caring nothing
for the bursts of Ack-Ack shells that formed beneath
his track.

> " And even the ranks of Tuscany
> Could scarce forbear to cheer."

There was plenty of room in the air that evening.

Such a violent attack on balloons was generally the
prelude to a retreat on Fritz's part, and in this instance
the retreat of August followed.   It ought to be added
that our air service nearly always took stern revenge
on the enemy's balloons for these attacks, and that
an attack on a practically defenceless balloon, though
in hostile territory, is not considered by airmen too
difficult a performance.

It was through a Boche 'plane that we sustained
our only casualty at Franvillers. About eight o'clock
one morning when our men were firing at one, the
merest speck up in the blue sky, a knob from an

Ack-Ack shell dropped through the canvas roof of one of the dug-outs, fell on Newland, still recumbent, happily or unhappily, and broke one of his ribs.

From July 1st to 3rd our team took a spell of work up forward to relieve A Sub., who were much weakened by the influenza epidemic ; our appearance there led to ironical inquiries from the " fighting " Subs. as to whether the noise of our guns gave us shell-shock. People will try to tweak the lion's beard. About July 8th the claims of work were presented to us again, for it was we of the Left Section who had to go up forward to dig a sap. So we found ourselves engaged for some four or five hours a day (every two days rather, since we worked in shifts) picking, shovelling, and hauling the earth in sandbags up to ground level—steady, rather back-breaking work. These saps are some twenty feet or more deep, and consist of a gallery fifteen or twenty yards long, with an ascent of twenty-five steps at each end ; the whole cavity is lined with stout timber planks. For most of the time Aussie sappers were in charge of the work, rough, vigorous chaps, with whom we became very friendly. We shall not soon forget that Socialist orator whom we could so easily induce to dilate on his sufferings and his views when we didn't feel in a mood for work, nor shall we forget his lurid-tongued pal who worked with diabolical energy for an hour, and had to take the rest of the time off. We started three saps along the Albert road as the battery moved progressively backward, but while we were engaged on the third, the Aussies, to our regret, moved away from our front ; we saw no more those slouch-hats every-where, and those rough, generous fellows with their free men's stride. Some R.E.s took charge of us and our sap, and rapidly and efficiently completed the work.

CHAPTER XIII

THE BEGINNING OF THE ADVANCE

SOLDIERS spoke often of their memory being affected by the life "out there," but, however that was, certain dates they never forgot. July 31st, for instance. "You remember the stunt that day," one would ask another, "the day we meant to get up to Passchendaele"; or again, "Were you there on March 21st, when the Boche made his push?" Classed with these days, indeed the chief of all, stands now August 8th, that day when the British started their series of "hammer blows," which was to continue irresistibly for three crowded months, and to end only when the broken enemy sued humbly for peace.

Throughout the whole Army there was an expectation of this great effort for weeks before it actually commenced. The Boche had been making a last desperate effort on the French front—the Rheims-Soissons sector. We had followed it with bated breath; wondered whether it was, after all, more than Foch could hold; whether Foch had indeed said, as the Poilus reported, "I give the Boche till the end of June, then I shall begin"; then one day we rushed to tell one another the great news, "Foch has struck." July 22nd was that memorable date, which one felt to be the turning-point of the war. Now on those peaceful fields above our little dug-outs at Franvillers we pored over the map of the salient in front of Château-Thierry, rejoiced in the day-by-day progress of French and Yank, and wondered how soon it would be our turn to join in the game.

For it was clear enough that the turn of the British was coming. Early in August the trenches behind our Franvillers positions suddenly became crowded with troops—young English lads, most of them. Fresh to this part of the country, they picked, as we had done, handfuls of apples off the trees by the roadside, and found, as we had done, that they were cider apples, " no bon ! " They knew they had come up for some big stunt—on a thirty-mile front, they thought. And we, of the Left Section, had personal grounds for suspecting this, for on August 2nd we were ordered to move forward to the position originally held by the other sections along the Albert road, and abandoned after the death of Mr. Edmondson. So at length came to an end our delightful stay at Franvillers. We left with regret those quiet slopes and cool caverns, where we had consumed so much milk and so many eggs, and where our guns had been so blessedly and consistently silent.

It was a dull evening, that of August 2nd, after heavy rain. The ground was very slippery, and, to form a track for the guns as we pulled them out, we used for the first time strong wicker mats, which were very satisfactory. Arrived at our new position we found the gun-pits fully prepared for us, through the

efforts of " Bish," our new sergeant-major, and we
toiled away contentedly, pulling in the guns, till the
small hours of the morning.   At a time like this, when
it's nothing but the monotonous order, " Together—
heave ! " for hours on end, little jokes please one, and
the pretended efforts of a couple of men (whom no one
in his military senses ever thought capable of winning
a stripe) to commend themselves to the potent S.M.
by making obvious suggestions in a loud voice, amused
themselves if no one else.

During the next day or two hundreds of shells came
up to the position, the invariable prelude to a big
stunt.   As, however, we were in a position with which
the Boche had already shown his acquaintance, the
guns were kept carefully camouflaged and silent until
the great occasion.   But Fritz wasn't inactive.   From
time to time he shelled the 60-pounders on our left,
and, despite all our tactful silence, about five o'clock
on the evening of August 4th, droning through the air
came the old sound—roar—smash ! and then the
hissing of bits past us.   It was a shoot of half a dozen,
apparently for purposes of registration on us—a plus
in the cornfield behind, a minus on the grass in front.
We all cleared safely away, and that night and subse-
quently slept in the splendid, roomy 4·5 sap.   Fritz
continued his attentions from day to day.   He gave
us a short 4·2 shoot on the 5th, and about dawn on
the morning of the 6th Jumbo Symes, who had per-
sisted in sleeping on the surface, came down the sap
to warn us there was gas about.   Down there we
heard practically nothing, smelt nothing, and went to
sleep again ; but when we came up for breakfast we

saw holes of little and medium size, gas and H.E., scattered over the area, there was the pungent smell of mustard gas about, and it was clear Fritz had engaged in a fairly thorough area strafe. This we didn't mind, as we were fighting him, but we were moved to bitterness next day when, being down on rest at the old billets, we saw him bombarding the village of Franvillers, and the pillars of destruction steadily rising from amongst the homes of our friends, the kindly Frenchwomen. Heilly, too, on our other flank, was under much fire ; we saw the burst here and there on the grassy slopes as he searched the roads. Amidst these constant shocks on both sides of us, our billets were untouched as before. When we went for the milk that evening, " Oui, m'sieu'," said our pretty little friend, " nous avons dû descendre dans la cave cinq fois aujourd'hui. Le brigand Boche ! "

But equally our artillery preparation was taking place now. We ourselves had started a long shoot at 4.40 this morning of August 7th. We had been rather wroth when Jumbo had had us up at 3 a.m. " Well, we've got to fuse twenty or thirty shells, and get the gun on the line," he said. " Confound it, you Oriental tyrant," we protested, " we could have done all that in an hour, and had nearly another hour in bed." We were, indeed, well up to time in this shoot, but had not much to spare, and really we were all glad that our first shoot with Jumbo was so creditable. Originally a gunner in our Sub., he had wandered away from us, giving other Subs. the benefit of his energy and knowledge, but as sergeant he had come back to us, and a cheery time we all had together on most of our stunts

that fine summer—Jumbo, so full of vitality, raging,
with mock ferocity, at one or the other of us; H. Vick
affecting a pleasantly acid style at the expense of his
less expert chums; Uppy (if I may be allowed the less
offensive corruption) saying something silly and
looking something solemn, and making even his " pie-
faced " butt laugh; Bill genially anathematising any
who did not get on with the work; and all the others—
yes, " a merry crowd were we." Just before we
started firing on this occasion a Boche 'plane came
flying back, very low, and dropped two bombs on the
other side of the road, killing a poor fellow on the
8-inch battery.

Firing was more or less continuous during this day
and night. Many men climbed the ridge on our right,
and could see from there the effects of our firing—
the steady bursts of the shells just beyond Morlancourt. It was not till the very end of this day that
we had the first intimation that the great attack was
just about to be launched, for at midnight the order
suddenly came through for twenty gas-shells to be
fused on each gun. (The danger if gas-shells were hit
was so great that they were never fused until just
before being fired.) Some natural tears we felt like
shedding as we turned out of the blankets simply to
fuse shells—and we had had a long spell of shell-humping during the evening; but all was forgotten, except
for the irremediable weariness of limb and eye, when
we had to take part, three or four hours after, in what
was at last the great stunt. " At 4.20 a.m. on August
8th," writes Sir Douglas Haig, " our massed artillery
opened intense fire on the whole front of attack, com-

pletely crushing the enemy's batteries, some of which
never succeeded in coming into action. Simultaneously
British infantry and Tanks advanced to the assault."
So this was what those gas-shells were for! The
fatigue was indeed worth while. With heavier fire
in those first hours after dawn, and harassing fire, less
intense, throughout the day, our battery did its part
in this commencement of the Allied triumph. The
batteries we fired on were 5·9's and 7·7's in Bois des
Tailles and Gressaire Wood, well behind Morlancourt;
after the advance we were able to inspect the ground
we had shelled, and were satisfied to find our M.P.I.
(mean point of impact) in the centre of our target.
There is no need to recall how definite the British
superiority was from this very first day, when on our
right our men advanced nearly seven miles, and
captured Harbonnières and all that part of the Amiens
outer defence line.

Our guns did not go forward that day, but on the
evening of the 9th we pulled them out by seven
o'clock in readiness for moving. There was an electric
feeling in the air that night. We, of course, were
jubilant, yet were wondering a little seriously what
might now await us in this move into the unknown—
"omne ignotum pro terribili." But as two of us
made our way down the great cornfield to fetch some
camouflage from B gun, it seemed as if we could
detect the Boche's extreme nervousness. Up in the
steely blue heavens we heard continually that deep
purring of his Gothas, saw the line of his tracer bullets
spurted forth, heard the crash of his bombs and the
rattle of the machine-guns directed at him as he

moved about from one part of the sky to the other, drawn by the flashes of the guns whose fire he was vainly endeavouring to keep down. Yes, Fritz was now the attacked, battling for his life against the strong assault of the British Army ; infantry, airmen, artillery—by any means whatsoever he must try to ward off this terrible onslaught.

All our preparations were made by ten o'clock, but orders for moving had not yet been received. So we went into the misshapen little dug-outs where during these last few days we had had not too bad a time, and, a bit chilled, for our blankets were already packed up, we got a poor doze in. Just on one o'clock came the order to move. It was a fine, clear night. We travelled back along the Amiens-Albert road, up the slope past the Centre Section's position, turned to the left on the crest, and so down to Ribemont. Then to the left again, and straight forward, the cold moonlight showing us a dusty white road, with dull fields on our left, but on our right the wooded course of the Ancre. Now into a village, whose ruins stare grimly at us. " What place is this ? " we ask one another, and only one or two can suggest that it is Buire. We pass just out of it ; the F.W.D.s are taking us over grassy ground, and chalk banks are rising on each side of us. We halt ; we are at the new position.

Descending from the lorries we unlimbered the guns, and then worked steadily through the night, making a good plank platform, laying the gun on its proper line, and fusing shells. They are hard times, these nights of unbroken exertion, but we were in good spirits, and it was still with considerable gaiety that about six o'clock we saw the cooks preparing to make tea for us. While we toiled on we were talking about the position. " Not a bad one, eh ? Pretty well sheltered, you know, in this pit."

" That's all against it ; don't you think the Boche knows we're likely to use a position like this ? "

" Well, if he does, we've got two good saps here, they say."

" Oh, have we ? Well, I hope they're good enough to sleep in, for the dug-outs round here are horribly dirty places."

Soon it was light enough for us to see our situation. The main street of Buire runs straight beyond the village for some distance, and, at about a hundred yards from the last house, cuts in two an old chalk-pit. Four of our guns were in the hollow on the right-hand side, and here too was a sap in which some of the men lived ; in the hollow on the other side was another, bigger sap, where most of the men and officers lived ; on this side, too, was the cookhouse. We certainly were sheltered here, the wall of the chalk-pit being twelve feet high in front of us. To our rear the pit became two small fields, of corn on the left-hand side, of grass on the right-hand side of the road. Both fields had a dirty, unkempt air ; there were old tins about, and old dug-outs, and the chalk brought out when the saps were made lay, a great bank, in the left-hand hollow, camouflaged with a vast piece of netting which disappeared when we disappeared. Fifty yards in front of us ran the " Emu " trench line, and the ground there was cut up by small

shells, while in our hollows were larger holes which
served us for cartridge-recesses. The village behind us
was ruined by shell-fire, mere walls and frameworks of
houses standing amidst their own débris, just as part
of the tower of the shattered church rose out of a
mass of the white chalk of which it had been
built.   The railway ran along the bank on the right
of our position ; both the little station and the rail-
line had been heavily shelled, and warnings were
posted about that no troops were to march along the
line.

In our eyes, however, Buire was a position hardly
less satisfactory than Bonnay. The weather was fine,
and often we spent a lazy hour out on the grass.   If
the ammunition troubled us sorely through its habit
of coming up each evening just after we had retired
to bed, yet we were almost compensated as we beheld
the strenuous mental labours of the two worthies who
superintended this department, " George " and White.
They generally entangled themselves quite sufficiently
for our amusement with their calculations, their note-
books, and their pathetic queries, " Yes, but how many
shells did you have before I started counting ? "   But
if they didn't, some unkind gunner would ask them
to help us lift the shells, and then we should indeed
be diverted ! We had a good deal of shooting by
night as well as day.   However, the chalky ground
took the spade of our trail splendidly, we could pull
the gun in and out with the least of efforts, and a gun
was easily worked with three men. How different
from the mud-baths of Ypres ! And then—a great
feature to commend a position to us—the Boche did

RAILWAY STATION, BUIRE-SUR-ANCRE

not send a single shell into the chalk-pit during our stay there.

We enjoyed at Buire—what was lacking in many other positions—a good water supply, and doubly welcome was this in that hot existence amongst the chalk, where, every time we fired the gun, we were enveloped in a cloud of chalk dust. Water could be pumped out of a sap in the chalk-pit, or—drinking water this—obtained from a pump on the railway station on the edge of the pit. Very soon too we tracked out a swimming-place ; we crossed the railway line and a marshy meadow, and came to our old friend, the Ancre, a narrow, swift little stream, and it was a decided pleasure to plunge into its keenly cold waters.

The Right Section did not come up until a couple of days after the rest of us, and some of us were bidden to prepare a lodging for them—the cellar of a house, already badly shelled, on a level crossing. It was a dirty job, for the cellar was half-full of coal dust, and we had to take turns getting some fresh air outside. Soon the Boche started shelling the village—a frequent performance of his. We looked out. " Oh, a hundred yards away ; no need to move for stuff like that." The next was a little nearer, but evidently all were meant for the more distant objective, and they were no enemies of ours, with the exception of bursts of shrapnel intended for the level crossing, which three or four times made us dash quickly down into the cellar. I had a tin hat, " Billie," as usual, only a soft cap. These we kept on exchanging like comedians, so as to have the advantage of the tin hat when we stood outside, and the lighter cap when we worked

amidst the coal. What a crime indeed if Billie's
coiffure had been spoilt by coal dust ! Or even mine !
The Right Section guns were placed in a garden along
the road which ran across the rear of our position. It
was from a shell that fell short of the village and
burst between these two guns that our only casualty
at this position occurred, Roberts being wounded.
Other men were on the guns at the time, and must be
considered to have had miraculous escapes.

Living in saps was a new experience for us. These
were broad, roomy saps, smelling horribly of medica-
ments when we took them over. A double layer of
wire-beds was soon fixed up, and we lay there reading
comfortably at night, a score or more of men, nearly
every one with a candle-end by his side. Once the
framework of a bed in the upper tier gave way, and a
" Nen C.O." found H. Vick precipitated on him. As
he was not killed, he merely condemned his guest and
the man who had put up the beds.

The system of reliefs every two days was still maintained, the rest-billets being our old dug-outs along
the Albert road, and, curiously enough, the Boche now
made these more unhealthy than the gun position,
which seemed pretty unreasonable of him, since all
the time the guns had been here, he had not shelled
the road. On our first evening on rest, when we were
just sinking into slumber, there came a sudden plonk !
near us, and the earth shook. Obviously it was an
H. Vick, for there was not the preliminary roar of a
howitzer shell. We waited ; in a moment another
came, equally near. " Why, the brute's shelling the
road ! " Three more came over ; then a pause, and

then again he sent over five, higher up the road. A message reached us from the Captain to take shelter in the sap, and there most of us clustered for an hour or two, and cursed the hour when these were taken as rest-billets. They didn't improve, for regularly each evening, the Boche sent over a few shells just on this portion of road. At length he dropped one into our cookhouse, and another into the B.X.,[1] and one or two of our men were a bit battered by them.

Even the journey to the rest-billets was not without incident. On one occasion a man, instead of accompanying the others along the Ribemont road, elected to cut across the hill—a shorter route. He was told that the Boche had direct observation on this, but comforted himself as he set off with the reflection that the relief party had just arrived by this route. He went along easily until he came to a cross-country road, when shrapnel started bursting nearly overhead. "Hullo!" he thought, "it does seem to be under observation." There was no one but himself on the road. Was he really having a little strafe on his own? Hastily, as the bursts continued, he dashed off the road and into a delightfully narrow little trench near by, and lay there just as small as he could make himself, while shrapnel pattered all about. When the sky was clear again, he cut off quickly, on to the road, now, that the others had taken, and arrived at the billets half an hour late, to find them growing anxious lest the bursts which they had observed had caught that "silly fool."

It was now that we heard of the tragic death of

[1] Battery Exchange—mainly a telephone office.

12

Billy Williams, our corporal-artificer, who had been
attached to us since the battery came out. A good-
natured, humorous Irish lad, he looked the embodi-
ment of health ; but he fell sick, was sent to England,
and was drowned when the *Warilda* hospital-ship was
torpedoed. A sad end to you, Billy ! We lost a good
chum in you.

To return to the actual shooting at Buire. We
registered on Bécordel, a village a mile or two behind
Fritz's line, and were then liable to be called out at
any hour of the day or night for a shoot. " Five
rounds rapid with such-and-such angles," would come
the order. " The first round a salvo ! " Rapidly the
layer gets the gun on to the proper line. " Touch
that trail over to the right ! " " Oh, too much !
Touch her back ever so slightly ! " Rapidly the shell
is brought up, rammed home, the lanyard affixed.
" No. 1 gun ready, sir," reports the bombardier in
charge, with a little smile of triumph at being ahead
of the other guns ; and then, these having reported
ready, there comes the order, " Stand by for salvo."
" Salvo, FIRE." With almost one sound the great
bursts come from the five guns ; then, before the
sound has died away, the bustling figures are round
the gun again, and in half a minute she is again ready
for firing. Gun-fire now—that is, each fires the
required number of rounds on its own as quickly as
possible. There was often keen rivalry between the
guns to finish the shoot first. Once, so eager were the
men on E gun, they fired while one of their number
was crossing—a risky action—in front of the gun.
With unique celerity he dived down as he heard the

fateful word, " Fire," and only his hat was blown off. When he spoke of the matter to the other men, it became clear that he was not willing for his gun to carry off the palm for rapidity of firing at the expense of his head.

Our chief task was to neutralise batteries between Bécordel and Fricourt. We sometimes wondered about those poor Boche beggars, for we knew what it was to find shells dropping about us. Had they cleared at the first shot ? Had we caught any as they served that gun ? One thought, for instance, of the mild, bespectacled Boche student, suddenly encircled with war's hurricane of noise and splinters. Sometimes, too, one pictured the effect of our harassing fire on roads. We knew what that meant too—to be marching or riding along a road, when crash ! comes the burst in front of you. Had we caught men or lorries coming up that road ? How many poor horses lay now stretched in agony or madness along the roadside ? Of the results of one shoot we had vivid details. It was an N.F. call that came from an aeroplane while we were engaged on another important shoot. We were consequently half an hour late in getting on the Boche battery, so that we caught them limbering up, and infantrymen who occupied the ground soon after, reported that horses and men lay dead there, and the gun was left behind.

At length our front was to move forward. Throughout the day of August 23rd there was an air of expectancy about. The officers, we understood, were out looking for a new position. A nice one too they had found ! After they had been on the spot a few minutes

Jerry opened out on it, and drove them well away. A poor prospect this, taking the guns up under fire ! An advance, however, was expected, though nobody knew definitely when "zero" hour was to be—and the general secrecy observed as to the attacks at this period was, without doubt, one of the great factors in their success. However, as we got into our blankets that night, news came through that showed us we might as well banish the thought of sleep for a good many hours. "Zero at one o'clock ! " "One o'clock ; that's a queer hour for zero ! " "Yes, but there's a fine moon now, and the lads are going over by moon- light." Good enough ! We turned out about mid- night, spent an hour preparing, then at one o'clock the clear, peaceful night becomes suddenly a tempest of roaring guns and shrieking missiles—the attack goes forward.

Albert had been captured a couple of days before. It was the Battle of Bapaume in which we were now taking part, and the fall of the town followed in a few days. We fired a few shots on the morning of the 24th, but we were nearly out of range, and imme- diately after dinner came the expected order, "Pull out guns, and pack up stores." This is quickly done, early tea is provided, and at about five o'clock away we move.

CHAPTER XIV

THROUGH OLD BATTLEFIELDS

W E were moving the guns now in daylight—
almost the first occasion on which we had
done this, though it was now to be habitual
with us—and we were able to observe the country
through which we were passing. A couple of hundred
yards and we were over the Ancre, its marshy meadows
plentifully besprinkled with the shell-holes of recent
fighting. Then through Ville-sur-Ancre, poor wreckage
of a village, worse even than Buire. "See what those
devilish Boches have done to the place," remarked
one man to his neighbour. "Dunce," came the reply,
"these shell-holes are as much our work as theirs,"
and, indeed, our own battery had taken a hand in the
capture of the village on May 19th. Four or five kilos
along the Ancre valley we went, Albert and Morlancourt out of sight on our left. We passed some of
our own trenches, then, a couple of hundred yards
further on, surely this was Boche wire ! We looked
more closely ; here indeed was a Boche trench. We
had got into their territory at last ! Here was tangible
proof that we were driving them out of what they
fain would hold. The great advance was before our

eyes ; what might it not bring to the warring world—
to ourselves ?   One gladly risked one's life again to
help in driving this blow home.

And just then, near Méaulte, we halted. Dernancourt,
where our Centre Section guns were already placed,
lay a few hundred yards further along the valley—a
dusty mass of ruined houses.   We of the Left Section
drew in up a track on the right of the road, and unlimbered in a meadow that sloped gently upwards
for a hundred and fifty yards till it met a low ridge.
We laid our platform carefully in the grassy earth.
" D'you see that balloon over there ? " suddenly
remarked one of the fellows ; " that's a Boche balloon.
He can see everything we do." Not a comforting
thought this.   It would not have surprised us at any
minute to hear the big stuff dropping about us.
Apparently we were acting on the policy dictated in
Sir Douglas Haig's recent order, in which he had
urged the relentless pursuit of the enemy at whatever
cost, and the taking of risks which previously would
have been forbidden.   All ranks and branches indeed
of the Army found that this policy affected them.
With us it meant that in future we were generally less
than a mile from the front-line trenches, instead of
being three or four miles behind, as previously. Being
so far advanced, we were naturally able to do highly
effective work on Fritz's batteries, and in hindering
his retreat.   But from the personal point of view we
sometimes pulled long faces as we came to our new
positions ; our splendid 6-inch guns seemed to be
mere trench mortars ; we almost felt that we had the
dangers of the infantryman's life without the shelter

of his trenches. Here, at Méaulte, we were only 1,500 yards from the front line.

However, Fritz was apparently too keenly concerned about his own retreat to afflict us much that night. We toiled hard for some hours, and it was a " sweat " comparable to the exertions of Trois Tours days to carry our hundred shells for each gun through a field of standing corn ; one fellow slipped under the weight of one, and when we came to him, " My nose is broken, isn't it ? " he queried phlegmatically—but it wasn't. About half-past nine the monotony was broken by crashes and flames near by. Fritz, flying past, had dropped three bombs on the further side of our ammunition dump. He set some cartridges on fire a hundred yards away, but the only injury was a scratch to one of our column drivers.

Ten o'clock was now come, and food we must have. We obtained biscuits and cheese, ate them voraciously, and, as we sat about the guns, discussed where we were to sleep that night. The Major slept on a stretcher in the open, some men under the camouflage that draped a gun, but some of us, in E Sub. at any rate, set to work at that late hour to dig a " bivvy " in a sunken road that ran along the rear of the position. We cut vertically down the bank, levelled the floor, sloped a tarpaulin across, and at 12.30 seven of us crawled under this covering, and huddled ourselves side by side in a space twelve feet by six. Nothing much to grumble at in that. But how soon we were out again ! We had hardly listened to the few H. Vicks which Fritz thought fit to splash about the area, had hardly fallen asleep, when it was 2.15 and

we had to turn out for zero at 2.30.   It was another
glorious moonlight night, and we sent the shells off
with great good-will.   A little incident occurred now
on our gun which might have ended calamitously for
us.   The empty shells of firing-cartridges, little pieces
of metal, had a trick, when ejected after a round had
been fired, of flying on to the shell-tray, and entering
the bore of the gun with the next shell ; if this was not
discovered in time, a "premature" would result.   On
this occasion we had actually rammed the shell in, but
only lightly, for, fancying that more effort was needed
than usual, one of those ramming said, "Hold on !
there seems to be something in the bore."   The
sergeant characteristically seized a rammer, and,
thrusting it down the mouth of the gun, tried to drive
the shell back ; a little more strength exerted on the
fuse which he was striking, and there would have been
an end to that gun-team.   But the shell wouldn't
move.   So the staff sergeant had to be roused from
his downy bed ; he came up in his leisurely, taciturn
way, applied a simple instrument or two, coaxed and
urged the shell out from the breech, displayed the
offending cartridge-shell, and strode away down the
moonlit slope as impassively as he had come.

We fired steadily for a couple of hours, and then the
gradual dying down of the firing in the grassy area
around us seemed to indicate to us, sensitive as we
could not but be to the signs of the course of the
battle, that away in front those invisible infantrymen
with whom we were co-operating were driving the
enemy far before them.   That, indeed, was the splendid
news that greeted us when, after another three or

four hours of sleep, we rose at nine to another beautiful, sunny day. Jerry was steadily retreating. No thought of further shoots from this position; we leisurely packed up, and then lounged about on the grass. But the best of the day was past by the evening, when we limbered up the guns in readiness for moving. The weather had become singularly dull, a drab gloom settling upon the disfigured countryside; H. Vicks were darting about on the road to our rear, where was a water-point; the humanity that was about seemed influenced by the sullen skies; the R.F.A. drivers trying to make their way along the crowded road were harassed and short-tempered, the infantrymen marching up to they knew not what looked fed up. And now heavy rain began to fall. The two guns that were to move forward had to wait a couple of hours on the roadside until the volume of traffic had diminished, and all that time the teams squatted in the F.W.D.s, familiar but never attractive home, and wondered irritably, some of them, how much longer they would have to wait there, and asked, " In heaven's name, get a move on;" or defied the atmosphere, others of them, and bravely roared out some of the old Army songs.

And while we are waiting, a remark or two may be made, occasioned by these constant moves of ours. At first they surprised every one acquainted with big guns, for these are not appliances to be lightly moved, or quickly placed in position. But it was a natural consequence of this remarkable advance that an effort should be made to assimilate them to the lighter horse-drawn field artillery, and their positions were therefore changed from day to day ; if necessary, they were pushed close up to the front line ; they were even, at Le Cateau, used to a certain extent for the creeping barrage. From August 8th, indeed, 6-inch Howitzer Brigades were attached to divisions, whereas previously their orders had come direct from Corps ; with orders coming to us through a shorter channel, we could get on to targets more quickly, obviously an advantage when we had to fire on " fleeting opportunity " targets, such as a column on the road. The divisions to which our batteries were in turn attached were the 25th and the 12th.

The rapidity of the advance had another technical consequence ; it made it impossible to man and use recognised O.P.s. The shooting was done mainly on areas indicated by Brigade as likely to be occupied by enemy batteries. However, F.O.O. parties went up from each position, consisting of an officer (forward observation officer), and some men, and if any information was obtained a gunner came back with it, for of course no wires were laid. This work took the parties into the scenes of the most recent fighting, and they came back with souvenirs, and with vivid and saddening tales.

At length about ten the engines began to throb, and we moved forward. It was a slow journey of nearly four hours ; we were too sleepy to notice anything more of the country than that it was rolling chalk land, defaced everywhere by marks of war, nearly all Boche—Boche trenches, ugly heaps of Boche barbed wire, and ugly Boche signposts, " Nach Bécordel," and the like. At Fricourt we turned to the right down a sunken road, and the guns were placed in position on the low right-hand side of the road. The " bivvies " were dug in the bank on the other side of the road, just as they had been dug at Méaulte the previous evening, gun-mats being used for flooring over the wet grass, and what with gun-platform-making and bivvy-digging, we did not get to bed this night till four o'clock. And then, a couple of hours after, Fritz, who had been shelling the area pretty steadily, dropped one five yards from E Sub.'s dug-out ; out we had to tumble, pull down the tarpaulin, and rig the whole affair up in a less exposed position.

On the 26th three other guns came up, one of them— C gun—to fire a single round, which had been rammed home by mistake, and then to go right back to the workshops. The blow over these old battlefields was being pressed home, and at five o'clock on the 27th we turned out for yet another zero. This was a comparatively short affair of some forty rounds, for the Boche apparently could not make any stand in these parts, and our Third and Fourth Armies were pressing on to Bapaume and Péronne. It was interesting here to observe the difference between the use made of us and of the lighter guns. A battery of 18-pounders had drawn up in front of us on the 26th ; they started firing, like us, at zero hour, but after an hour and a half they ceased, rapidly limbered up, and dashed away up forward after the retreating enemy. As for us, we learned that our guns were out of range, leisurely packed up and waited sedately till, about midday, the order came to move forward. No account of this Fricourt position would be complete

which failed to mention the breakfast our new,
scholarly cook had prepared for us after the zero
stunt. It was Gargantuan, a breakfast *ad lib.*, and
almost *à la carte*—bread, bacon, tomatoes, jam,
pickles, "umteen" cups of tea! Talking of it, in
reverent tones, six months afterwards, men could
think of no other explanation than that, on this
unique occasion, the officers' stores had somehow
become mixed up with the men's. The only drawback to perfect enjoyment was the strong effluvium
from a dead horse a score of yards away from the
cookhouse.

Our new position was near Carnoy. Here was a
wide stretch of fairly open country, which drops on
the left towards Mametz, while a mile away on the
right is the Ancre valley, in which Suzanne stands.
But that view was hidden from us by the dark,
thick mass of Billon Wood, and it was not until
one had made one's way through the high trees and
tangled bushes that stretch for a quarter of a mile,
and had gone still further along the Boche trench line,
showing all the marks of recent occupation and
hurried retreat, that one could look down on a great
brick barn which bore the German mark, in big white
letters, "O.U. Suzanne." Normally this must be a
fair piece of country, but now the hand of war was
upon it. Many of the once fine trees which lined the
high road were withered by shell-fire. Of the railway
station and buildings on our left, little but the framework now remained, and on the station were strong
concrete dug-outs into which the Boche railway
officials had fled during our bombing raids. A

Y.M.C.A. hut, relic of our stay here before the Boche onslaught of March, stood, battered and broken, but still displaying its red sign, by the roadside. Shell-holes, big and small, tripped one up amongst the grass. Running right through Billon Wood was a deep trench, full of strong Boche dug-outs ; our artillery had found them out, wrecked a side here, a roof there, and uprooted trees and destroyed bramble bushes looked pitiful in the sunshine falling upon that fair green spot. It was an awful place, that wood, when we first came into it ; dead horses lay about in it, and in the trench were corpses of Englishmen and Germans. Out in the open, too, was the saddest of sights—eight of our poor fellows lying dead in a group, several in the act of thrusting their gas-masks on ; close by was a man's head and shoulders (gas-mask on here also), the other part of his body twenty yards away. What object on earth was sufficient to justify depriving these men of the life they had enjoyed ? We cursed the war, and the men who talked and wrote so glibly of it, as we looked on these lifeless faces. For those who encourage hatred and war, damnation ; but as for these poor lads—God rest their souls ! Afterwards we used these Boche dug-outs as rest-billets for a week or two, and provided one did not dwell too much on the tragic sights round about— and one could never afford to do that in war—one could live comfortably enough in the depths of the greenery, doing a little cooking for breakfast or supper, and dropping in at the canteen for a convivial hour or two, while several times we went further afield and bathed in the cold water of the Ancre.

But this is to anticipate somewhat. We still have
the guns at Carnoy. Not, indeed, that there was
much shooting done there. A score or two of rounds
were sent off during the night from one to three, and
then on the 29th we once more packed up in readiness
for moving. But the Boche had now retreated with
a vengeance. A position was selected for us five or
six kilos from Carnoy, and then, ere we could move,
the order was countermanded : the position was
already out of range. A little time after, we got ready
again for the move, again the order was countermanded, and for the same reason. Fritz " could not
be found." Finally it was decided to spend the night
at Carnoy, and we went comfortably to bed, only to
be awakened at three o'clock for breakfast. An
odious game it was, slipping along the damp paths of
the wood in the darkness, and sliding down into the
trench where the cookhouse was. Mournfully I
remember how, clambering back to the level, with
mug of tea in one hand, and bread and bacon in the
other, I slipped and dropped my bacon. I picked it
up, and brushed the dirt off, resolved to make the
best of it, but a minute later tripped over a bramble,
and down on the damp clay it went again. There let
it rest ! I slid back in disgust to the cookhouse,
told my tale of woe, and was courteously granted
another piece.

We hung about by the lorries for a long time ;
dawn came about five, and then we could move off.
A long, interesting ride followed through the undulating chalk country, at first on the main road, then
we turned off towards the Maurepas area, unkempt

and scarred through three years of war. The forms of
our friends and our enemies lay, stiff in death, along
the roadside. Down a long slope we pass—on which,
alas ! is already an English military cemetery—and
then, near the top of the corresponding rise, we turn
along a track to the right, and a couple of hundred
yards down it, halt and unlimber the guns. We have
just asked the cook about making us a cup of tea—it
seems a long while since breakfast—when over come
two or three Boche shells. Hurriedly we clear to an
old trench just behind ; two or three times he sends
over bursts of eight or ten, which force us to take
cover as many times ; apparently they are intended
for the road running along the depression behind us,
but the minuses are pretty close to us. It is decided
to change the position to a little nearer the road, and
we are just unloading the stores again when over
come a gas-shell or two, and drive us behind the banks
on the roadside. One man thought himself gassed,
and we had to chaff him out of it. " If you spit two
or three times, and the third time it's green, be sure
you're gassed," we tell him. However, we get on
with our work, and soon the guns are well in position.
The hot, still afternoon we passed in squaring out some
of the big holes already made in the chalky ground,
and so constructing fairly commodious bivvies for
ourselves. We slept there comfortably enough, doing
but little firing. The next morning, just when a long
queue was lined up for breakfast, a chance shell
dropped near by, and there was a hurried flight—of
all except one canny man at the end of the queue, who
saw his turn providentially come, stood his ground,

obtained his breakfast, and was not blown to pieces. We were, indeed, in a rather warm area here. Besides the road behind us, the Boche was particularly anxious about the road along which we had come, and at intervals he would plant half a dozen shells up and down it, generally stopping, however, at a bend a hundred yards in front of us. Two of our stalwarts, who wandered off exploring, got caught in a strafe, and had to crawl under a limber for cover. Yet we had only one casualty on the guns here (at Maurepas, as this position was termed)—Morison, of F Sub., who was wounded in the leg on September 1st.

Every day now, without any great push, our troops were continually gaining ground. We asked them as they came down, walking wounded : " Have a cig., chum ?   How's it going up there ? "

" Oh, we took Hospital Ridge, a couple of miles in front, this morning.   Then this afternoon we went over again."

" Is Jerry putting up much of a show ? "

" No, he doesn't wait for us.   It's mostly machine-guns with him.   Copped this from a machine-gun."

It was time, therefore, for us to move forward again, and we did so on September 1st to a position near Le Forêt, known as Hospital Farm. E and F guns were on the right-hand side of the road, where the ground was fairly level, the other four guns were on the other side under the shelter of a bank ; the teams slept in " bivvies " in a trench that ran in front of the position. As the men were working about the guns in the evening, there came a lightning rush through the air, and the tremendous crack of a bomb exploding. They threw themselves flat on the ground, and none too soon, for three other bombs fell almost simultaneously a score or two of yards behind the guns. Apparently the Gotha had shut off its engines, and crept silently along like some transcendental cat, attracted perhaps by the cigarette points of light ; it was wonderful good luck that nobody was hurt.

But now, on September 2nd, came a sad loss. Mr. Elliott had been attached to us for some weeks as senior lieutenant, and we had quickly learned to appreciate his ability and coolness. On this day he had gone out with the Major after breakfast to look for a new position. About eleven o'clock they were standing with some officers from other batteries on the Bapaume-Péronne road, when the enemy apparently spotted them, and sent some shells over near them. The first one caught Mr. Elliott in the neck. The Major and Essex, one of the party, immediately searched for a stretcher, while the other officers bound Mr. Elliott up. Alas ! the wound was mortal, and he died a few hours afterwards.

Péronne, to our right, having been captured on September 1st, an attack was now to be made on the Drocourt-Quèant switch line to the north of us, and in co-operation the whole of our particular front was to move forward. Accordingly, 5.30 on September 2nd saw us engaging in yet another zero stunt. The only exceptional incident in this was the use one Sub. made of a fourteen-feet lever ; their trail sank hopelessly into the ground, and, after nearly every shot, they were to be seen—we watched them sympathetically, of course—working like giants with a weaver's

13

beam to get their gun into position again. Firing
continued on and off during the day, but our attack
had been highly successful, and Fritz was withdrawing
along the whole front to the outworks of his Hindenburg line.

There was therefore little doing for us until, on the
morning of September 5th, we got on the road once
again, passed at a corner a sign-board, " Bouchavesnes," but saw nothing there save a few bricks and
the mouth of a cellar in what had once been a garden,
and, proceeding a little further along, pulled in the
guns on a track to the left of the road. We had been
forestalled, so the tale was, in coming up here, for it
was reported that one sister battery had appropriated
the position, and another the billets, we wanted. It
was a dull spot here—a wilderness of rank grass,
nettles, thistles, and shell-holes lying by a white,
dusty road. We seemed to be following up a little
too fast, for the Boche soon treated us to a storm of
H.E. and gas, which drove us to an old trench and a
good sap dug therein. One of our limbers was put
out of action by a shell bursting near, and a lorry
stranded on the road was damaged. But if we were
close up, what of the 6-inch guns, with double our
range, which now, practically for the first time, we
saw on a level with us ? We did but little firing here,
and our only loss was that of a " compressor," in the
abstraction of which—an appliance weighing a couple
of hundredweight—the Army habit of scrounging
surely reached its highest point.

We moved off from Bouchavesnes on September 6th.
It was a night move, and brought us again that not

unpleasant experience of working all through the cool hours of dark on grass moist with dew. Behind us there showed up a broad white line which turned out to be a chalky track, but we could see little more than this of our situation ; one had the general impression that we had ruthlessly brought engines of war into a countryside that knew, and asked for, nothing but peace. As dawn came we saw that we were in a valley, with a high, steep ridge in front of us, and though the place continued to be as quiet and unfrequented, save by us, as during the night, shell-holes here and there, and some rusting Boche guns on the face of the ridge, showed that the tide of war had in fact recently flowed over it. Moislains, a couple of kilos away, was the nearest village to this position. After our night of toil we were glad to lounge about in the morning in the hot sun, and we were not too disappointed that that toil was wasted—for we fired not a shot here—Jerry was still retreating—and in the afternoon it was " Pack stores, and limber up," and on again once more.

Up that steep slope the F.W.D.s and the guns with difficulty climbed, then came a straight run over a high tract of land, passing on our right a tremendously " strong point "—a great, low earthen mound, with barbed wire thick around it (yet this the Boche had apparently evacuated without resistance), then down a pleasant, shady lane, leaving ruined Templeux le Fosse on our left, and then, turning to the left, we proceed some half-mile along, and draw the guns into a meadow of rich grass, with tall elms on the further side like any English country scene.

But this time we took one risk too many. We had
indeed got well into the habit of drawing in in full
daylight, but it was unwise to do it, as we now were,
under Boche observation—for there above the slope
in front of us, and not by any means so small an object
as usual, was a Boche balloon. We had hardly unlimbered the guns, men were up in the lorries handing
out the stores, when swirling it came through the air—
crash ! " Any one hit ? " " No." We looked
about for cover, made, some for a sunken track,
some for a trench on the left-hand side of the field,
and, even as we dashed off, ran into that pungent
odour ! Gas ! Another shell quickly came over to
place the matter beyond doubt—it was mixed H.E.
and gas. We got clear, and crouched low, while for
ten or fifteen minutes Fritz angrily searched the
area. Danger and the shadow of death had suddenly
descended upon the brilliant autumn day and the
fair landscape. But once again good fortune was
ours, and though several had had mouthfuls of the
stuff, only one man was reported gassed. It is not
pleasant to sit, breathing with difficulty through your
gas-mask, and to reflect that only that frail piece of
rubber is between you and torment.

When the strafe was well over, we repacked and
limbered up with exceptional speed, and drew away
out of the Boche's sight. We went back a quarter of
a mile along the road, and pulled in once again in a
pleasant grassy valley ; behind was a beautiful dark
wood, and at the mouth of the valley stood a wayside
Calvary. There was a deep trench just in front of
the guns, and in this we made our " bivvies." How

rapid was the advance nowadays may be gathered from the fact that, according to the original plan, it was the infantry, not we artillerymen, who were to have occupied the trench this night. We gave the Boche a little harassing fire during the night, just to improve his temper as he tried to retreat along his roads choked with transport ; then the next morning, September 8th, a dull, dispiriting morning, it was the old drudgery of packing and limbering-up, and off we moved again, along the straight road, past ruined Longavesnes on our right, and so to a position destined to be of sinister associations for us—Villers-Faucon.

CHAPTER XV

OUR position was in an incomplete valley, formed by a long ridge, thick with shrubs and brushwood on the right-hand side, and on the left by the gradual rise of the ground towards our rear, a copse crowning the slope and redeeming it from bareness. In front, too, the ground rose, and Villers-Faucon itself lay hidden from our sight on the further side of the hill. The road by which we had come—a road much used for traffic—ran right through the valley, and parallel with it was a Decauville railway on which, at our arrival, stood a dozen German railway trucks, the mines placed in them by the Boche not yet removed. Between the Decauville and the road was a settlement of battered, rusty-coloured Nissen huts.

Inauspiciously sombre looked the greenery of the valley as we drew into it. The dull morning had turned to rain, which was drizzling across the landscape, and, just as we halted, gas-shells were coming over, descending on the sodden ground with a soft thud that sounded harmless enough, in curious contrast with the baleful white vapour that heavily rose from them, and with the pungent smell that came in

whiffs to us. Stoicism was the only mood, as, leaving
lorries and guns, we took shelter, with gas-masks
ready, under the ridge, and watched the gloom induced
by Nature and the foe.

The fire ceasing, but not the rain, the F.W.D.s
brought the guns in from the road, and we worked
them into position towards the forward end of the
valley under a screen of shrubbery. The Nissen huts
had been suggested for our billets. We looked at them
dubiously. Frail structures, they offered little protection even against splinters, while their size increased
the danger for their occupants. Most of us did indeed
accept them as the only habitation, but some took
the precaution of digging a slip-trench just outside.
The officers and a few of the men found old hutments
at the foot of the ridge opposite.

We had not been asleep that evening above a
couple of hours when we were awakened by the noise
of bursting shells in the valley. Here, there, up and
down the valley they fell almost continuously. It
was not good to lie there in the dark and wonder
where the next one was coming, and to reflect on the
useless roofing above. " Is anybody clearing ? " one
asked, and though most in our hut preferred to stick
it where they lay, two of us, when a shell sent débris
sputtering on the hut, betook ourselves to the trench
outside, and stayed there for twenty minutes, yet
then, when we returned, found that the shelling was
by no means finished. Clear moonlight fell upon the
grass and the foliage, and it was wretched to have
the peace of the night destroyed by the bursts that
made one crouch down in the damp soil.

Nobody was hurt that night, but the next morning it seemed advisable to most of us to set to work to make dug-outs safer than these Nissen huts. It was a curious one that three of us constructed. Near the base of the ridge were four or five circular turf walls, tents having evidently at one time been erected on the spaces enclosed ; two of these walls nearly touched, and we dug a six-foot trench between them, joining two others of equal length which were dug along the two walls as they diverged, so that the shape of the dug-out was that of the Isle of Man symbol. The roof, of strips of corrugated iron, was level with the earth, and camouflaged with earth and grass. So " each in our narrow bed " we lay, with our feet touching, and concluded that it was as uncomfortable a dug-out as we had ever had ; but safety had to be among the first considerations at Villers-Faucon. Yet we did not deem this dug-out too well sited when an officer pointed out to us that we were directly in the line of the Boche's shells, most of which came from over the ridge on our right ! Deep slip-trenches, including one for the officers, were also dug under the lee of the other earthen walls.

This day after all seemed passing off quietly—for though we had done some shooting, we had had no shells over—and we began to think consolingly, " Well, he only means to disturb us at night." During the afternoon there had been a sharp shower of rain, but the sunset was calm and impressive, the brilliant orange and red moving in the western skies like the workings of the glorious countenance of some divine being. We had withdrawn to our different billets for a quiet hour or two before sleeping, when suddenly, near by, crashed a great shell. A few yards away from our dug-out was the officers' cookhouse, in which, at the moment, were C. E. Smith and Godden. The shell burst fifteen yards from them, stunned Godden and wounded him in the shoulder, and caught poor Smith in the neck; unconscious and bleeding profusely, he was taken by the officers into their slip-trench, and succumbed almost immediately. Meanwhile another great burst had taken place near by, and most of us deemed it best to clear to the further end of the valley. Out we dashed, slantwise across the valley, thinking that Fritz's line of fire was alongside the ridge; but we had misjudged: just when we were out in the middle of the valley, there came another horrible roar through the air; we had hardly time to fling ourselves on the ground when it burst— we saw the flash—twenty yards away, covering us with mud. A narrow escape indeed! Up we picked ourselves and ran, panting, and throwing ourselves down every time that warning roar was heard, until we reached the further end of the valley, which was not this night within his target. When the strafe was over we came back to our billets; Mortlock was wounded, and we found one big shell-hole just outside E Sub.'s dug-outs; and our minds were uneasy now, after the casualties suffered, and the evidence that our position was a definite mark for the Boche. Some digging of trenches was undertaken at the less shelled end of the valley—dispiriting work in the dark, and soon abandoned.

This strafe was one of many that the Boche afflicted

us with here. Whether he knew that a battery was actually in the valley, or merely argued that it was a likely position for one—at any hour of the day or night three, seven, or more shells would come over, with all the consequent discomfiture, for this was by no means a wide " area strafe " ; it was upon our own position. Officers and men shifted their berths from one spot to another, but it was hopeless—shells fell by them all. We kept up our spirits during the day ; men like Jumbo and Challis and Denby, perturbed by nothing, were a tower of strength, but our nerves got on edge with the subconscious but constant alertness for the sound of that threatening roar through the air. One fell asleep worn out, yet woke instantly at the noise of the shell's flight alone, before it had actually crashed. Our casualties, deplorable as they were, were miraculously few, for any man who spent those days at Villers-Faucon was in jeopardy not once, but many times.

Jumbo had a marvellous escape on the 10th. We had to turn out for a shoot just after dinner, at 1.30. He went down to the gun about 1.20 ; we were filing down some fifty yards behind him when we heard that roar through the air. Down we flung ourselves. Heavens ! peering up from the ground, we saw the explosion right by our gun ! Jumbo—what had happened to him ? Quick as the thought chilled our blood, his form, lightly jumping over the trail, emerged from the cloud of smoke, and he ran, smiling cheerily as ever, up towards us. Assured that he was safe, we started running back, but his voice came to us, " The old bastard's hit me ! " " Hit ! where, old

boy?" as we ran to him. "In the back, but it's
nothing much." Great, indeed, was our relief when
we found merely a bad bruise. A splinter, too, had
ruined his gas-mask, and this apparatus perhaps saved
Jumbo's life, for he had carried it, not slung across
his body, but carelessly hanging down from his left
shoulder. That shot was an almost inexplicable one—
the only one on this occasion, and practically an
O.K., for it had fallen a couple of feet from the trail
of the next gun to ours, scattering the limber-box in
fragments over a space of fifty yards. Had the other
gun-team turned out as quickly as Jumbo, they must
all have "copped out." We could only surmise that
the Boche layer had been doing a trick of which one
of our men had been rather fond : sending off the
last round of a shoot at a bigger range than that given,
to "put the wind up some blighter not in the
picture."

On this evening of the 11th Fritz started one of his
shoots at the rear end of the valley, and travelled
down towards us in jumps of about a hundred yards ;
no cheerful sight to stick your head out of the dug-
out, and see them coming along the base of the ridge
towards you. They didn't after all reach as far as
our E Sub. dug-outs, but one fell near the cookhouse,
and Bacon and Essex were caught there out in the
open. They fell flat as the burst came near them,
and Bacon was only scratched, but Essex was mortally
wounded. Captain Chattey, Jumbo, and Keen ran
up to him, and carried him off on a stretcher ; he was
conscious, and showed wonderful self-control : "It's
no good saying I've got a cushy wound, chaps," he

said ; " I'm badly hit, I know."   He died shortly after reaching the dressing-station. He was one of the quietest, and one of the best of men, and had always remained cool under the heaviest fire.   Bert Hayward was wounded this night also.

There were some queer doings the next day, for once or twice, immediately we had sent the first round off, shells started dropping about us. Some imagined there was a spy hidden in the bushes on the hillside, but probably the fact was that the Boche knew of our activity by sound-ranging, and tried to quell it.   One shoot in particular stands out in one's memory. Ten o'clock, and a very dark night, the splutters of fire from Boche field-guns darting about like fiery serpents in the bushes in front of us ; a shout through the darkness from the officer behind us, " He's dropping gas fifty yards further back ; how are you men ? "   Jumbo's suggestion, " All right, sir, but I think we'd better clear to the left for a bit."   After a few minutes the Boche ceased, and we resumed our shoot, then, worn out, crawled away to bed, and were hardly asleep, it seemed—really it was three hours later—when roaring through the air they come again. " Shall we clear ? " we three in our dug-out ask one another.   " It's useless ; he's up and down the valley ; stick it out here."   Crash ! the earth rocks, the narrow space is filled with dust, the candle-flames disappear, convulsively we crouch down ; then, still alive, " Are you hurt, chaps ? "   " No—nor you ? Heavens, that was a near one ! "—it was within the tent-rampart in fact, not three yards away. And then from a hut a little way up the ridge, where he and his men are sleeping, comes Keen's voice: " You chaps below, any-body hurt ? " A longer shoot this was than most of those we had endured here—a wretched business alto-gether. A and B gun-teams were sleeping in the Nissen hut furthest up the valley, and had cleared when this strafe started to a slip-trench at the rear of the hut; very lucky this proved for them, for a shell dropped right at one end of the hut, blowing blankets and other kit all over the place, the slip-trench collapsed with the explosion, and Leuty was buried up to his chest. One man was laughing wildly with shell-shock, another, blown flat by the wind from a burst near by, was hardly able to control himself, and the others had to divide their energy between attending to these and extricating Leuty from the earth pressing on him. And now gas was coming over, and we had to put our gas-masks on as we sat miserably in the dug-outs or crouched in the slip-trenches.

It had been proposed that our rest-billets as well as our gun-position should be at Villers-Faucon, but the Boche had not retreated so quickly as was anticipated, and the argument from strafing convinced the authori-ties that some healthier spot was needed. So, on the 12th, relief-teams came up, and men gladly betook themselves to the quiet of the hills near Moislains, where they could brace their strained nerves by dips in the cold waters of the Canal du Nord.

It pleased the Boche now to send shrapnel over as well as H.E., venomous-looking black bursts up in the sky, which drove us quickly into the slip-trenches, and Jakes was wounded by a shrapnel bullet. One burst caught a party of men working on the road ;

plenty more was coming over, but Challis and Hammond immediately went to their aid, and took them to the dressing-station, and it was for this brave deed, not merely for good conduct—if I may here correct a certain misconception—that the Military Medal was awarded them.   Keen also won the Military Medal by his plucky conduct through this time of stress.   Fritz gave the valley itself a little more rest now, but constantly was strafing either the slope to our left rear or the ridge on our right.   Through most of the night we could hear the shells going over on the former area—a kind of whistling through the air, with a new gas-shell that he was now using—and ere the sob of that burst had died away, evilly whistling came another.   It was with the explosion of great H.E. shells, however, that the ridge shook far too frequently ; we learned later, when we could see from the positions Fritz was now holding, that he had direct observation on the track that ran along the ridge, and when he saw field artillery or transport using the track, he would time his fire to catch it as it reached a certain point, apparently just above our dug-outs. We crouched down as we heard the big stuff coming over, then heaved a sigh of relief as it burst above us, " Good, he's on the ridge."   Dirt flew over the valley, and bits of metal went singing through the air.   Up and down the ridge he went, smoke-pillars rising at regular intervals.   The ridge sloped down abruptly just by our guns, and the crest here was a particular target for Fritz ; to the end he did not cease to batter that poor dumb shoulder of Mother Earth.   We were fusing shells one afternoon when he opened out with a shell right home on it. If he switched but a few yards he would have O.K.s on our guns, so we jumped into our slip-trenches ; but no ! his objective was not the valley—it was nothing but that crest, and on it during the whole afternoon he dropped his heavy shells at two-minute intervals. The bursts resounded through the valley, but it was perfectly safe for us, choosing our time just after a burst, to move from the trench to the more commodious Nissen huts further away.

Now, too, at night Fritz was busy on the track above us, so that, after a heavy and perhaps bad day on the guns, we should hear, as soon as we tried to sleep, the Gothas purring above us, and then the venomous crack ! and explosion of great bombs. It was, indeed, a dog's life there at times. Fritz seemed bitterly suspicious that another great push was coming off, and he was doing all he could to bar the roads to traffic. One night, the 17th, we heard a shell come over, though not too close. We looked out. " Oh, nothing to trouble about ! He's taken to putting them on the road—that corner by the guns." It was, indeed, worth getting out of one's blankets to see that curious sight—a continuous stream of horse-traffic cutting diagonally across our grassy position, while Fritz's shells dropped steadily at the corner they were thus avoiding.

Another assault was, in fact, about to be made by the armies on our front. In the ten days we had been at Villers-Faucon the line on our left, which at first bent slightly backwards, had been straightened by the capture of Trescault and Havrincourt on the 12th, and by the corresponding advance made on subsequent days. Epéhy, which lay nearly in front of our own guns, had already been proved to be a terribly strong position. But now, September 18th, was to see another grand general attack, aimed at carrying us well past the formidable outer approaches of the Hindenburg Line.

We were up late on the 17th receiving ammunition, and, after the usual noisy night, were on the guns again by six the next morning. It was rainy, wretched weather ; H. Vicks were already darting about the position, and it seemed as if our last work here might be not the least unfortunate episode of all this troubled time. Happily, however, there were no casualties. Our bombardment was a long and heavy one, lasting from seven o'clock until the afternoon ; on E gun alone we sent off over two hundred rounds. The sloppy weather—rain soaking down on us, mud to slip about in, mud to carry 100-lb. shells in, mud to clean off those unwieldy brutes—doubled the fatigue, and even a teetotaller may believe, as some men averred, that, after these days and nights of strain, it would have been impossible to keep going but for a generous rum-ration that was served out. But it was all worth enduring, if only in our own interests, for before the end of the day Epéhy and the surrounding district had been taken, and Fritz was no longer in a position or mood to trouble seriously our much-harassed valley and selves.

CHAPTER XVI

THROUGH THE HINDENBURG LINE

I WAS not in the artillery work which closed our active stay at Villers-Faucon, for on the night of the 17th I was told that the next morning Denby, Perkins and I were to accompany Captain Chattey and Mr. Underhill on their search for a new position. It was the only experience of the kind I had had, and an account of it may not be without interest to the reader. One wondered as one fell asleep what this venturing into the unknown would be like. " Very interesting," said Jumbo comfortingly; " what's your home address ? " But, old hand that he was, he advised me as to taking rations and water, and noticing carefully landmarks and cross-roads on the way.

Up at five, therefore, not too reluctantly, for in war the quiet excitement quickly overcomes one's natural lethargy in these early hours ; a good breakfast out in the cold, damp morning ; soon the guns in the neighbourhood are booming away, and at about six we set off, carrying with us short signposts, " 309 S.B. reserved position." Quickly across the road on our left—no place for wise men, a road on the morning of a stunt—and then we walked through fields, up and down one or two ridges, and got well in front of our guns. We were away from the booming of our heavy artillery; the air instead was filled with the sharp whistling of the missiles through the air, shrill, irritable sounds, and with the rapid crack of the field-guns; it was as if armies of bitter females were shrieking venomously at one another across the empty spaces. The Boche fire was flagging. A gas-shell burst here and there in the area we were traversing; Fritz had put up already a heavy barrage of shell-gas, and we continually smelt the lingering traces of it. Now and then it seemed advisable to walk along a trench, and once we had to take shelter in a strong sandbag dug-out in a little wood, known as Capron Copse. Very quickly we came across parties of " walking wounded." It was pitiable to see them— mostly small, young fellows—one with a wound in his hand; another limping along, having stopped a bullet in his ankle; while one poor lad, with a wound in his upper arm, was almost fainting. We gave what assistance we could, but they seemed to have a fearfully trying journey in front of them before they would find a dressing-station. At length, bearing to our right, we came to St. Emilie, and made our way to a road that leads out from it on the east. A couple of hundred yards behind, and almost parallel with the road, lay the railway line, and the Boche was shelling this with short bursts of 4·2 stuff—splendidly accurate shooting. About a quarter of a mile from the village we came on some old British gun-pits and dug-outs, well constructed, in the bank on the right-hand side of the road. They might have seemed the

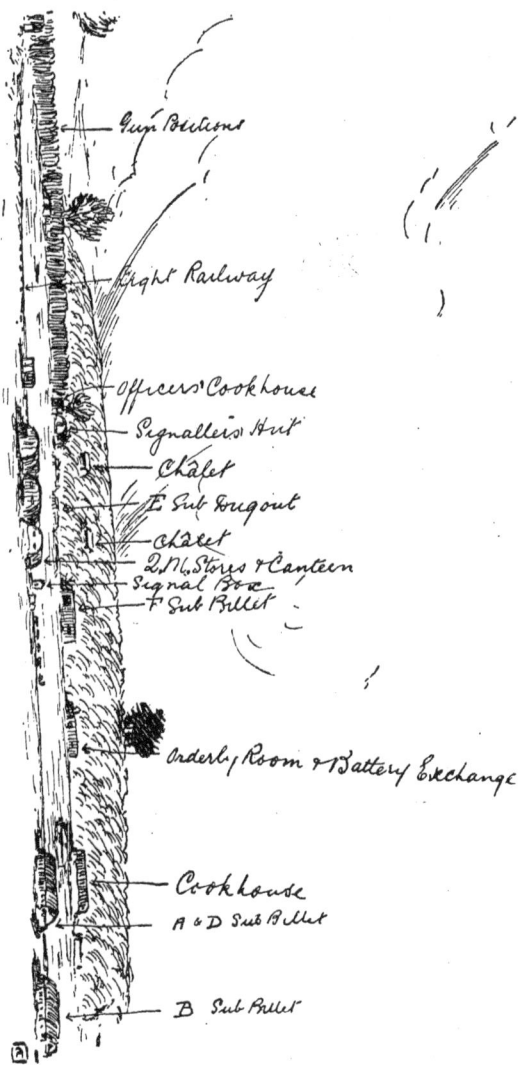

VILLERS-FAUCON

Gun Sections

Light Railway

Officers' Cookhouse

Signaller's Hut

Chalet

E Sub Dugout

Chalet

Q.M. Stores & Canteen

Signal Box

F Sub Billet

Orderly Room & Battery Exchange

Cookhouse

A & D Sub Billet

B Sub Billet

very thing, but there was significance in the question the Captain put to us : " Well, do you men think this would be too windy a position ? "

" We don't like old positions too much, sir," we said. " He knows all about them."

So the Captain went further along the road, which, a hundred yards on, bent to the right, a group of tall elm trees lining the corner. We were left behind for the time. The Boche sent an H. Vick now and then in the grass between the road and the railway, and at intervals he dropped low-bursting shrapnel—two or three ugly black bursts of smoke—at the bend where the trees were. We pulled out our rations ; while we were eating some bread and cheese a company of machine gunners came along, halted a little, then passed on. Two or three minutes after a young fellow coming back stopped to chat to us. His mouth was bleeding and bandaged.

" How did you get this ? " we asked.

" Why, don't you remember ? You were eating some cheese. We'd just gone on, and Jerry dropped some shrapnel at the corner. I stopped a bit."

There were some young infantry lads resting there who had gone over the top that morning. " Took our first objective—the railway line behind us—without a single casualty ! " And then came that question for ever on men's lips, " When do you think it will end, chum ? "

Not so cheerful were three other older infantrymen whom we found in one of the dug-outs. Two were gassed and exhausted, yet not considered bad enough to drop out of the fight ; they had to rejoin their unit as quickly as possible. Yes, our infantrymen did marvels in this long advance, but they paid for it.

Meanwhile, the two officers had been absent nearly an hour, and had not returned. We heard machine-gun bullets swishing the grass in front of us, and began to feel anxious for them ; but at length they came back. They considered, after all, that our present position was the best one, but, to be on the safe side, we had to go a thousand yards or so along where they had been, and plant our signboards on another favourable piece of ground. Arrived there, we found some R.E.s in a group under the shelter of a bank. " Siege guns coming up here ? " they said sceptically. " You'd better go back to bed, chum. Why, we can't go round this corner except on our hands and knees. Jerry's sniping at it." No place this for an artilleryman to go further, nor happily did duty demand it. Yet the remark illustrates the risks that the heavy artillery were now taking—risks that the event showed were well worth taking—in following up the advance.

When batteries are ordered to take new positions there is often laughable competition between them. A captain of another battery came along, and saw 309 chalked up all over the gun-pits on which apparently he had set his mind. He became angrily ironical. " How long have you had these up, eh ? " " Oh, about half an hour ; you're sure you didn't put them up at six this morning ? " Yet if we had forestalled him, others outwitted us. Beside the dug-outs on the road there were four others in the field between the road and the line. We had meant to appropriate these, but didn't at first chalk our number on them. Going to them after an hour's rest we found an officer of 312 in possession, and that number visible everywhere. Knowing the weakness of our position, but braving it out, we—two mere gunners—pointed out to him that we had a prior claim to these dug-outs. " You're talking to an old soldier," he said. " Is that your number chalked on them, or ours ? "

That evening three guns came up to the old gunpits in the position already described, and the two others followed a couple of days later. St. Emilie, near which we were, was one of the typical ruined villages of these parts, grey, drab, battered and broken, its great sugar-refinery no more than a collection of twisted iron work and rusty boilers ; it seemed to forbid any thought of restoration, seemed to ask for no future save as a necropolis of industry. The advance was again held up for a time. In front of us were exceedingly strong machine-gun posts, including the famous " Knoll," which it was hard to take. The Americans made a great attack on this sector ; they displayed their wonted dash, but we heard sad tales of the price they had had to pay for their inexperience ; they had gone ahead, so our infantrymen said, without " mopping up " the machine-gun nests, which had caught them in the rear ; the Americans were between two fires, and thousands of fine men lay dead. We did a good deal of firing on strong points, as shown in the accompanying map. It has seemed useful to indicate also what our general areas of fire were from three or four positions on the advance, so that the reader can see how our work from the one position helped to clear the way for the general advance the next day or so. We engaged, with a view to destruction, posts such as Little Priel Farm, The Knoll, Ossus Wood, and we harassed the exits from Vendhuile. A machine-gun post might be a mere pit six to ten feet deep in the ground, camouflaged generally with branches of trees ; but in the most important posts, there were generally strong underground saps, which only our heaviest guns could really damage. Beyond Vendhuile, for instance, lay Richmond Quarry, a chalk-pit with tunnels and dug-outs, serving as a splendid site for a machine-gun post. Heavy guns blazed away at it for hours, but when our men tried to take it, it was hardly damaged ; Fritz came up from his burrows, and held our men up. At length a 12-inch battery was put on it ; the tunnels gave under the terrific shells, the place was ruined.

For three days and nights a couple of our guns were engaged continuously at a slow rate of fire, battering away at three Boche strong points, Below, Tino and Vendhuile trenches, on which we ranged with aeroplane guidance. Over 2,000 shells were used up on these targets, and the battery was required to justify this heavy expenditure, so, as soon as we took up our next position, we inspected these places and found them obliterated.

The Boche on his part treated us to varieties of evil things at St. Emilie. On September 19th Lilley was wounded by shrapnel, the bullet piercing the iron roof of the dug-out in which he was at the time. On the night of the 24th gas-shells came over, and from one that burst under B gun, the fumes blew into the adjoining dug-outs, where the men were asleep, and Keen was gassed before he was really awake. On the evening of the 26th, too, Fritz gave us a most unpleasant time. He started with some 4·2's near the wooded corner of the position, and soon most of us cleared towards the village. The officers, however, remained in the B.X., on which a strong false-roof of rail lengths had just been placed, and the cooks, too, Schollar, Sansom, and Espeland, stayed behind, tired with their day's work. The heavy stuff came whirling over, shaking up the position, now here, now there; there was no one to be seen on that road and green meadow, you may be sure. One poor Yank, who was caught in an early burst, was killed outright. The cooks counted the bursts up to sixty-seven, then they stopped, with their dug-out tumbling about their ears, and the shock of an 8-inch burst in the cook-house adjoining. It seemed best to clear to the B.X., but, once here, they immediately volunteered to go out and make sure that no men were left in the dug-outs. A salvo of four greeted them as they emerged; they pushed on, dropping to the ground with each burst near them, until Schollar was hit in the leg. Sammy went for a stretcher, and on the way was blown up the bank by a near burst. They carried Schollar towards St. Emilie, hardly expecting ever to reach it alive, found as they came to the cross-roads that the shelling was particularly heavy there, and dashed across right into a tangle of barbed wire, in which, cursing strongly, one assumes, they had to lie perdu for twenty minutes. The other two took Schollar to

the dressing-station, and on their return were advised
by an officer of another battery not to venture by
the cross-roads if they valued their lives, so they
gladly accepted his offer of a billet for the night, as
Jerry was still bumping the position heavily. Amongst
other damage he destroyed C Sub. dug-out, and
ruined a canvas water-point on the position.

Our spirits were pretty high at this time, though
our position was a moderately warm one. It seemed
as if our enemies were at length crumpling up. Bulgaria
was seeking peace ; the Turks had lost in prisoners a
number that quickly rose from thirty to ninety
thousand ; Fritz himself was unable to stand before
us, as we could see for ourselves. This continuous
big push, on which we had now been engaged since
August 8th, was achieving its purpose then. The
sacrifices of four long years were to end in triumph.
It was cheering to think so.

While the guns were at St. Emilie our rest billets
were at Villers-Faucon. Fritz could still reach this
with his H. Vicks ; he dropped some troublesome gas
on the ridge at first ; then one morning he suddenly
played about the valley with half a dozen shots all
over the place. It was like old times to have to cut
into our funk-holes. The canteen merchants had by
now brought their goods up to this position, and were
occupying a Nissen hut. Popular humour always
associated them with the piping times of peace ; but
here was a big H. Vick hole suddenly gaping a few
yards away from their hut, and the building itself
shaken by the burst. Chocolates, biscuits, tinned
milk neglected, out they fled ! I still laugh immo-

derately at the mental vision of Whaler's bulky figure, buff waistcoat and all, careering madly round the corner of the Nissen hut to a strong funk-hole behind. Another morning too, when on rest here, we saw a very interesting incident. At the rear end of the valley an observation balloon was now stationed, and a Boche 'plane dashed down towards it while it was actually on the grassy ground. There was the usual flurry of machine-gun fire all about, a natural scurrying away of the balloon men ; in a moment the Boche soared aloft, and the balloon passed upwards— metamorphosed—for the last time. The valley was now a big shell-dump, a fact which did not commend itself to us, since shell-dumps were a great target for Fritz's bombs. But nothing evil happened to us during this part of our stay at Villers-Faucon. It was a quiet, pleasant time, much appreciated after the strain of recent weeks—a strain which now showed its effects in the minor ailments that beset many of us, the rare sight being seen one morning of our stalwart E Sub. sending no less than six men to the medical officer with septic thumb, sciatica, gas in eye, nettle-rash, and the like.

But the move had to be maintained—the blow driven home. September 29th was the date of the next attack. Our zero hour was 5.50. It was a fine, cool morning. We landed them over with great goodwill ; the time passed quickly, with a cup of tea at 6, a cigarette now and then, and chaff and fun running free after the first half-hour, when the firing was at the leisurely rate of one every two minutes. We were ready for the good breakfast provided at

7.30. An hour or so afterwards our walking wounded commenced to come down the road. Eagerly we question them. " How's it gone, chum ? "

" Oh, well enough. Jerry fought a bit, but he's on the run. The Yanks ? Oh, yes, they fought jolly well."

Our firing ceased at 11, and quickly came the intimation that we were now out of range, and must get ready for moving. Then, half an hour after, we had to shoot, with third [1] charge too. What was happening ? The explanation, I think, was that though the general line had gone well forward, certain strong points had been left behind—" masked," as it were—which we now must help to smash up.

So it was not until two days after—October 1st—that two guns moved forward, followed the next day by the other two, to Ronssoy, a distance of 3,000 yards. The road, sloping gradually upwards, passed through the usual desolated country—wasted grass land, which stretched wide towards the horizon, slashed about as if in contempt with dirty trenches, pitted here and there with dark dug-outs, encumbered with coils and tangled strips of rusty barbed wire, and showing, for human habitation, only tents that stood coldly unattractive in the sharp air, or ruined houses amidst the heaps of bricks that now represented Ronssoy ; a dull grey sky overhead, with leaden clouds, forming the proper counterpart for such a hopeless landscape.

But we could not allow ourselves to be depressed ;

---

[1] The charges for propelling howitzer shells are of four different weights, the fourth, or heaviest, charge of course propelling the shell furthest.

we had work to do. It required all our energy to pull the guns over the grass, here cut up with shell-holes, amidst which a 76-cwt. gun needs careful steering. Our position was on the further side of a line of trenches beyond Ronssoy, in the area known as Basse Boulogne. Fritz sent a few shells over, but we all avoided them, and they caused rather less trouble than did the disappearance of a tarpaulin which had been intended to shelter the slumbering officers that night. What a scurrying and searching! What a series of recriminations! and how violently " Bish " had to maintain that he could not include responsibility for scrounged articles amongst the multifarious duties of his office! At length an innocent gunner, emerging from a cellar he had been cleaning, remarked to " Bish," " Oh, I've got a tarpaulin put aside for you." " The devil you have!" quoth the astonished sergeant-major, " why, that's the one we've been looking for this last hour ! "

We spent the night in the trench, very comfortably. Fritz shelled a bit in the area ; set an F.W.D. alight on our right front, which burnt for an hour or two, a bright flame in the darkness, and sent up two boxes of our cartridges between the guns and the trench. From the bivvies to the cookhouse the path ran across a meadow used both by British and Boche for a cemetery. The dead lay there now on the opposite sides of the meadow, " Kanonier " and " Unter Offizier " in the same plot of ground with " Private " and " Gunner," the keen enjoyment of life, the fear of, the struggle to avoid, death, over for them.

We did a few shoots at Ronssoy, chiefly on the exits from Le Catelet and Gouy, two places to which the Boche was still clinging. He could not hold on long. The British push was a continuous one, and after a couple of days at Ronssoy we had to turn out for another zero stunt. It was easy enough, for our team at least, for the gun was working very well, and as soon as the shoot started, one member of the team was sent off the gun to prepare, as a " private stunt," porridge for breakfast. The attack appeared to be thoroughly successful, judging by the hundreds of prisoners who soon came marching by us ; in fact, Le Catelet and Gouy we,ᵤ both captured this day. There was but little more for us to do from this position, and on the 4th the guns went forward to Bony.

But now came in a blessed rest for the author and his friends. For the first time in this year's campaign E Sub. gun was so disabled that it had to go to the workshops. Such an event had happened at some time or other to each of the other Subs., and the reader may wonder what these dozen or score of gunners, fine, stalwart men, used to do to end the war under these circumstances. Well, work is generally found for them ; they go forward and help to make gun-positions and dug-outs for the other Subs., or build dug-outs for the officers. But on this occasion our services were not required, so while our relief team was " on rest " at Villers-Faucon, not less were we on rest at Ronssoy. We slept in a couple of cellars there, the larger of which served as a cookhouse, and the smoke from the fire was more than compensated for by the luscious grub which our good cook " Sammy "

—the best cook the battery ever had—prepared for us. We had plenty of time to write letters, read, play chess and cards, and " chin-wag " with some R.E.s who were sleeping in the smaller cellar. Some walks we took too, along the long low ridge that runs across the road from Ronssoy to Bony, where we found scores of bodies of our gallant men who had fallen in the recent fighting, and saw too several of our Tanks which had met their fate through the anti-Tank mines which the Boche, in desperation, was now using. The war had not quite finished here, for even on the 6th three or four H. Vicks came over. They seemed quite uncalled for. We were strolling along the road to the cookhouse about ten o'clock, when " pip ! bang ! " came the old sound near us, and a column of smoke sprang up a score of yards away. We were at peace now, and weren't asking for things like this, so we got near our cellar. But only a couple more came over—one a hundred yards further on, the other a quarter of a mile on—all in one line, but apparently a blind shoot, born simply of unreasoning ill-temper on the part of the Boche.

Meanwhile the guns had been installed at Bony, well in the Hindenburg Line, and our men were accommodated in its trenches and saps. Our short stay at Bony is chiefly remembered for a novel " descensus Averni " during an H. Vick shoot in which the Boche indulged. An officer was sitting dozing at the mouth of a sap when a shell burst near him ; he awoke, started backwards, and tumbled down the thirty feet of the sap, his descent happily being softened by the bodies of the sleeping gunners which lay thick down the sap. We did the usual harassing fire from Bony, and on the 5th took part in a zero stunt at six o'clock, this being the operation in the course of which the Third Army established itself across the Scheldt Canal. Harassing fire followed during the day, and on the 6th we made a long move forward to Estrées.

We were now travelling in a more north-easterly direction than hitherto, heading for Le Cateau, which was to be one of our principal objectives in the next few days. The country through which we went was the usual undulating grass land, utterly waste, devoid of any normal human interest ; it was just an area in which war had exacted its damnable toll, and our dead fellow-men lay along the roadside. Approaching Bellicourt we were passing through the Hindenburg Line itself. A wire entanglement of exceptional depth, with strong trench-lines behind, stretched on either side of our road, and at intervals were the air shafts of the great canal tunnel, which, six thousand yards long, had afforded shelter for thousands of the defenders of the Hindenburg Line. Bellicourt and Bony had been strong points of the line, and it had taken both Australians and Americans to capture the former place in the great attack of September 29th, while as for Bony, that held out till October 1st. As we went through the ruined villages we saw there, resting, many of the troops who had stormed them a few days before. A little further on we passed through Nauroy, and at length came to Estrées. The Boche was very lively as we entered, shelling over the whole village, and driving us into an elaborate German sap under one of the billets. The Major had already been similarly greeted on his visit of reconnaissance, finding himself in the midst of a strafe in which an artillery captain across the street lost his life.

Our guns were placed in a narrow sunken track at the further end of the village ; all around was a level stretch of country. We registered the following morning on Bronk's Farm, a building supposed to be occupied by the Boche, and shells came up by the hundred for a great stunt the next day. For the Hindenburg Line having been passed, an attack was now to be made on the Cambrai-Le Cateau line. Victory was in the air ; that we should advance where we wished was unquestioned. So it proved on October 8th. Zero hour was 5.10 a.m., and at first we were shelling Bronk's Farm again. Afterwards we helped to put up a barrage round Serain, to hinder Boche retreat from there. Good news rapidly came in. Cavalry, it was said, were pursuing the retreating enemy ; Serain was captured. For ourselves, the immediate result was a move forward in the afternoon to Bronk's Farm. Bivvies were made in a trench here, and we had a nasty time at night when the Boche was bombing horse-lines near by for four hours or more, relays of the brutes coming over, for in his bombing activity appeared now to lie the Boche's only hope, his forlorn hope, of hindering the British attack. But the pursuit continued. We fired only a few rounds from Bronk's Farm, and though the guns remained there until the 11th, the majority of the men went back at once for a rest of indefinite length at Estrées. The Boche retreat had become so rapid that a minimum number of heavy guns like ours were

now required in action, and it was judged that, after
being in action continuously since May 19th, our
battery had now some claim to a rest.

We were now, therefore, enabled to look at the
district a little more closely. It was of peculiar
interest after the devastation of the Somme battle-
field ; it was the first area to which we had come
which showed signs of the normal activities of life
under the Boche régime of the last four years. Behind
the village, instead of a wilderness, were cornfields
and pasture, cut up now, of course, by the tracks of
men and guns, and there were some pretty little
orchards, in one of which our sister battery, 146, had
had its position. What particularly pleased us, however, was to see houses with roofs still on—only a
slate or two gone—the whole building, indeed, practically intact, though the interiors, deserted as they
had been for some months by their inhabitants, were
waste and dirty. Little, old-fashioned cottages, bigger,
well-built houses, we looked at them with grateful eyes
after two months during which we had seen, for buildings, only heaps of rubble and shattered walls. Of
course the village was knocked about by shells and
bombs ; the proportion of more or less undamaged
houses was perhaps one in three. It had evidently
been a billeting centre for the Boche ; on every house
were to be seen the legends, " Fliegerschutz—(6)
Offizier, (4) Mann," and here and there the phrase,
itself a tribute to the work of our bombing 'planes,
" Keller für 15–20 Mann."

It was very pleasant for all the battery to be together
again now—in particular, for each gun-team to be

AERIAL PHOTOGRAPH OF A SECTOR OF THE HINDENBURG LINE

complete again, for, when in action, half the gun-team normally sees the other half only in the few minutes during which the relief is taking place. We could now talk over the doings in which we had separately been engaged.

" What a rotten trail-pit you left us at Ronssoy, you Wabbits," was our first remark to our E Sub. relief.

" Rotten ! You've got a fine right to talk ! Look at the state the rifles were in when you handed them over to us at Villers-Faucon ! "

" No, no ! But, really, we'd had a rough time there."

" So had we at St. Emilie just before we came to Ronssoy. What time had we to dig a trail for lazy chaps like you ? "

With such friendly recriminations we greet our helpmates in the great war. And then we speak more seriously of the various experiences through which we have recently passed.

It was a treat to live once again in houses instead of stuffy dug-outs. In them we found Boche wire-beds, in stout wooden frames, sometimes a double tier of them, and as many as a score in one room. We rather envied the care displayed for their unworthy bodies ; even in rest-camps we had had but the floor to sleep on. It surprised us perhaps to find how much the Boche had loved his bed, since, at certain positions, he had seemed to be keeping awake all night, particularly for the purpose of disturbing us. In one of the rooms occupied by E Sub. only one wire bed was brought in, and discussion raged round it for days. Should it remain in the centre of the room ?

15

It blocked the way. Should it be removed into a corner ? The man already there didn't want to lose his berth. One man thought the problem could only be solved, in a root-and-branch manner, by throwing the bed out altogether, and its owner with it if necessary. Time brought its own solution in the end.

"Ye gentlemen of England that sit at home in ease," ye ladies, too, who, in choosing a new house, have to spend so much time considering how many bedrooms will be needed, and whether this or that room is big enough for three to sleep in ; ye upholsterers who would persuade your clients that a brass bedstead, fine palliasses, a thick carpet, curtains, chairs, all are necessary for the bedroom of it may be a single man, how would you view being turned into a room such as we had at Estrées, and being told, "There's the billet for you twelve " ? It was a ground-floor apartment some twenty feet by ten, the windows were all broken, and a shell had fallen on the roof and shaken down most of the ceiling, which lay in heaps of plaster and dust on the floor. There was but a thin partition, too, between us and the sergeants' mess, and we perforce had to listen to the sound of their wagerings, compliments, and discussions of the abstruse points of artillery work. We could see that room turned into a comfortable enough billet, however. We shovelled and swept the débris into the courtyard outside ; put a great tarpaulin up over both windows, and even found a stove which we fixed up in one corner. Then we dumped our kit in the particular spot that pleased us, and found everything "très bon."

But now we come to the sad story of the demon, Gas. We were settled down after tea on our kits, writing and reading, when one fellow sneezed violently a couple of times. He went on writing, but—" Ertishoo!" he was off again. And somebody else had to blow his nose violently; in fact, in a minute or two nearly everybody was blowing his nose, or sneezing, or doing the two together. " Are you like it, too ? " says one to another. " No, I'm——" Ertishoo ! Ertishoo ! " No, you're "—Ertishoo !—" not, of "—Ertishoo !— " course." What malignant fiend is about ? Our handkerchiefs are wet already. Has somebody sprinkled pepper all about ?

" No, I'll tell you what it is," cries a brainy one. " That shell "—Ertishoo !—" that hit the roof must have been a gas-shell, and some idiot's been walking about upstairs and "—Ertishoo !—" stirred the filthy stuff up." It's still all sneezing and nose-blowing ; a sorry set we look, with reddened faces, convulsed with these paroxysms, and with tears, not of mirth, helplessly rolling down our cheeks ; one or two even seek relief by putting on their gas-masks for a few minutes. The atmosphere cleared at last, but afterwards we very quickly cursed off anybody else who seemed exploring the upper story, or— for possibly here was the gas imprisoned—stirring up the old straw in the courtyard beneath our windows.

That first evening we were at Estrées the Boche, as indeed we had noticed on many recent nights, seemed to be making tremendous efforts with his bombing 'planes ; in point of fact, it has since become clear that these were by now the only 'planes which he could use to any advantage, for his fighting and scouting 'planes, besides being greatly reduced in numbers, dared not show their wings near the Allied lines. But that night, some half-mile away from us, it was the old sound, " Woof ! " " Woof ! " " Woof ! " He was shovelling them out again. In the courtyard outside a lorry driver spoke to us, and said that up the road Fritz had " caught " a lorry and its drivers. Evidently he was desperately trying to hinder our traffic. After the first two nights here, however, we did not hear these unfriendly sounds, the moving forward of our line giving him targets well removed from us.

At the back of the yard already referred to was a big building which the Boche had evidently used for a stable. It now became the cookhouse for us and another battery. The six guns were hauled through the yard and parked by the side of the building—two lines of three, dressed by the right, and all religiously cleaned each day, so that the rain which fell all too frequently might have bright surfaces to work on. At the gate of the yard lay, when we first made our billet here, a dead horse. A fatigue party was called out next morning, and dug a big hole in a garden on the opposite side of the road. Then a drag-rope was put round the poor beast's neck, but it slipped badly, and the team sat about on the road. Gilbert, the lorry-driver, that facetious man, put it on again ; dignitaries like " Tan," the Quarter Bloke, the cooks, and Bombardier Billy Williams stood by to crack jokes at another failure ; but this time, with a steady pull,

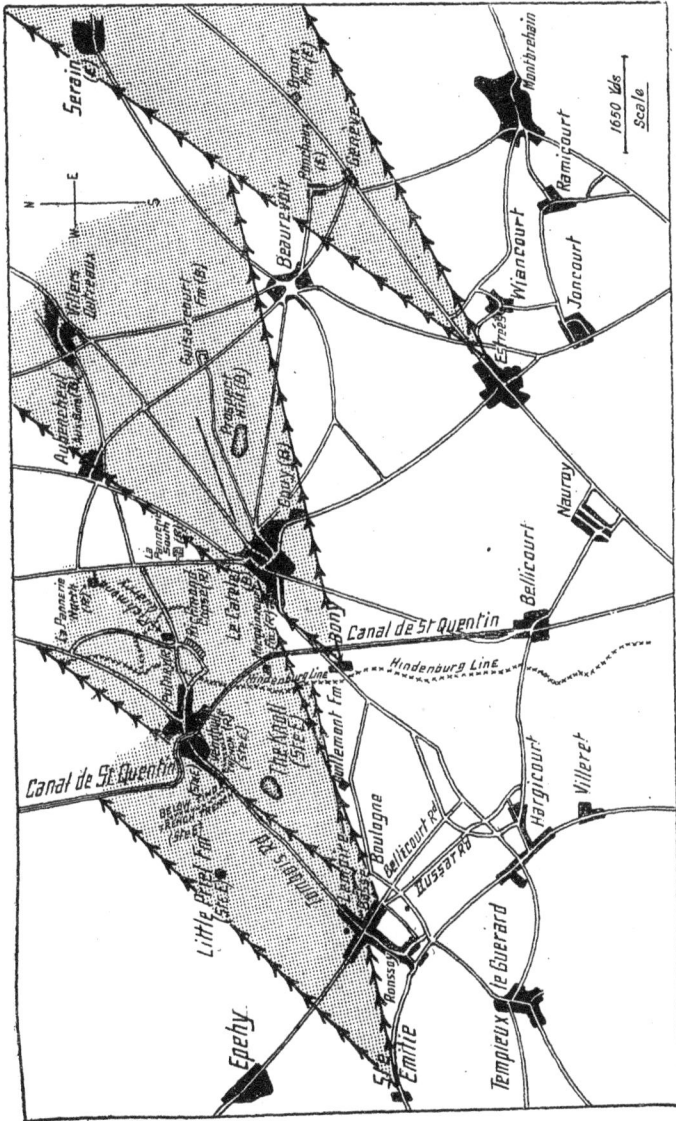

MAP OF A SECTOR OF THE HINDENBURG LINE TO ILLUSTRATE OUR "ARCS OF FIRE" FROM VARIOUS POSITIONS

we got our burden across the road, and into its grave. Qualms as to the pleasure it would give to the owner of the garden when he started digging there were partly set at rest by the throwing of a liberal supply of lime on the carcase.

We didn't do much at Estrées, nor did we want to. It was pleasant enough to be even in this battered village, to be away from the sound of guns and shells for a bit, to have no painful lifting of shells to one's shoulder, no heaving on the drag-ropes to do. We relaxed our limbs and our minds. Sergeants' faces became less grim, less serious; bombardiers forgot the cares of picket-lamps and passing the angles on to one another, and joked, while the signallers, those " bons viveurs," of course settled down like boys to a merry time. And however dull might seem our surroundings, there was a general uplifting of spirits, for peace seemed at last returning to the earth. The Bulgarians had surrendered unconditionally; the Turks had been routed by Allenby's force; Austria was evidently at her last gasp; and the Boche himself had been humbled to ask for our peace terms. We talked of these things continually as we sat about in these bare rooms. Hope ran high; bets were exchanged that we should not fire another shot. And we began to anticipate a prolonged stay at Estrées. One or two men came back from a morning's jaunt with the news that after going forward a few kilos on lorries they had come to an inhabited village, Maretz! Houses untouched by war—many civilians there—even wine sold! We could hardly believe it. We asked again and again about it, and were filled with strange pleasure to be getting back at last to some semblance of civilisation.

Divine service was conducted by the Brigade chaplain, Rev. C. H. Matthews, in the loft above the cookhouse on the morning of October 13th. In the evening a debate was held downstairs. It was desired to provide some entertainment for the battery; a concert could not be arranged in time, so four men were asked to allow themselves to be butchered to make a soldiers' holiday. Freddy Parr and the unhappy author were ready to discuss any subject, and especially favoured " Love in a cottage ; " but weightier men asked for a less ethereal subject, so we fought over the proposition, " That the total prohibition of the manufacture of alcoholic liquors would be for the benefit of the universe." It was a unique scene ; the bare, discoloured, broken-windowed hall, in darkness save for the further end, where, behind a long counter, sat the Captain, as chairman, with us protagonists and the officers on either side of him ; on the counter, half a dozen candles that rapidly burnt and guttered away, threw a flickering light on the rows, seated and standing, of our chums. Along the centre of the hall were stout piles to which but a few days ago our enemies had tethered their horses, and one's thoughts would not but wander from the debate to the stern war in which we were still engaged. I proposed, and Fraser seconded the resolution ; Parr, seconded by W. W. I. Jones, opposed. (N.B.—None of these items is to be used in evidence against any of us in civil life.) It was a fairly lively evening. The voting ? Oh, some 60 to 12 against.

After the debate came a momentous announcement—
the Boche had accepted President Wilson's fourteen
points ! The war seemed as good as over ! Our own
hardships were near their end ! In an access of joy
we let ourselves go, cheering and singing the National
Anthem ; we broke up discussing, not prohibition, but
peace, animatedly, sanguinely, and a rare rum ration
was served out to all who wanted it, including the pro-
hibitionists.

The debate having apparently reawakened literary
tastes, it was now proposed to publish a harmless
battery magazine, which the Orderly Room undertook
to type. Events defeated us at the time, but immediately after the Armistice we turned out the " Squib,"
which no doubt excited general odium during its
career of four issues.

And then after all to have to go forward again !
For that was the order for the Left Section the very
next morning, Monday, 14th. Why ever was it, we
asked indignantly ? Wasn't the Boche's submission
just what we had been asking for ? Wasn't it good
enough ? Something of a natural, if illogical, revul-
sion of feeling set in as we contemplated going into
battle again. Yet, as we thought of the firm, keen,
yet humane strain of President Wilson's notes, we
reminded ourselves that our affairs were in good
hands. So to the guns once again !

Before we went, however, we were cheered by the
most remarkable sale of goods that even our canteen
ever carried out. We formed a long queue outside
the canteen room, and came away laden with sandbags full of tinned milk, fruit, marmalade, cigarettes,

and other luxuries, always longed for, rarely seen
nowadays.   And life's little ironies !   One who had
posed as an ardent prohibitionist the night before,
now, as a member of the canteen committee, had to
help to obtain for our column men some of the canteen
supply of beer.

CHAPTER XVII

THE GREAT CONCLUSION

THE battery's last three weeks in the war stand out in the minds of most of us as a totally separate phase from all that had gone before. We worked at our tasks as energetically as before, but our minds were keyed to a different note. Suspense, anticipation—they were our moods in these days. It seemed but a chance that peace had not yet come; the angel of peace had all but covered us with his wings, and then been driven away; he might return at any minute—we longed for it. We had risked our lives willingly enough, but now we wanted not to lose them when the war was practically won. Short-sighted, selfish, such views doubtless seem to those philosophically surveying the whole wide field of the war; but we were not statesmen or generals, with impersonal viewpoints, not writers free, with the detachment of mind that safety at home gives, to urge a never-ending war; we were simply men whose lives were endangered day by day.

Far forward was our move this time, a distance of twenty-two kilometres. It was a fine, clear evening when we rolled away with our two guns and accom-

panying lorries.   Twilight had come on, but we could
see how different this cultivated country was from
the barren, neglected lands to which we had so long
been used.   Our eyes rested with surprise and
pleasure on the regular strips, brown tilled earth or
green vegetables, and on the undamaged, splendid
trees.   And then to come in the mysterious dark to
Maretz, a village of inhabitants and intact houses,
like those we dimly remembered from former days ;
still more, a village that for four years had been under
the rule of the Boche, and from which at long last
he had unwillingly been driven !   One felt that the
reconquest of this village symbolised finally the defeat
of the mighty German power.   It was for such a
liberation that many we had loved and lost had
fought during the past weary years.   Ah, would that
they were with us now to see the goal of their toil !

The Boche had mined various of the cross-roads
along the route we were taking ; we saw the great
circles in the surface, filled with rubble and other
unusual material, and in some cases the adjoining
houses had been shaken down—" abîmé," as the
French expressively put it.   We passed through
Honnechy and Reumont, and turning to the right at
the further end of the latter village found ourselves
on a cross-road, which, at a little distance down, sank
between banks some twelve to fifteen feet high.   We
hollowed out dwellings in these chalky banks ; and,
for another Sub. that joined us next day, we dug a
bivvy near the top of a damp, sloping field.   This
dug-out was not well sited, for a diary of one of the
occupants that night reads : " Sleep in bivvy in open

field. Strafed all round bivvy ; also flooded out by rain. Next day made bivvy by side of road." So they joined us in the chalk.

It was a dull time, this at Reumont. The country was pleasant enough, the guns being in a green meadow, but the weather kept us for most of the time in our chalky recesses, and we sat there in the gloom on our rolls of kit, yawning and taciturn, while the rain pattered down on the tarpaulin, one's chief interest being so to arrange that poor roofing that, if the rain did drip through, the other fellow had the benefit of it. With peace so much in the air, thoughts of our homes and our futures would obtrude themselves upon our minds ; and yet here the war had closed in on us again. Not that we were shelled much, nor had we much work to do ; we were simply bored, and a little tantalised. The cooking was not too good at Reumont, and one who " never complained " was actually seen taking a plateful of exceptionally watery, discoloured rice up to the Major for inspection. Yet we had pity and an odd tin of bully or two to spare for some of the infantry chaps who lay in support alongside of us. Poor beggars ! their holes in the bank were still less comfortable than our dug-outs, and for warmth they had only their jerkins and groundsheets—no blankets, no overcoats. But they seemed to take it philosophically enough. " You see, chum," said one, " overcoats 'ud be in the way when we go over the top."

The Boche was holding strongly Le Cateau, three kilos in front of us, and the general line of the Selle, before which our advance, which started on October

8th, had stopped. This was now to be resumed. It
was a raw, foggy morning, that of October 17th, when
we turned out before 5 for the stunt ; the picket-lamp
could not be seen in the fog, and another one had to
be placed at half the distance. At 5.20 out roared
and flashed all the guns once again in their great zero
chorus ; yes, and over came half a dozen H. Vicks
from an obviously nervy enemy. He did our men no
damage, however. Through the early hours of the
morning we worked steadily at the guns, refreshed
about six o'clock by a cup of tea and a huge slice of
cake from a lucky man's parcel. It was not too good
news that we heard during the morning, for the fog
had prevented our infantry from fully getting their
objective of Le Cateau. So the next morning another
" zero " shoot took place, with an extended range,
and on this second day, as we learned afterwards,
our men took Le Cateau and pushed far beyond it,
to the Sambre-et-Oise Canal, in fact. It was not till
the 19th, however, that our guns moved forward.

   In the alternation of work our relief gun-teams had
meanwhile come up to take our place. They had
covered the whole distance from Estrées—a feat on
which, in their civilian ease, they will, beyond a
doubt, ever look back with pride and disgust, for,
laden with kit and blankets, they had had to travel
the twenty-two kilos as best they could. They had
picked up lorries for most of the distance, but they
had footed a good deal ; their instructions had not
been clear, and some had wandered about and cursed
mightily, so that, when they arrived, sweating and
bending with the weight of their kit, they were a

sight to move the stoniest to tears. Having, through
faulty arrangements, eaten their tea, we left them as
quickly as possible. We, happily, had but to get
back as far as Honnechy, some four kilos away. We
trudged up the hill into the village, noticing curiously
the few civilians still about that evening, and then
we found—a score of us at any rate—that we should
do best to appropriate on our own the schoolroom as
a billet. An infantry division was due in the village,
and we had quite a keen little argument as to whether
it was well to risk being ignominiously expelled by the
town major. We resolved to, anyhow, and it was
well, for we had a very comfortable two days there.
The Boche had fitted the big double room with tiers
of wire beds, on which we reposed most comfortably.
Then the next morning it was delightful to go round
the village and see the houses ; in particular one fine
old farmhouse, with turrets and high terrace above
its great yard, and the suggestive date 1793 on its
front. At Honnechy we first met with people who
had been under the Boche these last four years. We
looked at them with sympathetic curiosity. How
had they endured the long strain ? They had lived
under conditions of which during these years we had
heard evil reports, but had known little definitely.
They seemed still nervous, the fear of the tyrant who
might enter at any moment had not worn off ; even
their liberation could not restore to them their natural
good spirits. There was an intense bitterness in the
way they spoke of the Germans, telling us of their
neighbours who had died of starvation through the
Germans taking the good white flour sent out by the

Relief Commission, and giving instead their own wretched blackish stuff ; and they stirred our emotion when they told us of the heartless treatment our own countrymen had met with in this very place. These good people made us very welcome, entertaining us with coffee, and being hardly persuaded to accept any payment for the washing they did for us.

After two days, however, the rest-billets were moved to Reumont, to the hither end of the village, not that nearest to our guns. There were a number of civilians in Reumont, but some of these were considering evacuating it, for the Boche was now developing the habit of shelling—ostensibly at least for military purposes—the villages he had been driven from. The poor fellow who lived at our billet might well have lost his nerve, with a couple of big 5·9 holes in his garden. If the other Subs. were as comfortably billeted at Reumont as E Sub., they were in luck. We had a large room, with a double tier of Boche beds in it, eight in each, and a good stove. We looked at the quarters appreciatively when we reached them that morning, threw our kits on the beds, and then learned that we were not to spend a night there ! Only two days' rest after three days on the guns—it seemed monstrous. However, there was nothing for it but to obey orders, and, in the event, we gained rather than our relief team, for it was they who had to go through the experiences of October 23rd.

As soon as we took over, on that afternoon of October 19th, we had to move forward with the guns. It was as great a struggle to get them out of the field as it had been to get them in. And that was not the only experience of the kind that afternoon. The new position was hardly a mile forward ; we went down the cross-road, turning on the high road, by a well-known bridge, in the direction of Le Cateau, and a kilo or so along drew three guns in, in fields on the other side of the road. The fourth gun was taken into a further field, lower and damper, and then it was found that it would have to be moved ! Oh, the tugging and heaving of men, the panting and whirring of the F.W.D., the bitterness of our spirit as we pulled ourselves to pieces that damp October afternoon. Dark came on, and still we had not succeeded ; we left the brute stuck in the field, in position, if needed, only for firing on our rest-billets at Reumont, and finally a great " caterpillar " hauled it out.

. This new position of ours was near the river Selle, which runs through Le Cateau. From the guns we walked down a little lane amidst damp orchards, and in a couple of minutes came to a sheltered corner of land by the rushing waters of the stream. A high ridge just on the further side of the stream cut off Le Cateau, with its towers, from our view, and a similar ridge ran along on our right. Here stood Chapel Mills, a big, red-brick structure, with its barns adjoining, and its owner's house, now merely a burnt and blackened shell, and with all the chaff and litter of a mill lying about the yard. An attractive place, as a mill is to any right-minded person ; only we couldn't help wondering, since it was so obviously suitable for billets, and since a building of this sort was bound to be marked on the Boche maps, whether

he wouldn't drop a few shells over while we were
there.   But he didn't, though he shelled frequently
the ridge on our right.   So we had an exceedingly
" bon" two days here.

Our first view of the interior of the mill revealed a
scene of comfort as we came out of the darkness into
the bright light of many candles.   The flooring was
of clean cement, the room would have been spacious
but for the wooden shafts, part of the machinery,
which rose to the upper stories.   These formed, as
it were, irregular groups of pillars in the room, and
the different Subs., half hidden from one another, were
clustered about in different corners.   To get to one's
corner, one had to step delicately over half a dozen
other people, and squeeze oneself round one or two
of these big square shaft-casings, and holding on to
an iron bracket, lower oneself gently on to one's kit.
Some little tables and chairs had been scrounged, and
a number of mattresses for sleeping on, or one could
climb on to the pile of hay at the further end of the
room, and make one's bed there.   Here we sat and
rested and smoked and chatted ; soon " Primuses "
and " Kampites " were got out, and here half a dozen
men were having coffee together, and there some others
were making porridge, or a tin of bully-beef was
being opened.   " Who's going to share it with me ?
It's Fray Bentos, jolly good stuff, you know."   Thus
we made our frugal suppers, had a hand at cards
perhaps, and fell then to a good night's sleep, all
except the wretched gas-guards.

The next day was rainy, and there was nothing to
do on the guns but dig a slip-trench.   We climbed the

upper story of the mill, admiring the fine machinery—
German—and we inspected the gun-pits and piles of
shells which showed that one of Fritz's own batteries
had been placed in the orchard a few yards away.
One of our N.C.O.s, a well-known marauder, explored
Le Cateau, and came back with an account of a barn
in which were 300 barrels of wine, with no one guard-
ing them. Not just yet, unfortunately, did we go
in search of them! In the afternoon three long,
sturdy members of F Sub. proved their heroism by
a swim in the cold waters of the mill-stream. We
settled down again in the evening to quiet and rest,
and a good night's sleep. But in war-time this easy
existence could hardly continue for long, and it was
no surprise to us when next day, the 21st, we had to
pack stores and move forward in the afternoon, a
change due to the success with which the general
situation had been developed on our front. The attack
on the 17th-18th had given us Le Cateau and the line
of the Selle ; one made on the 20th had given us the
same line north of the town. A further advance along
the whole line was now planned.

Our battery's new position was in Le Cateau itself.
The capture and the pathetic welcome to our troops
had been the subject of vivid descriptions in the
recent newspapers, and we looked at the town with
keen interest. The outskirts naturally had a dull
and battered appearance, a house here and there
ruined by bomb or shell, and many cut or chipped by
the fragments of shell, but the main streets were not
too badly damaged. There were only a few people
and children to be seen about the streets, and our

16

comrades of other units seemed well in possession of the town. At the centre of the town we turned up a broad, cobbled side street ; it finished in a chasm two hundred yards up, where the bridge across the railway line had been destroyed by the Boche. About half-way up on the left-hand side was a cemetery, which a railway cutting adjoined, and beyond this was a low wall. Here was to be the battery position, the most difficult for handling guns in that we had during the whole advance. One gun—F Sub.'s—was actually drawn some yards along the railway line in the cutting, crowbars being used to pull up a length of railway for it. That was portentous labour, and men hoped it would be worth while, for the cutting, rising to a yard or two at each side, afforded a kind of natural defence. For the other guns holes were knocked in the wall, a fairly easy matter ; but what was not so easy was to cut out the bank behind the wall and haul the gun into this rough kind of gun-pit. It was all done, however, at last, and the guns were better screened and sheltered than if they had been pulled in on the level other side of the road, which it would have been much easier to do. There were a few small houses on this latter side, which were taken over for billets, the cellars being viewed with a certain amount of favour, for a town like Le Cateau was an obvious target for the Boche. Intermittently now he was dropping a few over, and when the " stunt " took place, the battery was to have the worst single strafing it had had on the whole advance.

The first day at the position there was no firing ;

but at night all preparations had to be made for a big bombardment. This started at 1.20 a.m. on October 23rd, and almost simultaneously the Boche opened out all about our position. The bad weather which, in these last two days, had confined us to Chapel Mills had had the rather more important effect of making it difficult for our airmen to locate the enemy's batteries, which consequently were not so well kept under by our artillery fire as was usual on zero mornings. He threw heavy and light stuff over, and even machine-gun bullets came whistling down, for the battery, being only some 1,500 yards from the front line, was well within reach of a machine-gun barrage. Our men stuck to the guns, but it was warm work ; crash ! and then a little more distant crash ! they kept on coming ; in the intervals between getting each round off, it was well to crouch down behind the wall. The cookhouse on the other side of the road was an unlucky spot. An old boiler just outside it was blown to bits, and a little later a gas-shell, landing not far away, blew the doorway in, and Sammy, the cook, was slightly gassed. But probably the most marvellous escapes were those of F Sub. They were working the gun when a shell fell on the left bank of the cutting, not a couple of yards away, and at about shoulder-height ; yet not a man was hurt, not even the sergeant, Hay, who, as layer, was on that side of the gun. Another shell fell soon after, only a yard or two further away, and the splinters knocked two nuts off the cradle of the piece. And still another shell, falling in front, damaged the "lands" of the muzzle. Nasty work that, out in the dark and danger, stuff

falling about from you knew not where; but it had
to be carried on, and it was carried on, and in recognition of the fact the Military Medal was later awarded
to Sergeant Hay, Bombardier Griffiths, and Bombardier Slinn. About 4 o'clock breakfast was served,
and it was now that the Boche strafe slackened. Ours,
however, went on for some hours longer, and it was
of a particularly interesting type from the artilleryman's point of view, for it was the nearest approach
to a creeping barrage that our battery took part in.
In these barrages the lighter guns lengthen their
range every four minutes, and we were instructed to
do similarly. We were, however, fifteen minutes in
advance of them—that is, at the time the stunt
started, we fired on the line which came under their
barrage fifteen minutes later; and another difference
was this—that whereas they maintained a more or
less unbroken curtain of fire all along the front of
attack, we bombarded only certain areas, such as
woods and the cross-roads at Pommereuil.

All justice should be done to our signallers for their
work on this day. They had had warm enough work
lately, particularly from St. Emilie, but the work
from Le Cateau proved warmer still. The O.P. from
here was an isolated house in our front line, and when
our fellows were laying their wire, the Boche started
shelling it. They happened to be in the front garden ;
he dropped a 5·9 in the back. They took shelter in
the house, and his next shell dropped in the front
garden. They cleared ! The following day, that of
the zero stunt, our line was continually cut by his
heavy fire, but Billy Williams and Burdett, that

inseparable and priceless pair, worked out in it, repairing the line, nearly the whole morning. Their
parts were equal; Billy Williams was awarded the
Military Medal. Another signaller, R. P. Green, had
also gained the Medal just previously for good work.

It was splendid news we heard during this day,
October 23rd, of our men's advance. They had gone
well forward along the whole line, and more particularly in front of us they had driven the Boche out
from the Bois l'Évêque and the village of Pommereuil.
In later days we went " salvaging " over the ground
taken on this occasion, and could picture the scene.
Where there was a cutting or a sunken way beneath
the crest of a slope, one would find the little Boche
dug-outs, little Boche holes, too, all along the banks
of the roads, and here and there a corpse still lying
about; Boche machine-gun posts lower down the
slopes and behind hedges, with half-empty cartridge
bands; short lengths of trenches: and everywhere,
everywhere, our shell-holes, thinly scattered perhaps
over this field; fairly abundant along the roads and
roadsides, and particularly around cross-roads; close
together up this slope where, for some reason, concentrated artillery must for a few moments have
maintained a blasting storm of fire: mainly the marks
of field artillery, but many of the holes those made
by the siege guns, a silent demonstration of the scien-
tific precision and terrible power of the British artillery. One poor young fellow there was, I noticed,
lying dead in an open field; he was running, apparently, from the advancing barrage, and a bit caught
him. The same fate has menaced every combatant

in this war, and, enemy though he was, one felt sorry that he had not missed that brutal splinter of iron.

After the morning stunt there was no more firing for us to do on this day, for our guns were out of effective range, and we were to move forward the next morning. In the evening Jumbo Symes proposed a walk to two or three of us. We went up to the higher end of the road, and dropped down into the railway cutting. How strong a position it had been for the Boche! There were dug-outs all along the banks, machine-gun posts at the top, in one of which—one of these simple, grave-like holes—lay crouched up one poor beggar, caught in his refuge. The cutting had indeed been heavily shelled by us, and the line was broken everywhere. Further down, where the railroad emerged on level ground, deep belts of barbed wire were set across the grass in front of the machine-gun posts, and one could realise that the Boche, despite his continuous retreat, had yet placed obstacles before our infantry lads which it needed all their gallantry to overcome. The railway station, too, was badly damaged, and we noted with interest the fearful note of the German orders printed about as to what was to be done when the three whistles announced the approach of the English bombing 'planes. And now, just beyond the station, we arrived at what was one at least of our objects in coming this way—the store containing the 300 barrels of wine. Alas! it was over two days ago that we had been told of it. Then it was to be had for the taking. Now there was a guard on duty at the place; behind him we could see those tempting rotundities, but no cajolery (and there was a high dignitary in our party) could obtain us access to them.

Up at five the next morning, the 24th, to get the guns ready for moving. F gun came out far more easily than she had gone in : not that the blasts from the shells falling twenty-four hours previously had loosened her seventy-six hundredweight, but an F.W.D. was skilfully backed into the railway cutting and drew the gun out. From away forward came the dull booming of another zero stunt, the infantry were again advancing ; they reached this day the out-skirts of the great Mormal Forest, and completed victoriously the Battle of the Selle River. The Boche was indeed being relentlessly pushed these days. We were full of hope that all these labours would soon have their result in his submission, and the war—for we were building on this now—would be over. We were cheerful indeed as we rode off on lorries, limbers, and guns about 8 o'clock that fine, sunny morning. A good mail came up just after breakfast—always a welcome thing, especially when, as on this occasion, one of your Sub. immediately cuts up a rich home-made cake for your consumption. At the further end of the town a railway viaduct had been blown up, and the surrounding houses reduced to ruins, and others further away burnt out ; but soon we got out on the high road, and breathed the pure air and looked on fields and fine trees. We turned to the left along a secondary road which took us through undulating country to the village of Pommereuil. In a newly made cemetery on the right, just before entering the village, the victims of the recent fighting,

British and German, were being buried, many of the
latter together in one great grave. We went to the
further end of the village, which is set amongst
pleasant agricultural country, well wooded, with
many orchards, and with hedges separating the fields—
a rare sight around Le Cateau—and we drew the four
guns into a field and an orchard adjoining the last
house in the village. C Sub. gun, indeed, was placed
just by this house, and its team had to wear their
tin hats quite as much when they were shelling the
enemy as when he was shelling them, though the
missiles in this case were only the tiles shaken off the
roof. Fancy having a bath out in the open with
your tin hat on ! This is what one of their number
had to do, a man creditably famous for not missing
his cold bath one single day out at the front.

We looked out billets in the empty houses near by,
and made ourselves pretty comfortable, keeping good
fires going in the stoves or open fireplaces ; indeed,
some billets looked quite homelike, with blazing fire,
chairs and table, and the men seated comfortably
about, chatting or playing cards. E Sub.'s was one
of the more Spartan billets—a big bare room with
two doorless doorways. We improved it by scrounging a big door to go roughly over one doorway—sometimes the man going in or out nearly suffered the
fate of the sparrow trapped under a tile—and we used
our big tarpaulin as a carpet. There was but little
work to do, and it was quite nice to sit out in the
pleasant green orchards behind the houses, or chat
with the infantrymen in the place. Some civilians,
sent away by the Boche just before he cleared out,

were already returning, old ladies whom it was pathetic
to see greeting one another as they went back to their
ransacked houses.

And, really, they seemed to be returning too soon
for safety. That first evening the Boche dropped a
few gas-shells, apparently by the other end of the
village. Then about half-past ten we had a shoot
of twenty rounds on. From E Sub. only four men,
under Usher, went out to the gun ; we heard the
reports of about a dozen, and then there was a Boche
shell crashed near by, and another nearer still. A
minute after, in rushed Usher and his team : " No
good out there at present," they said ; " that last one
dropped on the roadside by our gun." None of
them was hit, and how fortunate they were was plain
next day when we saw on the other side of the road
the corpse of a poor infantryman, killed by that very
shell, which had dropped in fact nearer to our team
than to him. The next night, the 25th, as ammunition
was being unloaded, a shell suddenly came over, and
killed Corporal Temple, of our column, and wounded
Corporal Theobald and Tomsett. The men of our
column were, throughout, a set of good chums, and it
was sad that, at this late stage of the war, these
casualties should be sustained amongst them. That
the Boche, by sound-ranging, had some idea as to
where our guns were, seemed more than likely, from
the fact that two or three times he opened fire almost
immediately after we had started. A brigadier-
general quartered near by was apparently convinced
that this was the case, for, when we were engaged on
a shoot another evening, he sent a request that we

should cease, ostensibly on the ground that our noise interfered with the work of his staff! But whether we fired or not, the Boche used to show his hate on the neighbourhood. I remember how one evening, when I happened to be gas-guard, having had the luck to win the earliest shift, I was standing in the dark, brick-strewn yard outside the B.X. when I heard a big shell crash up in the village. The next one fell a little nearer, and the third still nearer; the Boche was evidently "sweeping." Happily the third one was the limit of his traverse, and the fourth and fifth bursts sounded with diminishing noise. One soon came to look and listen a bit before walking down the street! Every night as we lay in our blankets we could hear at one hour or other the steady whistle of his gas-shells, and their soft thud. But it was mainly the road at the further side of the village that he was troubled about; we sank comfortably to sleep with that thought. The cooks had their equanimity disturbed one night when a shell dropped in the yard and shook their cookhouse about. But on the whole it was a pretty healthy, good time at Pommereuil: we didn't anticipate being at this game much longer; it was fine, sunny weather again, and we chaffed one another in good spirits at meal-times as we lined up in the yard to see what grub the gods might provide for us.

Our rest-billets all this time continued to be at Reumont. Reumont is a village lying pleasantly on a side-road amidst fields and orchards. We were comfortably billeted in empty houses there, and I have before mentioned how pleased we of E Sub.

were at the first sight of our billet. When we returned to it one evening after our spell up forward we
inquired as usual all about the place.

" Well, Tommy, you scarified base-wallah, what's it
like down here ? "

" Oh, less of your prolixity ! We've saved tea for
you, it's on the stove, and here's the bread and stuff."

We dipped our mugs, clean or dirty, into the dixie,
half full of brown, acrid liquid, picked up one of the
bits of bread from the litter of crumbs, cups, tins, and
flickering candles on the table, disentangled a chunk
of margarine from its clinging paper vestments,
scooped out some jam, and resumed the catechism.
" Well, anything doing here ? "

" Yes, there's a Church Army hut down the road ;
nothing in the canteen, but Whaler keeps on saying
he's getting in some wine from Bordeaux. What's it
been like up forward ? "

" Good enuffski. Gas-shells over in the village at
night, but nothing much else. Where are you off to
now ? "

" Honnechy. There's a splendid pierrot troupe
there—25th Divisional. You go to-morrow night.
It's not at all bad down here now. You can get
coffee next door. Cheerioski."

This sounded quite good, and after tea and a smoke
we strolled out. Next door was a house we had
noticed—a pretty, neat house in a well-kept garden,
still with lovely dahlias in it, and when we went there
for coffee, we met four of the kindest little ladies one
could come across. To get in their warm, clean sitting-room was a pleasure in itself, and they received

us most kindly, so appreciative were they of the
British Tommy after their four years under the Boche.

"But you, did you stop here all the time?" we
asked, for, a rare sight, furniture and other articles
seemed all complete.

"No, we went away for a fortnight to escape the
bombardment, but we locked up the house."

"And didn't you lose anything, m'am'selle?"

"Yes, two coverlets were taken, but we have
recovered one. The other one was a very good one."

Yet they were lucky not to have lost more. But
Boche medical officers had been quartered on them,
decent men, whose presence had doubtless saved them
from loss of furniture.

We left them, arranging to call for a bath in the
morning. The first man, we heard, who had gone
there for a bath, a reverend man of great pudency,
had found the tub arranged for him in an unscreened
corner of the sitting-room, where the normal work
was going on! When we went we found that a screen
had been provided—two tablecloths hung around the
corner of the room, so that standing in the tub, one
could chat with one's chums or hostesses over the
tablecloth. It was great fun; the hot water, and
after that the cup of coffee and cigarette, were deli-
cious. And the pierrot concert party at Honnechy
more than exceeded expectations. We heard it again
at Le Cateau and elsewhere, and never found reason
to alter our opinion. The brightly dressed troupe,
with artistic background on the stage flooded with
light, the splendid orchestra rendering music, airy or
classical, in a way that appealed to all, the clever

fooling, the perfect ensemble of pieces like the capti-
vating " Yea, yea, verily yea," Newton, the tenor,
with his powerful and expressive singing, and striking
poses, all united to give a delightful glimpse of the
happy world of music and theatres, of comfort, in
short, that we were at present denied. To come out
from the concert hall, with its brightness and artistic
attraction, was suddenly to feel one's spirits fall ;
beyond the mile's walk were not the pleasures of home,
but the dulness of the bare billet. True, we had been
in far worse places. " Better than a year ago, anyhow. You remember the mud of the salient." But
music and art had led us into the familiar home atmosphere, and how distant all that seemed again ! " Aye,
it's a foul war," we agreed, as we strode glumly homewards. But the good spirits engendered by our own
robust health soon asserted themselves, and glumness
soon gave way to—shall we say ?—badinage and
persiflage. And, getting near to our billets, variety
was provided by a few H. Vicks which the Boche sent
over in the village. Yes, we must certainly keep
cheerful, and return him a little hate as soon as we
were on the guns again.

Another morning Vokins and I undertook a jaunt
to Serain, a score of kilos away, in quest mainly of
tobacco, for all the autumn there was a horrid dearth
of this. We lorry-jumped that distance ; it was a
great boon at the front that lorry-drivers, except
the wretched majority of the R.A.F. people, would
nearly always give one a lift, and one could thus get
to almost any spot within a thirty-kilo radius in a
day. Of course, passes were supposed to be asked

for. We had a quick ride to Serain, and with luck bought 1,000 cigarettes at a canteen that was just moving ; then we tried at a Divisional canteen, where there was a big crowd, and the vendors didn't want to serve us, on the ground that we weren't in their division ; we spun them a dit, however, " Oh, but we're just down from the line ; we cover your infantry, you know ; put up the barrage for them. Let's have some cigarettes, chum," and our tenacity and their good-nature won us another 500 cigarettes. Oh, the content in my companion's face as he lit one of these luxuries ! We sat on a Boche timber-cart in a dirty yard, and made a dinner off biscuits and two twopenny tins of Maconochie's meat paste, and then we had a grand ride back, for we found a lorry full to the top with new blankets and uniforms, and by the kindness of the Infantry Q.M.S. in charge were allowed to ensconce ourselves at the rear of this, and travel in softness and luxury the whole of the way to Reumont. The 1,500 cigarettes were disposed of immediately we returned.

While the guns were at Pommereuil there was no big attack on our front, as we knew through there being no " zero " stunt for us ; but after the capture of Valenciennes (which fell on November 2nd) a great stunt was to take place along the whole line. Opposite us was the Forest of Mormal, a formidable obstacle, It was judged advisable that our guns should go yet further forward, and, as a preliminary, on October 28th ten of us under Jumbo were detailed to go up and make dug-outs. It proved rather an exciting afternoon. Carrying our picks and shovels we strolled

leisurely along the road and across the fields, green
and pleasant in the clear sunshine, and dug away
with zest enough. There was no bank to dig into,
just a sloping meadow in which we easily cut out
three or four oblong cavities. However, about
2 o'clock Fritz opened out before and behind us—
nasty heavy things that seemed most evilly and in-
congruously to bring destruction into that fair landscape and quiet air. We soon noticed that he had
definite targets 150–200 yards from us, probably roads,
we said to one another, and we could proceed with
our digging fairly undisturbed, though we felt that
one that dropped on the country-road along the
side of the meadow was a little too close. It was only
a short shoot, and about 3 o'clock it was repeated.
Soon after, Jumbo, moving about the dug ground, hurt
his ankle badly, and that " warrior, famouséd in
fight," and most honourably so, had to go down early,
in the light car in which some of our officers had come
up to inspect the work. We packed up tools at
4 o'clock, and set off down the road. Alas ! we had
forgotten Boche regularity. The hour was up. We
had not gone 200 yards, were just at a point where
our road converged with another, when s-ssh-s-sh it
came through the air, and crash ! almost before we
could throw ourselves on the ground. The smoke
rose a score or two of yards behind us ; we picked
ourselves up, and ran for all we were worth. Ssh—
crash ! and again we had to collapse into the depression at the side of the road ; then up again, and while
some were by this time away from the point of danger,
four others had to stay in a little trench, happily

discovered, while he kept on dropping them at the
road-junction for four or five minutes. We breathed
with relief when it was over, and getting out of the
trench walked down the road again, noting with
approval little holes dug by infantrymen in the low
banks, and we had gone a couple of hundred yards
and were just quietly passing another cross-roads
when our hearts suddenly stood still, there was that
roar right above us, that crash ! almost before we had
hurled ourselves, flattened ourselves, out upon the
hard road. The rush of air beat on us like a
great sea-wave, a splinter brought blood from one's
chin, and one at least, as he slowly gathered his
limbs together, felt sure that the other three still
lying prone had been hit ; we could hardly believe it
when we all rose and found none was hurt. Later on,
but not now, we saw the shell-hole, a 5·9, less than
twenty yards away ; down we now dashed along the
road, along which Cuthbertson was coming back, fear-
ing for us. A salvo of two, it appeared, had been
fired ; the second had fallen a hundred yards down
the road ; we hurried quickly past that hole, and at
length felt a little safe.

It will not be wondered at that when, next morning,
having drawn the guns out from the Pommereuil
position, we rode along with them to the new site, some
of us felt pretty windy when we drew near to these
two cross-roads of infamous association ; however,
he was dropping nothing over at this time. Yet we
did not envy the men of 156 who were billeted at the
building by the converging roads ; we knew too well
the meaning of the big shell-holes all round this

point.   And as a matter of fact our reliefs coming up
that afternoon found the Boche shooting again, and
had to flop and run, flop and run, just as we had the
previous day.

We felt more sylvan in this, our last position, than
in any position we had occupied since Curlu.   Irregular green meadows and orchards lay about on each
side, with trees and fine hedges screening from our
sight even that nearest house already referred to.   In
front of our dug-outs, at the foot of the field, the ground
was marshy, reedy ; it was quite in accord with our
rustic mode of life that a deserted cow should be
wandering about here, and be milked by some of our
men.   There were blackberries still to be picked from
the russet-tinted hedge by our dug-outs, and the guns,
when they were fired, shook down, like gales of autumn,
the dying leaves.

The position was variously called Tilleuls Farm,
from the building with a row of fine lime-trees at
the cross-roads behind, or Fontaine-au-Bois, from the
village which lay, near Landrecies, a mile in front of
us.   The field in which the guns were was a shallow,
broad one, extending from one to the other of the
converging roads mentioned before, and they were
at first placed nearly in the centre of this.   An 8-inch
battery, however, came in the field just behind, and
it was clear that all our guns, except the one on the
right flank, were too near the blast from these guns
for comfort, so openings were cut in the hedge in
front of our field, and the guns pulled forward, right
in these.   The actual platforms were raised some
inches above the ground, and it seemed as if we should

17

never be able to haul the guns up that small elevation—
the wheels kept on slipping—but " dogged did it."
By this time, three o'clock or so, our reliefs had come
up, and very indignant were we when informed that
we had still to stay until a hundred rounds had been
brought to each gun. We did grouse! Our rulers
said it was for a stunt next morning, and this mollified
us for a time, but as five o'clock came and went, and
the new teams had their tea, and there was none for
us, our indignation grew apace. The two bitterest
men were two senior N.C.O.s of B Sub., whose canny
team had cut off immediately the reliefs hove in sight,
while they had been detained by a stern sergeant-major
to supply their deficiency. About 7 o'clock we were
at length allowed to board a lorry and go down. But
our labours were not yet ended, for we were ordered
to go to Pommereuil and clear that position of shells
ere we proceeded to the rest-billets at Reumont. Some
of us, however, did go straight on to Le Cateau. The
Boche was bombing over on the left, and at each great
bang the sparks burst out above the ground, like some
broad-cupped flower suddenly springing forth in the
darkness. At Le Cateau nobody was in the streets;
it was a common target for Boche bombers, and, some
little time before, they had killed there two members
of the concert-party we had heard at Moislains. So
we passed on, and, pretty fagged, at length reached
the rest-billets. Our chums did not arrive till the
morning, and it was a dolorous tale they told. They
had got to Pommereuil all right and found, of course,
no rations there, though the kindness of a few other of
our men there saved them from utter hunger. Similarly

they had no blankets, and had had to spend the night there in cold discomfort. The one useful thing they had was their gas-masks, for in the night the Boche had shelled this end of the village more continuously than during all our stay there ; he had thrown much gas over, and they had had to descend to the cellars for safety. Such was the beginning of their spell of rest! However, in our battery things were " evened " out as much as possible, so that when our team returned to the guns, some of these men were allowed to stay behind on rest an extra night.

But up forward there was nothing very arduous to do, only a small, harassing shoot now and then. On fine days it was tolerable up there in that green spot, but there was a good deal of rain, and then it was pretty depressing to squat in our cold square holes in the earth for hours on end. It was worse still to crawl out from under the wet tarpaulins and go up to the top of the field to fetch one's grub, for there one slithered about as in a small quagmire, and when one brought it back, one nearly upset it handing it down into the hole, and then one slopped down into the hole oneself. And then we'd light our pipes and try to drive our thoughts from the temporary to the permanent—that is, to the peace which we hoped was coming. But it needed a tot of rum in the evening to warm our bodies and cheer our spirits sufficiently before getting into the blankets. Yes, peace did seem nigh ; we talked of it now all the time. " Got any rumours ? " " Yes, the Germans have asked for an armistice." " Hurrah ! well, surely we shall give it them." "Oh, I don't know!" How our faces fell! "They say we're asking extraordinary terms." Living in those rabbit holes we loathed the men who would delay the coming of peace an instant longer than necessary ; but President Wilson, we felt, wasn't of that sort.

We were not shelled at this position, though Fritz continued his operations on the cross-roads. Sometimes his missiles fell short. One night one shell dropped apparently a hundred yards or so away from us. Thinking of some of our men who had constructed dug-outs by the side of the marshy ground, we murmured contentedly, "That's put the wind up them," and fell asleep. Another evening four men had a wonderful escape. They were playing cards in our dug-out when a shell, falling short, burst just on the edge of it. The splinters tore the tarpaulin in a hundred places, so that in the rainy weather afterwards the floor of the dug-out became a veritable pool, but not one man was even scratched.

All this time we were expecting a big "stunt" to come off. When we took over from, or were relieved by, our other gun-team, the question was, "Any stunt yet ?" and down at the rest-billets we compared notes as to whether that bombardment we had heard in the early hours of the morning was really heavy enough for a big stunt. It seemed delayed day after day. At length we came up on the evening of November 4th, and heard that the stunt had actually taken place. Our zero hour had been 6.15 ; we had put a creeping barrage over the Forest of Mormal, and after it had finished we fired no more, for Fritz was once

THE BATTERY IN FRANCE, 1918

again out of range. Terribly effective, too, we gathered
the artillery-fire had been in that forest, shearing and
wrecking trees in its methodical progress, and not
sparing—such are the exigencies of this foul warfare—what human habitations were there. But it
helped our lads to get forward; they took Landrecies, and pushed right to the other end of the
forest.

These were the last shots we fired. The Boche
played about on the cross-roads that afternoon with
a few H. Vicks, their sudden spurt causing us a hasty
dive into our ground-holes, but when that was done,
we had finished being shelled, equally with shelling.
The guns were left on the position for two or three
weeks longer, under the charge of a small guard, but
the battery went back into rest-billets at Le Cateau.
Events were moving quickly now, and we hopefully
awaited the news of peace. On Sunday, the 10th,
all were elated by the news that the Germans had
accepted terms for an armistice. Yet when, on November 11th, the great moment came, there was but little
outward celebration. At Le Cateau we were inspected
by Major-General Wellesley, and a church service was
held. To those of us who were on guard up forward,
billeted in the big room of a wayside estaminet, this
talk of peace seemed not wholly real, even as late as the
Sunday evening, and at dawn on the Monday morning
the dull rumble of a distant bombardment appeared
certainly to contradict it. But some one came in at
breakfast with the tale that a dispatch-rider going past
had said the armistice was to begin at eleven o'clock.
The news was corroborated by another, and we quietly

read or cooked the dinner during the morning, making
certain as late as 12 o'clock that the news was true
by inquiries from dignitaries such as a quartermaster-
sergeant who went past. Later, learning how the
occasion was to be officially celebrated, we sent a
willing messenger down to Le Cateau to fetch our
issue of rum.

So the war, then, was finished ! Finished our hardships, our cave-dwellings, our nights of strafes and
journeyings and pullings-in ! Finished our dangers
from the Gotha that purrs at night, from the 5·9's that
drop by night and day impartially, and from the
H. Vicks that dash about when these other troubles
are o'er ! Finished the ordeal from which we have
emerged whole, but which has taken from us too
many good comrades, and grievously maimed too
many more ! But a little time remains, we hope,
before the khaki itself is doffed, the quasi-eternal
stew and rice are left behind, and we resume our
natural lives again. Yet, for us who have come
through, this life has not been all waste. Through
its very primitiveness and its nearness to death
it has taught us better to know ourselves, to understand one another, and to know the true worth of
things.

None of us has liked war, none of us but hopes that
never again will that accursed mode of settlement be
employed in this world's affairs. Many men have
suffered under it for longer than we—all praise to
them ; yet, more than any human being ought to be
called on to endure, even we have endured. But,
man helping man in the greater demands of life, and

THE GREAT CONCLUSION 263

equally by the warmth and brightness each put into his daily intercourse, we have seen such good aspect as there may be to a life inherently so damnable. We have done our part. By God's good grace we have come through. *Deo Laus.*

APPENDIX I

COMPOSITION OF THE BATTERY ON ACTIVE SERVICE

Original Battery—arrived in France, April 26th, 1917

(A) OFFICERS

Major Edmondson, A. J.
Capt. Knox, J. H.
2nd-Lieut. Mortleman, W. R.
    ,,   Baylis, G. H.
    ,,   Medhurst, H. F.
    ,,   Wintle, C.

(B) MEN

B.S.M. Stokes, W.O.	Cpl. Seton, G. R.
S. Sgt. Wheeler, F. W.	,, Rayns, F.
B.Q.M.S. Mordin, A.J.	Bdr. Booker, C. W.
Sgt. Pullen, W. H.	Gnr. Sutton, A. H.
,, Williams, T. A.	Bdr. Woodcock, F.
,, Thiele, H. F.	,, Lyons, S. L.
,, Jeffreys, E. A.	,, Parsons, G. L.
,, Turnage, P. S.	,, Sands, J.
Cpl. Tansley, H. J.	,, Bird, C. K.
,, Vassie, C. F.	,, Fletcher, H. L.
,, Barratt, H. B.	Gnr. Wells, J. C. M.
Sgt. Daines, A.	Bdr. Goodman, H. J. G.

Bdr. Fulford-Brown, N.
,, Lindsay, K. M.
,, McNeil, G. H.
,, Cundell, H.
,, Newland, R. W.
Cpl. Fear, C. H.
Bdr. Heller, G. P. K.
,, Cooke, W. R.
,, Ives, F. H.
,, Brooker, B. J.
,, Curtis, W. D.
Tptr. Whitaker, A.
Gnr. Denman, G. W.
,, Edmunds, H. J.
,, Emson, F. J.
,, Fairgray, C. J.
,, Fitness, H. E.
,, Hayes, W. A.
,, Hill, R. S.
,, Johnson, C. E.
,, Moss, R. W.
,, Perrett, H. V.
,, Pink, C. H.
,, Simon, A. J.
,, Smith, F. R.
,, Staples, A. E. V.
,, Storer, H. M.
,, Turney, A. S.
,, Bastow, L. G.
,, Bocking, E. F. C.
,, Brownsill, J. W.
,, Carter, A. C. J. H.
,, Clark, P. H.
,, Clarke, J. M.

Gnr. Cranham, R. W.
,, Rix, R. G.
,, Baker, R. G.
,, Earley, C. H.
,, Upsdale, D. R.
,, Coston, A. J.
,, Hyde, C. F. W.
,, Watkins, S.
,, Hayward, A. A.
,, Batt, L.
,, Brown, J. B.
,, Burnham, W. C.
Cpl. Bishop, S. C.
Gnr. Clark, A. S.
,, Dixon, R. A.
,, Fogden, G. L. A.
,, Green, T. H.
,, Hanhart, H. H.
,, Hoyle, E.
,, Jones, H. J. H.
,, Mould, H.
,, Morris, W. C. E.
,, Phillips, K. S.
,, Nicholls, P. S.
,, Taunton, D. B.
,, Akers, S. F.
,, Barber, W. L.
,, Brock, F. G.
,, Burdett, H. F.
,, Danvers, E. V. J
,, Graves, H. G.
,, Hone, D.

Gnr. Hayman, L. S.

,,   Heathcote, F. P.

Bdr. Hussey, R. E.

Gnr. Hutchings, W. H. H.

,,   Longcroft, R. S.

,,   McFarlane, D.

,,   McMillan, D.

,,   Massingham, R.

,,   Millen, A. H.

,,   Parr, F. T.

,,   Read, C. E.

,,   Sellers, G. H.

,,   Thomas, D. M. E.

,,   Usher, F. E.

,,   Whales, O. O.

,,   Boundy, F.

,,   Burningham, A. W.

,,   Brown, M. A. P.

,,   Challis, A. S.

,,   Collier, E. C. W.

Gnr. Doyle, F. C.

,,   Godwin, F. H.

,,   Green, W. W.

,,   Gillott, J. H.

,,   Greenwood, J. W.

,,   Hammond, H.

,,   Hopkins, P. H.

,,   Kirk, S.

,,   Miller, C. St. C.

,,   Rolfe, W. H.

,,   Sherwood, J. H. V.

,,   Schofield, G. B.

,,   Stokes, E. W.

,,   Simco, P. G.

,,   Trice, W. G.

,,   Wellington, S. H. A.

,,   Winans, J. W.

,,   Wright, S.

,,   Haigh, A.

Wheeler, T. Hinch.

Limber-Gunner Wilson, W.

Wireless Operator, Clarke, A., May 9th, 1917

,,   ,,   Manterfield, C. H., July 13th, 1917

,,   ,,   Reinstein, L., July 13th, 1917

(C) A.S.C. COLUMN ATTACHED TO THE BATTERY

2nd-Lieut. Bowley, A. M.

Sgt. Leaman, J. B.

,,   Stevens, E. J.

,,   Rex, F. C.

Cpl. Cox, F.

,,   Tilbury, G. S.

,,   Phillips, W.

Cpl. Tucknott, J.

,,   Temple, T.

,,   Theobald, T.

L.-Cpl. Sheppard, E.

,,   Slaney, W.

,,   Thompson, O.

,,   McVay, H.

L.-Cpl. Spits, T.
,, Kennedy, W.
Pte. Buck, W.
,, Birtwistle, E.
,, Cookson, T.
,, Davies, C. H.
,, French, T.
,, Green, W.
,, Gilbert, E.
,, Gooch, C.
,, Hammond, W.
,, Howarth, T. H.
,, Hustwitt, E.
,, Hill, H.
,, Hume, G. H.
,, Judge, A.
,, Kennel, C.
,, Keith, A.
,, Lowe, R.
,, Law, F.
,, Leaver, A.
,, McCullum, W.
,, McNulty, T.
,, Marshall, R.
,, Naylor, N.
,, Pirie, A.
,, Rawcliffe, W.

Pte. Rice, J.
,, Sanders, F.
,, Saunders, A. W.
,, Sawyer, R.
,, Smart, S. R.
,, Smart, J. W.
,, Smith, C.
,, Silburn, W.
,, Spicer, F.
,, Surtees, T.
,, Shimel, C.
,, Shearer, A.
,, Sirrell, D.
,, Scouler, T.
,, Stanton, A. E.
,, Sweet, A.
,, Taylor, J.
,, Thewlis, H.
,, Tucker, W.
,, Tyres, S.
,, Tomsett, A.
,, Topping, J.
,, Underwood, T.
,, Upton, J.
,, Vales, V.
,, Wedlake, H.

OTHER OFFICERS OF THE BATTERY

2nd-Lieut. Masservey, R.G.A., attached June 22nd, 1917
,, Forsyth, R.G.A., attached June 22nd, 1917
Lieut. Hickson, H., R.G.A., attached August 4th, 1917
2nd-Lieut. Edmondson, P. H., H.A.C., August 5th, 1917
,, Sheppard, G., H.A.C., August 5th, 1917

2nd-Lieut. Stewart, J. H., R.G.A., attached August 7th, 1917
   ,,   Chattey, A. S. C., H.A.C., September 15th, 1917
   ,,   Colman, J. C., R.G.A., attached September 30th, 1917
   ,,   Rawe, C. H., R.F.A. attached October 29th, 1917
   ,,   Tranmer, F., R.G.A. (ammunition officer), attached October 26th, 1917
   ,,   Hughes, H. L., R.G.A., attached November 16th, 1917
   ,,   Baugh, B. P. R.G.A., attached November 22nd, 1917
   ,,   Glover, J. B. H.A.C., December 3rd, 1917
   ,,   Twine, W. A., R.G.A., attached December 28th, 1917
Major Spooner, J. C. G., R.F.A., attached March 30th, 1918
2nd-Lieut. Underhill, S., R.G.A., attached April 24th, 1918
   ,,   Graham, E. I., R.G.A., attached June 18th, 1918
   ,,   Tomlinson, G., R.G.A., attached July 8th, 1918
   ,,   Mould, H., R.G.A., attached August 28th, 1918
   ,,   Elliott, W. R.G.A., attached August 3rd, 1918
Lieut. Hawkes, F. C., R.G.A., attached October 2nd, 1918
   ,,   Taylor, J. T., R.G.A., attached October 2nd, 1918
2nd-Lieut. Simon, A. J., R.G.A., attached October 9th, 1918
   ,,   Goodman, H. J. G., R.G.A., attached October 9th, 1918

REINFORCING DRAFTS

Joined Battery, June 17th, 1917

Gnr. Brimmell, H.	Gnr. Hoon, C. L.
,, Riley, F.	,, Heal, F. E.
,, Williams, S. G.	,, Oulsnam, R.
,, Lloyd, E. D.	,, Barnes, L. D.

Gnr. Reeves, C. E.
,, Vokes, H. J.
,, Johnson, H.
,, Behar, A. M.
,, Parkinson, A. T.
,, Moon, C. H.
,, Kydd, J. S.
,, Wackrill, H. R.
,, Janes, T. F. C.
,, Stephens, L. G.

Gnr. Peacocke, H.
,, Hughes, S. G.
,, Clayton, H. J.
,, Wilkins, S. C.
,, Vezey, A. W.
,, Cosier, C. M.
,, Wordsworth, G. H.
,, Edwards, J. G.
,, Seal, T.
,, Seal, J.
,, Ballinger, G.

August 11th, 1917

Gnr. Dyer, B. A.
,, Bull, W. C.
,, Culross, A.
,, Broadway, C. L. J.
,, Bailey, J. N.

Gnr. Elphick, J. W.
,, Curnock, P. E.
,, Colville, P. J.
,, Bannister, E. P.
,, Calver, R. J. B.

August 25th, 1917

Gnr. Pluck, W. F.
,, Hoggins, P.
,, Thiele, A. P.
,, Pollard, L. A.

Gnr. Green, P. A.
,, Matthews, C. H.
,, Mathews, J. K.

August 28th, 1917

Gnr. Galbraith, R. H.
,, McCarthy, C. T.
,, Spencer, W. A.

Gnr. Thurrell, C. C.
,, Siffre, A. L.

September 17th, 1917

Gnr. Boaden, E.
,, Hall, C.
,, Leuty, L.

Gnr. Schollar, R.
,, Taylor, P.
,, Charatan, B.

Gnr. Johnston, D.
  ,, Merry, W.
  ,, Smart, P.
  ,, Upperton, H. W.
  ,, Evans, C.
  ,, Knowlton, H.
  ,, Shoesmith, J.

Gnr. Hasler, E.
  ,, Lowe, W.
  ,, Porter, F.
  ,, Tuckett, J.
  ,, Smith, R. S.
  ,, Pierce, W. J.
  ,, Winckley, L.

September 25th, 1917

Gnr. Higgins, F. G.
  ,, Cheverton, G. C.

Gnr. Hornsby, E.

September 29th, 1917

Gnr. Cherry, F. C.
  ,, Hill, H. St. J. S.
  ,, Maylam, A. T.
  ,, Lillicrap, J. R.
  ,, Felstead, O. G.

Gnr. Lane, W. G. C.
  ,, Greenhow, R. O.
  ,, Lewis, W. P.
  ,, Butcher, F. T.
  ,, Cuthbertson, E. H.

October 5th, 1917

Gnr. Bennett, W. H. B.
  ,, Lilley, G. H.
  ,, Whiting, R. E.
  ,, Rendell, R. H.
  ,, Clarkson, P.

Gnr. Silvester, H. T.
  ,, Harris, H. M.
  ,, Watkins, G. W.
  ,, Joel, B. B.

November 4th, 1917

Gnr. Beaumont, B. G.
  ,, Coulter, W. C.
  ,, Battle, C. S.
  ,, Jones, H. J.
  ,, Rayne, H. J.
  ,, Cozens, R.
  ,, Kingham, W. R.

Gnr. Morison, A. J. P.
  ,, Godden, L. S. F.
  ,, Lauder, A. A.
  ,, Massey, R.
  ,, Jones, E. A. M
  ,, Moody, W. E.
  ,, Menzies, J. C.

November 29th, 1917

Gnr. Skilbeck, C. T.   Gnr. Symes, B. H.
 ,, Taylor, H. C. D.   ,, Vokins, W. H.
 ,, Taylor, A.   ,, Gibbs, R.
 ,, Wenham, S.   ,, Rickard, A.

December 9th, 1917

Gnr. Bartlett, R. W.   Gnr. Atkinson, R. V.
 ,, Shaw, L. R.

December 18th, 1917

Gnr. Ellis, P. H.   Gnr. Potter, F.
 ,, Gribble, L.   ,, Swinstead, J. W.
 ,, Little, B. S.   ,, Jones, W. W. I.
 ,, Bartlett, A. W.   ,, Light, R.
 ,, Grant, A.

February 6th, 1918 (*Centre Section*)

Sgt. Brundle, F. W.   Gnr. Butler, E. G.
 ,, Huelin, E. S.   ,, Camm, G. E.
Cpl. Hay, L. H.   ,, Craig, K. C.
Bdr. Williams, L. A.   ,, Dack, A.
 ,, Keen, P. M.   ,, Davis, F. L.
 ,, Green, R. P.   ,, Denby, H.
 ,, Ingram, D. C.   ,, Towns, J. F.
Gnr. Smith, C. E.   ,, England, J.
 ,, Adamson, J. L.   ,, Espeland, L.
 ,, Allen, R. O.   ,, Essex, F. G.
 ,, Ansell, E. W.   ,, Foulsham, R. H.
 ,, Aylward, T. R.   ,, Fraser, D.
 ,, Bacon, P. J.   ,, Fry, A. J.
 ,, Blundell, H. E.   ,, Gardner, F. B.
 ,, Brand, A. N.

Gnr. Gifford, H. A.
„ Guest, H. J.
„ Henderson, F. R.
„ Hurworth, B. J.
„ Jackman, F.
„ Jaques, B. C.
„ Knowles, E. A.
„ Leech, W.
„ Lockitt, J. W.
„ Loveridge, F. O.
„ Lucas, G. F.
„ McLoughlin, D.

Gnr. Medway, L. S.
„ Mein, J. B.
„ Peart, W. B.
„ Pepper, E. W.
„ Pollack, D. G.
„ Sansom, E. W.
„ Shaw, T. L.
„ Silvester, W. T.
„ Sutton, F. W.
„ Tremellen, H. C.
„ Weaver, G. W.
„ Webb, W. J.

March 3rd, 1918

(Temporarily attached to 109 *Siege Battery)*

Gnr. Walker, A. G.
„ Walden, G. L.
„ Williams, T. H.
„ De Weck, E. M.
„ Mackenzie, D.
„ White, E. D.

Gnr. Over, T.
„ Ring, G. F.
„ Lough, A. H.
„ James, C. E.
„ Davies, W. R.

May 16th, 1918

Gnr. Slinn, R. T.
„ Bradban, G. C.

Gnr. Frank, H. A.

July 6th, 1918

Gnr. Barwood, A. E.
„ Perkins, W. L.
„ Scott, J. C.

Gnr. Roberts, R. A.
„ Peacock, G. H.

APPENDIX I

July 18th, 1918

Gnr. Ames, S. G.
  ,, Bathurst, H. H.
  ,, Boys, H. C.
  ,, Bonser, F. A.
  ,, Bailey, H. N.
  ,, Gibbs, C. A. R.
  ,, Hayman, J. F.
  ,, Harris, A. T.
  ,, Heaton, W. H.
  ,, Jeffcoat, J. H.
  ,, Jones, L. G.

Gnr. Johnstone, R. W.
  ,, Knight, F. J.
  ,, Lewis, H. M.
  ,, Mortlock, E.
  ,, Oliver, R.
  ,, Pierce, G. E.
  ,, Roach, W. F. T.
  ,, Shinkins, H. G.
  ,, Strickland, W. M.
  ,, Willows, J. E.

August 15th, 1918

Gnr. Proddow, W. N.
  ,, Pearson, W. E.
  ,, Milne, E.
  ,, Loe, A.
  ,, Shearing, J. E.

Gnr. Jeffcoat, H. V.
  ,, Webster, J. L.
  ,, Turpin, F. G.
  ,, Murdock, F.

October 3rd, 1918

Gnr. Burn, G.
  ,, Barnes, S. H.
  ,, Carter, J. E.
  ,, Carter, L. J.

Gnr. Evans, T.
  ,, Hamilton-Heinke, H.M.
  ,, Russell, E. C.
  ,, Ward, W. W.

18

APPENDIX II

THE ADVENTURES OF A PARTY OF 309 MEN, TEMPORARILY ATTACHED TO 109 SIEGE BATTERY

A DRAFT of fifteen men for our Battery arrived on March 14th, 1918, at Villers-Faucon, the Headquarters of the 47th Brigade, the authorities at the Artillery Base from which they had come being apparently ignorant that 309 were still at Sailly-Flibeaucourt, a hundred miles or so away. Instead of being sent thither, the draft were temporarily attached to 109 Siege Battery, a chance which subjected them to the great German onslaught. Most of them went up to the forward guns, between St. Emilie and Ronssoy, to work through each night on the construction of a sap in the chalky ground. Not a shell came over on 109, until the morning of the offensive, Thursday, March 21st. Then, at dawn, a heavy bombardment, high-explosives and gas, opened out on this, as on other batteries. All men were called to work on the guns, and did work, furiously. Three 109 men were killed and several wounded or gassed, and at length all had to clear to the trenches behind. Mr. Scrimshaw, after a time, returned with half a dozen men to the guns, but they could fire off only a few rounds, for the Boche was machine-gunning the position ; the guns had to be abandoned, and the men fled. Baker, one of our men, was captured ; he died, later, in Germany. A striking incident now was Lough's journey from the O.P. to Brigade at Villers-Faucon—through continual shelling, from which it seemed impossible that he should emerge alive. However, he delivered his message—the first intimation to the rear of the depth of the Boche advance in this area (for all telephone-wires had been cut by the bombardment)—and he was awarded the Military Medal.

Meanwhile, the two rear-guns, near Saulcourt, were being shelled, though less heavily, and during this and the following night they had to move backwards from one position to another—Longavesnes, Bussu ; here, too, there was something of a *sauve qui peut.* But the guns were retained, and on the night of the 23rd to 24th were placed in a farm-yard at Bray, and to them was added one gun, all that was left of another battery. 109, like 309, had to make a hurried retreat from Bray, late on the 25th, and on the 26th the guns were placed near Bresle, just off the Amiens-Albert road. Here, being near the road-junction, they had thirty-five casualties before they moved, on the 29th, further down the high road. On April 3rd the H.A.C. men joined their own unit.

INDEX

www.ingramcontent.com/pod-product-compliance
Lightning Source LLC
Chambersburg PA
CBHW020808100426
42814CB00014B/369/J